Institutional Ethnography

THE GENDER LENS SERIES

Series Editors

Judith A. Howard
University of Washington

Barbara Risman
North Carolina State University

Joey Sprague
University of Kansas

The Gender Lens Series has been conceptualized as a way of encouraging the development of a sociological understanding of gender. A "gender lens" means working to make gender visible in social phenomena, asking if, how, and why social processes, standards, and opportunities differ systematically for women and men. It also means recognizing that gender inequality is inextricably braided with other systems of inequality. The Gender Lens Series is committed to social change directed toward eradicating these inequalities. Originally published by Sage Publications and Pine Forge Press, all Gender Lens books are now available from AltaMira Press.

BOOKS IN THE SERIES

Yen Le Espiritu, *Asian American Women and Men: Labor, Laws, and Love*
Judith A. Howard and Jocelyn A. Hollander, *Gendered Situations, Gendered Selves: A Gender Lens on Social Psychology*
Michael A. Messner, *Politics of Masculinities: Men in Movements*
Judith Lorber, *Gender and the Social Construction of Illness*
Scott Coltrane, *Gender and Families*
Myra Marx Ferree, Judith Lorber, and Beth B. Hess, editors, *Revisioning Gender*
Pepper Schwartz and Virginia Rutter, *The Gender of Sexuality: Exploring Sexual Possibilities*
Francesca M. Cancian and Stacey J. Oliker, *Caring and Gender*
M. Bahati Kuumba, *Gender and Social Movements*
Toni M. Calasanti and Kathleen F. Slevin, *Gender, Social Inequities, and Aging*
Judith Lorber and Lisa Jean Moore, *Gender and the Social Construction of Illness, Second Edition*
Shirley A. Hill, *Black Intimacies: A Gender Perspective on Families and Relationships*
Dorothy E. Smith, *Institutional Ethnography: A Sociology for People*

Institutional Ethnography

A Sociology for People

Dorothy E. Smith

ALTAMIRA
PRESS
A Division of
ROWMAN & LITTLEFIELD PUBLISHERS, INC.
Lanham • *New York* • *Toronto* • *Oxford*

For George, once more

ALTAMIRA PRESS
A Division of Rowman & Littlefield Publishers, Inc.
A wholly owned subsidary of The Rowman & Littlefield Publishing Group, Inc.
4501 Forbes Boulevard, Suite 200
Lanham, MD 20706

PO Box 317, Oxford OX2 9RU, UK

British Library Cataloguing in Publication Information Available

Library of Congress Cataloging-in-Publication Data
Smith, Dorothy E., 1926–
    Institutional ethnography : a sociology for people / Dorothy E. Smith.
        p. cm. — (The gender lens series)
    Includes bibliographical references and index.

ISBN: 978-0-7591-0502-7

    1. Ethnology—Methodology. 2. Ethnology—Research. 3. Sociology. I. Title.
II. Series.
GN345.S57 2005
305.8'001—dc22

                                                                    2005001013

Printed in the United States of America

♾™ The paper used in this publication meets the minimum requirements of
American National Standard for Information Sciences—Permanence of Paper
for Printed Library Materials, ANSI/NISO Z39.48-1992.

CONTENTS

Series Editors' Foreword   ix
Acknowledgments   xiii
Introduction   1

PART ONE
Making a Sociology for People

CHAPTER 1
Women's Standpoint: Embodied Knowing
   versus the Ruling Relations   7
Women's Standpoint and the Ruling Relations   9
The Historical Trajectory of Gender and the
   Ruling Relations   13

CHAPTER 2
Knowing the Social: An Alternative Design   27
Reorganizing the Social Relations
   of Objectivity   28
What Is Institutional Ethnography?
   Some Contrasts   29
Experience and the Ethnographic
   Problematic   38
Conclusion   43

PART TWO
An Ontology of the Social

CHAPTER 3
Designing an Ontology for
Institutional Ethnography   49
An Ontology of the Social   51
Institutions, Language, and Texts   68
Conclusion   69

CHAPTER 4
Language as Coordinating Subjectivities   75
Reconceptualizing Language as Social   76
Experiential and Text-Based Territories   86
Conclusion   94

PART THREE
Making Institutions
Ethnographically Accessible

CHAPTER 5
Texts, Text–Reader Conversations,
and Institutional Discourse   101
The Text–Reader Conversation   104
The Text–Reader Conversations
   of Institutional Discourse   111
Texts as Institutional Coordinators   118
Conclusion   119

CHAPTER 6
Experience as Dialogue and Data   123
Experience as Dialogue: The Problem   124
An Alternative Understanding of
   Experience as Dialogue   127
Experience, Language, and Social Organization   128

The Data Dialogues 135

Conclusion 142

CHAPTER 7

Work Knowledges 145

Work Knowledge of University Grades
and Grading: A Mini-ethnography 145

Work Knowledge as the Institutional
Ethnographer's Data 150

Work Knowledge 151

The Problem of Institutional Capture 155

Assembling and Mapping Work Knowledges 157

Conclusion 161

CHAPTER 8

Texts and Institutions 165

How Texts Coordinate 170

Conclusion 180

CHAPTER 9

Power, Language, and Institutions 183

Making Institutional Realities 187

Regulatory Frames 191

Conclusion 199

PART FOUR

Conclusion

CHAPTER 10

Where We've Got To and Where We Can Go 205

Where We've Got To 205

Expansion 212

The Collective Work of Institutional Ethnography 219

Glossary   223
Reference List   231
Index   245
About the Author   257

It is now more than twenty years since feminist sociologists identified gender as an important analytic dimension in sociology. In the intervening decades, theory and research on gender have grown exponentially. With this series, we intend to further this scholarship, as well as ensure that theory and research on gender become fully integrated into the discipline as a whole.

In their classic edited collection *Analyzing Gender: A Handbook of Social Science Research* (1987), Beth Hess and Myra Marx Ferree identify three stages in the study of women and men since 1970. Initially, the emphasis was on sex differences and the extent to which such differences might be based on the biological properties of individuals. In the second stage, the focus shifted to the individual sex roles and socialization, exposing gender as the product of specific social arrangements, although still conceptualizing it as an individual trait. The hallmark of the third stage is the recognition of the centrality of gender as an organizing principle in all social systems, including work, politics, everyday interaction, families, economic development, law, education, and a host of other social domains. As our understanding of gender has become more social, so has our awareness that gender is experience and organized in race- and class-specific ways.

In the summer of 1992, the American Sociological Association (ASA) funded a small conference organized by Barbara Risman and Joey Sprague to discuss the evolution of gender in these distinctly sociological frameworks. The conference brought together a sampling of gender scholars working in a range of substantive areas with a diversity of methods to focus on gender as a principle of social organization. The discussions of the state of feminist scholarship made it clear that gender is pervasive in society and operates at multiple levels. Gender shapes identities and perception, interactional practices, and the very forms of social institutions, and it does so in race- and class-specific ways. If we did not see gender in social phenomena, we were not seeing them clearly.

The participants in the ASA-sponsored seminar recognized that although these developing ideas about gender were widely accepted by feminist sociologists and many others who study social inequalities, they were relatively unfamiliar to many who work within other sociological paradigms. This book series was conceived at that conference as a means of introducing these ideas to sociological colleagues and students and of helping to develop gender scholarship further.

As series editors, we believe it is time for gender scholars to speak to our other colleagues and to the general education of students. There are many sociologists and scholars in other social sciences who want to incorporate scholarship on gender and its intersections with race, class, and sexuality in their teaching and research but lack the tools to do so. For those who have not worked in this area, the prospect of the bibliographic research necessary to develop supplementary units or transform their own teaching and scholarship is daunting. Moreover, the publications necessary to penetrate a curriculum resistant to change and encumbered by inertia have simply not been available. We conceptualize this book series as a way of meeting the needs of these scholars and thereby also encouraging the development of the sociological understanding of gender by offering a "gender lens."

What do we mean by a *gender lens*? We mean working to make gender visible in social phenomena, asking if, how, and why social processes, standards, and opportunities differ systematically in women and men. We also mean recognizing that gender inequality is inextricably intertwined with other systems of inequality. Looking at the world through a gendered lens thus implies two seemingly contradictory tasks. First, it means unpacking the assumptions about gender that pervade sociological research and social life in general. At the same time, looking through a gender lens means revealing how central assumptions about gender continue to be the organization of the social world, regardless of their empirical reality. We show how our often unquestioned ideas about gender affect the words we use, the questions we ask, the answers we envision. The Gender Lens Series is committed to social change directed toward eradicating these inequalities. Our goals are consistent with initiatives at colleges and universities across the United States that are encouraging the development of more diverse scholarship and teaching.

The books in the Gender Lens Series are aimed at different audiences and have been written for a variety of uses, from assigned readings in introductory undergraduate courses to graduate seminars and as professional resources for our colleagues. The series includes several different styles of books that address these goals in distinct ways. We are excited about the series and anticipate that it will have an enduring impact on the direction of both the pedagogy and the scholarship in sociology and other related social sciences. We invite you, the reader, to join us in thinking through these difficult but exciting issues by offering feedback or by developing your own project and proposing it for use in the series.

About This Volume

Through works such as the *Everyday World as Problematic* (1987), *The Conceptual Practices of Power* (1990), and *Texts, Facts, and Femininity* (1990), Dorothy Smith has developed a powerful feminist theory of what she calls the "relations of ruling." In the current volume, Dorothy Smith brings her work together into this compelling articulation of the social organization of knowledge. Smith begins with the premise that women have been and continue to be excluded from the ruling apparatus of society, a society that is manufactured by those in dominant positions—positions of ruling. These ruling institutions create forms of thought that structure how those who are societal members view themselves and the worlds they live in. Smith thus develops a critique of knowledge as ideology and addresses the subtle ways that women's daily material situations provide a distinctive epistemological perspective on the everyday relations of ruling.

In the first section, Smith lays out what she means by "women's standpoint" and locates that standpoint in the historical trajectory of the relations of ruling. Importantly, she also locates the place of sociology in enacting the relations of ruling and uses her own experiences as a practicing scholar—and practicing teacher, practicing mother, practicing wife—to illustrate the material realities of the everyday and their locations within the relations of ruling.

In the second section, Smith articulates a plan for designing a sociology that extends people's ordinary knowledges as practitioners of their everyday lives into realms of power and relations that go well beyond their everyday lives. This method is ethnographic but goes beyond most practices of ethnography. What she calls *institutional ethnography* builds knowledges of how the relations of ruling operate from the standpoints of the people participating in them and creates maps whereby people can see the workings of institutions and their own locations within them. She distinguishes institutional ethnography by emphasizing its practices of exploration and discovery; conventional ethnographies and other sociological methods are, according to Smith, profoundly constrained by a priori conceptual frameworks. Institutional ethnography, in contrast, resists the dominance of theory; it is an alternative sociology, not just a method of inquiry. Language is central to this model. Smith emphasizes language as the medium in which thoughts and ideas move reciprocally between individual people and the realm of the social. The forms of coordination that constitute institutions occur in and through language.

This then takes the reader to the third section of the volume, in which Smith illustrates institutional ethnography in action through analyses of texts. In a series of rich chapters, Smith articulates different institutional knowledges, text-mediated organizations, and how textual systems coordinate work and social relations and do the work of institutional power.

It has become a sociological truism that research aims for objectivity, a state in which the presence of the subject is suspended and knowledge is constituted as standing over against individual subjects and subjectivities, overriding idiosyncrasies of experience and perspective. Smith argues strongly against the claims of objectivity, using institutional ethnography as a method for realizing an alternative form of knowledge of the social, a form in which people's own knowledge of the world through their everyday practices is systematically extended to the social relations and institutional orders in which they act. Ultimately, what institutional ethnography seeks to achieve is to bring what is beyond individual experience into the realm of the everyday, into the scope of ordinary knowledge, so that people can integrate this beyond-the-everyday into their knowledge of and participation in the institutions in which they act. In the introduction to another Gender Lens volume, the editors write, "As sociologists, we believe that an accurate understanding of inequality is a prerequisite for effective social change." In the current volume, Dorothy Smith might reframe our words to say the following: For people to comprehend the institutions that create and enact inequalities, they must understand the fabric of their own everyday lives. Neither individual nor progressive social change can occur without this understanding.

Judith A. Howard
Barbara Risman
Joey Sprague

ACKNOWLEDGMENTS

Writing acknowledgments is difficult. I have so many to thank. I am afraid I might omit a name of one of those who has been important to me. While, as an old woman, I am forgiven if I do not always remember a name on the street, at a conference, or the like, the same tolerance is not extended to the printed page.

I have decided therefore not to acknowledge by name each and all of those who have worked with me as graduate students and who have contributed so much to what I now know how to do—however imperfectly that may be explicated in this book. The work of many of you has been referred to in what follows, though not all. If you do not find your work identified here, the reason is that I had to be selective in using people's research with regard to their illustrating particular points. I treasure the work of all those whose dissertations I supervised; I treasure the experience of working with you; and I treasure what I learned and continue to learn from your research then and what you are doing now.

In the making of this book I have many to thank, notably, the editors of the Gender Lens Series in which it appears. It is indeed an extraordinary and wonderful thing that there should be such a series, and I am honored to be included in it. Judith Howard, Barbara Risman, and Joey Sprague read drafts of the book in its early stages and gave valuable guidance. Drafts were also read by institutional ethnographers: Marie Campbell provided a detailed commentary, as did Tim Diamond—I hope the final version has been responsive to the care and thought with which they scrutinized the original topographically impossible early version. Tim also proposed and sketched the glossary. Susan Turner went through my original chapter 1 with fine stylistic attention that improved it immeasurably, and she later read the whole thing, making valuable comments and corrections. Liza McCoy helped me to get the passages describing her work more or less right (she is not responsible, of course, for my errors). Stephan Dobson has been with me all along, reading chapters here and there and bearing with reading and rereading those chapters that I simply could not get to work—one chapter had at least four substantial rewritings, each of which he treated with the same degree of thought and attention to detail that mark his editorial work in general. He read the whole in its final draft state, trapping muddles, repetitions, impossibilities, and stylistic horrors. It is also his excellent editorial skills that have produced the logically ordered index that I for one appreciate (I hate books without indexes, but Dobson's work in this respect is particularly fine). I learned of the identities of two of the official reviewers of the penultimate version of the book. They were Peter Grahame and Virginia Olesen, and both of them wrote comments that were invaluable. Again, I hope that this final version keeps faith with the work and thought all of these contributors have put in.

This book spells out what I have learned from working through an attempt to make a sociology from what I experienced as, and have argued over the years is, the deep opposition between the mainstream sociology I had learned as a graduate student at the University of California at Berkeley and what I had discovered in the women's movement.

Though the women's movement and its political practice of consciousness raising were foundational to what I—and others working with me—have developed as an alternative sociology, a sociology cannot be confined to a particular category of people. If it is a sociology that explores the social from women's standpoint and aims to be able to spell out for women just how the everyday world of our experience is put together by relations that extend vastly beyond the everyday, then it has to work for both women and men. It has to be a sociology *for* people, as contrasted with the sociology in which I was so properly educated, the sociology in which people were the objects, they whose behavior was to be explained. This book explicates institutional ethnography as a sociology that translates that concept into a method of inquiry.[1]

To write a sociology from people's standpoint as contrasted with a standpoint in a theory-governed discourse does not mean writing a popular sociology. Though it starts from where we are in our everyday lives, it explores social relations and organization in which our everyday doings participate but which are not fully visible to us. The work of discovery sometimes calls for research that is technical and conceptually outside the everyday language of experience; at the same time, it has been our experience that once the institutional ethnography is completed, it becomes a resource that can be translated into people's everyday work knowledge. Hence it becomes a means of expanding people's own knowledge rather than substituting the expert's knowledge for our own.

1

I emphasize, however, that institutional ethnography, as it is written here, is a *sociology*, not just a methodology (it tends to get assigned to qualitative methods textbooks and courses). It is not just a way of implementing sociological strategies of inquiry that begin in theory, rather than in people's experience, and examine the world of people under theory's auspices. I have described it as a "method of inquiry," and I know how that's a bit misleading. But I describe it as such because the emphasis is always on research as *discovery* rather than, say, the testing of hypotheses or the explication of theory as analysis of the empirical.

It is difficult to express in a sentence or two just how radical a departure institutional ethnography is from mainstream sociology. It has kin, notably in Marx—though not in the subsequent theoretical developments of Marxism—but also to some degree in ethnomethodology. What institutional ethnography shares with these is a commitment to begin and develop inquiry in the very same world we live in, where we are in our bodies. And because it makes language a key to the ethnographic discovery of how institutions are coordinated, it draws on the tradition of symbolic interaction originating in the work of George Herbert Mead, linking it with Russian traditions of thought on language, notably that of Mikhail Bakhtin, A. R. Luria, and Valentin Vološinov.

Once trained in sociology, as I was, one cannot easily shift into a different paradigm for making a knowledge of the social that is not reified and does not posit the social as existing over and above people. Institutional ethnography aims at a knowledge that is essentially an extension of the ordinary ways in which we know our everyday worlds into regions we have not been to, and perhaps could not go to, without the explorer's interests and cartographic skills. Understand, then, that parts of this book will not be easy reading, though some of the difficulties may be less a problem of the writer's style than of giving the reader entry to a different way of conceiving the social and imagining inquiry. What is involved is what has been called a *paradigm shift* (Kuhn 1970). It took me twenty-five years or so make it, and I'm asking you to make it in reading one book.[2]

Finding out how people are putting our world together daily in the local places of our everyday lives and yet somehow constructing a dynamic complex of relations that coordinates our doings translocally means that the project of inquiry is open-ended. It must be always subject to revision, as attention to actualities imposes corrections, takes us by surprise, forces rethinking, and works toward some better statement of what we have found. What I have written here is the product of the work of institutional ethnographic research and the discoveries that we have been making. It is open to being changed, expanded on, improved as research goes forward and as new regions of the relations that rule us are brought under ethnographic scrutiny.

The book is in four parts, with the fourth constituting a conclusion. The first part, Making a Sociology for People, describes the foundations of the project in the women's movement and differentiates it from other sociologies that have apparently similar political commitments. The second part, An Ontology of the Social, offers a much-needed ontology because the phenomena on which institutional ethnography focuses and on which it relies in writing descriptions, explications, and analyses happen in the actualities of people's lives. Actuality, however, does not itself tell the sociologist what is relevant to her or his project. Her or his inquiry needs a way of focusing her or his ethnographic attention. This is what writing an ontology is intended to provide. There are two chapters in this section: the first provides an ontology of the social in general, and the second assimilates the phenomena of language to the ontology proposed in the first. Introducing the idea of language as coordinator of people's subjectivities is essential if it is to be incorporated into explications of institutions as organizers of our everyday lives.

The third part of the book, Making Institutions Ethnographically Accessible, translates the ontology into a general framework for institutional ethnography as a practice. It addresses the textual bases of institutions and the characteristic workings of institutional discourse. A second chapter in this section takes up the problematic role of experience in the making of institutional ethnography, and the third examines just what aspects of people's experience are relevant to the project of mapping institutions. Then we proceed in the following two chapters, 8 and 9, to examine further the central importance of texts and how to recognize texts as entering into the organization of institutional forms of action.

Finally, there is a conclusion that maps the journey we have traveled in the book, suggests some possibilities of expanding exploration further into the extended relations of ruling, and, by recalling the political commitments with which this method of inquiry began, appraises how those commitments have been and may be realized in the collective project of institutional ethnographic research.

Notes

1. I recommend the briefer introductions to institutional ethnography by Peter Grahame (1998), Marie Campbell and Frances Gregor (2002), and myself (D. E. Smith 2001a).

2. George Smith and I used to call it the "ontological shift." I gave him a birthday T-shirt once with "I have made the ontological shift" printed on the front. He wore it to work.

Making a Sociology for People

CHAPTER 1

Women's Standpoint

Embodied Knowing versus the Ruling Relations

It's hard to recall just how radical the experience of the women's movement was at its inception for those of us who had lived and thought within the masculinist regime against which the movement struggled. For us, the struggle was as much within ourselves, with what we knew how to do and think and feel, as with that regime as an enemy outside us. Indeed we ourselves had participated however passively in that regime. There was no developed discourse in which the experiences that were spoken originally as everyday experience could be translated into a public language and become political in the ways distinctive to the women's movement. We learned in talking with other women about experiences that we had and about others that we had not had. We began to name "oppression," "rape," "harassment," "sexism," "violence," and others. These were terms that did more than name. They gave shared experiences a political presence.

Starting with our experiences as we talked and thought about them, we discovered depths of alienation and anger that were astonishing. Where had all these feelings been? How extraordinary were the transformations we experienced as we discovered with other women how to speak with one another about such experiences and then how to bring them forward publicly, which meant exposing them to men. Finally, how extraordinary were the transformations of ourselves in this process. Talking our experience was a means of discovery. What we did not know and did not know how to think about, we could examine as we found what we had in common. The approach that I have taken in developing an alternative sociology takes up women's standpoint in a way that is modeled

7

on these early adventures of the women's movement. It takes up women's standpoint not as a given and finalized form of knowledge but as a ground in experience from which discoveries are to be made.

It is this active and shared process of speaking from our experience, as well as acting and organizing to change how those experiences had been created, that has been translated in feminist thinking into the concept of a feminist standpoint—or, for me, women's standpoint. However the concept originated, Sandra Harding (1988) drew together the social scientific thinking by feminists, particularly Nancy Hartsock, Hilary Rose, and myself, that had as a common project taking up a standpoint in women's experience. Harding argued that feminist empiricists who claimed both a special privilege for women's knowledge and an objectivity were stuck in an irresolvable paradox. Those she described as "feminist standpoint theorists" moved the feminist critique a step beyond feminist empiricism by claiming that knowledge of society must always be from a position in it and that women are privileged epistemologically by being members of an oppressed group. Like the slave in Hegel's parable of the master–slave relationship, they can see more, further, and better than the master precisely because of their marginalized and oppressed condition. She was, however, critical of the way in which experience in the women's movement had come to hold authority as a ground for speaking, and claiming to speak truly, that challenged the rational and objectified forms of knowledge and their secret masculine subject (123). Furthermore, feminist standpoint theory, according to Harding, implicitly reproduced the universalized subject and claims to objective truth of traditional philosophical discourse, an implicit return to the empiricism we claimed to have gone beyond.

The notion of women's standpoint—or indeed the notion that women's experience has special authority—has also been challenged by feminist theorists. It fails to take into account diversities of class and race as well as the various forms and modulations of gender. White middle-class heterosexual women dominated the early phases of the women's movement in the 1960s and 1970s, but soon our, and I speak as one, assumptions about what would hold for women in general were challenged and undermined, first by working-class women and lesbians, then by African–North American, Hispanic, and Native women. The implicit presence of class, sexuality, and colonialism began to be exposed. Our assumptions were also challenged by women in other societies whose experience wasn't North American, by women such as those with disabilities and older women whose experience was not adequately represented and, as the women's movement evolved over time, by younger women who have found the issues of older feminists either alien or irrelevant. The theoretical challenge to the notion of women's standpoint has been made in terms of its alleged essentialism. It has been seen as essentialist because it excludes other bases of oppression and inequity that intersect with the category "women." The critique of essentialism, however, assumes the use of the category "women" or "woman" to identify shared and defining attributes. While essentialism has been a problem in the theorizing of *woman*, it cannot be extended to all uses of such categories. In practice in the women's movement, the category has worked politically rather than referentially. As a political concept, it coordinates struggle against the masculinist forms of oppressing women that those forms themselves explicitly or implicitly universalize. Perhaps most important, it creates for women what had been missing, a subject position in the public sphere and, more generally, one in the political, intellectual, and cultural life of the society.

Claiming a subject position within the public sphere in the name of women was a central enterprise of the women's movement in its early days in the 1970s and 1980s. A powerful dynamic was created. While those making the claim first were white middle-class women, the new subject position in public discourse opened the way for others who had found themselves excluded by those who'd gone before. Their claims were positioned and centered differently, and their own experience became authoritative. It is indeed one of the extraordinary characteristics of the women's movement that its continual disruption, its internal struggles against racism and white cultural dominance, its internal quarrels and angers, have been far from destructive to the movement. On the contrary, these struggles in North America and Europe have expanded and diversified the movement as women other than those with whom it originated gave their own experiences voice.

Women's Standpoint and the Ruling Relations

Standpoint is a term lifted out of the vernacular, largely through Harding's innovative thinking and her critique (1988), and it is used for doing new discursive work. Harding identifies standpoint in terms of the social positioning of the subject of knowledge, the knower and creator of knowledge. Her own subsequent work develops an epistemology that relies on a diversity of subject positions in the sociopolitical-economic regimes of colonialism and imperialism. The version of standpoint that I have worked with, after I had adopted the term from Harding (previously I'd written of "perspective"; D. E. Smith 1974a), is rather different. It differs also from the concept of a feminist standpoint that has been put forward by Nancy Hartsock (1998) in that it does not identify a socially determined position or category of position in society (or political economy).[1] Rather, my notion of women's (rather than feminist) standpoint is integral to the design of what I originally called "a sociology for women," which has necessarily been transformed into "a sociology for people." It does not identify a position or a category of position, gender, class, or race within the society, but it does establish as a subject position for institutional ethnography as a method of inquiry, a site for the knower that is open to anyone.

As a method of inquiry, institutional ethnography is designed to create an alternative to the objectified subject of knowledge of established social scientific discourse. The latter conforms to and is integrated with what I have come to call the "ruling relations"—that extraordinary yet ordinary complex of relations that are textually mediated, that connect us across space and time and organize our everyday lives—the corporations, government bureaucracies, academic and professional discourses, mass media, and the complex of relations that interconnect them. At the inception of this early stage of late-twentieth-century women's movement, women were excluded from appearing as agents or subjects within the ruling relations. However we might have been at work in them, we were subordinates. We were women whose work as mothers reproduced the same gendered organization that subordinated us; we were the support staff, store clerks, nurses, social workers doing casework and not administration, and so on. In the university itself, we were few and mostly marginal (two distinguished women in the department where I first worked in Canada had never had more than annual lectureships).

"Standpoint" as the design of a subject position in institutional ethnography creates a point of entry into discovering the social that does not subordinate the knowing subject to objectified forms of knowledge of society or political economy. It is a method of inquiry that works from the actualities of people's everyday lives and experience to discover the social as it extends beyond experience. A standpoint in people's everyday lives is integral to that method. It is integral to a sociology creating a subject position within its discourse, which anyone can occupy. The institutional ethnographer works from the social in people's experience to discover its presence and organization in their lives and to explicate or map that organization beyond the local of the everyday.

Examining Sociology from a Woman's Standpoint

The project of developing a sociology that does not objectify originated, as did so much in the women's movement, in exploring experiences in my life as a woman. That exploration put into question the fundamentals of the sociology I had learned at length and sometimes painfully as an undergraduate and graduate school student. I was, in those early times, a sociologist teaching at the University of British Columbia, on the west coast of Canada, and a single parent with two small boys. My experience was of contradictory modes of working existence: on the one hand was the work of the home and of being a mother; on the other, the work of the academy, preparing for classes, teaching, faculty meetings, writing papers, and so on. I could not see my work at home in relation to the sociology I taught, in part, of course, because that sociology had almost nothing to say about it.

I learned from the women's movement to begin in my own experience and to start there in finding the voice that asserted the buried woman. I started to explore what it might mean to think sociologically from the place where I was in-body, living with my children in my home and with those cares and consciousness that are integral to that work. Here were the particularities of my relationships with my children, my neighbors, my friends, their friends, our rabbit (surprisingly fierce and destructive—my copy of George Herbert Mead's *Mind, Self, and Society* bears scars inflicted by our long-eared pet's teeth and claws), our two dogs, and an occasional hamster. In this mode, I was attentive to the varieties of demands that housekeeping, cooking, child care, and the multiple minor tasks of our local settings made on me. When I went to work in the university, I did not, of course, step out of my body, but the focus of my work was not on the local particularities of relationships and setting but on sociological discourse read and taught or on the administrative work of a university department. Body, of course, was there as it had to be to get the work done, but the work was not organized by and in relation to it.

The two subjectivities, home and university, could not be blended. They ran on separate tracks with distinct phenomenal organization. Memory, attention, reasoning, and response were organized quite differently.

Remembering a dental appointment for one of the children wasn't part of my academic consciousness, and if I wasn't careful to find some way of reminding myself that didn't depend on memory, I might have well forgot it. My experiences uncovered radical differences between home and academy in how they were situated, and how they situated me, in the society. Home was organized around the particularities of my children's bodies, faces, movements, the sounds of their voices, the smell of their hair, the arguments, the play, the evening rituals of reading, the stress of getting them off to school in the morning, cooking and serving meals, and the multitudes of the everyday that cannot be enumerated, an intense, preoccupying world of work that also cannot really be defined. My work at the university was quite differently articulated; the sociology I thought and taught was embedded in the texts that linked me into a discourse extending indefinitely into only very partially known networks of others, some just names of the dead; some the heroes and masters of the contemporary discipline; some just names on books or articles; and others known as teachers, colleagues, and contemporaries in graduate school. The administrative work done by faculty tied into the administration of the university, known at that time only vaguely as powers such as dean or president or as offices such as the registrar, all of whom regulated the work we did with students. My first act on arriving in the department office, after greeting the secretaries, was to open my mail and thus to enter a world of action in texts.

I knew a practice of subjectivity in the university that excluded the local and bodily from its field. Learning from the women's movement to start from where I was as a woman, I began to attend to the university and my work there from the standpoint of "home" subjectivity. I started to notice what I had not seen before. How odd, as I am walking down the central mall of that university that opens up to the dark blue of the humped islands and the further snowy mountains to the north, to see on my left a large hole where before there had been a building! In the mode of the everyday you can find the connections, though you may not always understand them. In a house with children and dogs and rabbits, the connection between the destruction of the spine of my copy of *Mind, Self, and Society* and that rabbit hanging around in my workspace was obvious. But the hole where once there'd been a building couldn't be connected to any obvious agent. The peculiar consciousness I practiced in the university began to emerge for me as a puzzlingly strange form of organization. If I traced the provenance of that hole, I'd be climbing up into an order of relations linking administrative process with whatever construction company was actually responsible for the making of the hole; I'd be climbing into a web of budgets, administrative decisions, provincial and federal government funding, and so on and so on. I'd be climbing into that order of relations that institutional ethnographers call the "ruling relations." These could be seen as relations that divorced the subject from the particularized settings and relationships of her life and work as mother and housewife. They created subject positions that elevated consciousness into a universalized mode, whether of the social relations mediated by money or of those organized as objectivity in academic or professional discourse. Practicing embodiment on the terrain of the disembodied of those relations brought them into view. I became aware of them as I became aware of their presence and power in the everyday, and, going beyond that hole in the ground, I also began to think of the sociology I practiced in the everyday working world of the university as an organization of discursive relations fully integrated with them.

The Historical Trajectory of Gender and the Ruling Relations

My experience when I examined it as a woman, an act in and of the women's movement of that time, brought into view an order of social relations that enter into and may be observed in the everyday world of our experience but cannot be fully explored there. The objectified relations of ruling coordinate multiple local everyday worlds trans- or extralocally. The organization that was the matrix both of my experiences and my reflections on them itself arose in a historical trajectory of gender and the ruling relations.

The concept of ruling relations (D. E. Smith 1987, 1999c) doesn't refer to modes of domination but to a new and distinctive mode of organizing society that comes into prominence during the latter part of the nineteenth century in Europe and North America. The ruling relations are forms of consciousness and organization that are objectified in the sense that they are constituted externally to particular people and places.

The transformations that were accelerating rapidly at the turn of the nineteenth and twentieth centuries began earlier, with the invention of movable type and of the possibilities of widespread access to words from beyond those spoken locally. The availability of the Bible as a text printed in the vernacular and hence readable by people without the mediation of priests transformed not just the substance but the organization of Christianity in Europe. Government pronouncements could be replicated and distributed widely in the same form; news media emerged; opinion was vested in print; the novel emerged as a distinctive genre of storytelling (McKeon 1987); political and social thought took on the generalized form of ideology. Complementing and transforming the rapid development of capitalism as a mode of production were forms of consciousness and agency that were no longer identified with individuals. Marx, writing in the first two-thirds of the nineteenth century, theorized capital in terms of individual ownership. His conceptions of "consciousness" were also identified with individuals and what goes on in our heads (1973). By contrast, the ruling relations objectify consciousness: these new forms of social relations had not developed in Marx's time; hence, he did not incorporate into his thinking forms of social consciousness that were (a) differentiated and specialized as specific social relations and (b) objectified in the sense of being produced as independent of particular individuals and particularized relations.

Leonore Davidoff and Catherine Hall (1987) have described how, during the seventeenth and eighteenth centuries in England, the domestic sphere of the middle classes became increasingly isolated from the more and more exclusively male worlds of business, politics, and science. While women remained at work in the particularities of domesticity, men of the middle classes were active in businesses that connected them to the impersonal, extralocal dynamic of the market; they were also active in the public discourse that emerged in talk with other men in the clubs and coffee houses of Britain and Europe and in the saloons and places of public assembly in North America where the topics of journals, newspapers, and books were discussed (Habermas 1992; Ryan 1993), A radical division between the spheres of action and of consciousness of middle-class men and women emerged. The peculiar out-of-body modes of consciousness of the nascent ruling relations required a specialization of subject and agency. The formation of the middle-class male subject in education and ideology aimed at creating that extraordinary form of modern consciousness that is capable of agency in modes that displace or subdue a local bodily existence.[2]

According to Joan Landes (1996), women's exclusion from the emerging public discourse, associated with the Enlightenment and with the rise of capitalism as a general economic form of life, was essential to men's capacity to sustain what she calls "the masquerade of universality." The public sphere was defined by a gender order that excluded women. During the French Revolution and later, women's attempts to organize in public "risked violating the constitutive principles of the bourgeois public sphere. . . . [They] risked disrupting the gendered organization of nature, truth, and opinion that assigned them to a place in the private, domestic but not the public realm" (87–88). Men confronting men did not raise the specter of particularity whereas women bore particularity as their social being. Hence men associating exclusively with men could avoid recognizing "the masquerade through which the (male) particular was able to posture behind the veil of the universal" (Landes 1996, 98).

From the mid-nineteenth century and accelerating rapidly into the early twentieth century, the new forms of social organization enabled by print and other technologies for reproducing words and images expanded rapidly (Beniger 1986; Yates 1989). Developments in the bureaucratization of the state, familiar in sociological literature from the writings of Max Weber (1978),³ were accompanied by radical innovations in the management of business enterprises (Beniger 1986; Waring 1991; Yates 1989). The direct connection between individual owner and the capitalist enterprise largely taken for granted by Marx is progressively displaced by the invention of corporate ownership and control (Chandler 1977; Noble 1977; Roy 1997), which not only separates ownership from control, creating management as a distinct function, but also leads to the creation of what Alfred Sloan (1964) of General Motors called "objective" as contrasted with "subjective" organization. Objective organization relied on procedures for rendering the performance of the different divisions systematically accountable in terms of a financial accounting system oriented to the quarterly reporting periods of the stock exchange. The knowledge on which decisions were made were no longer in the individual manager's or owner's head; decisions were made on grounds warranted by the data rather than on the basis of guesswork and forms of reporting that had no objective basis in calculations. Relationships were no longer as they had been, for example, in the DuPont Company, where in the latter part of the nineteenth century the sons and sons-in-law of the patriarch lived in one house, ran the various plants, and wrote daily letters to the patriarch reporting on the day's doings (Yates 1989). The importance of the personal trust that familial relationships supplied, along with creating a community of interest in the family business, was displaced by regimes of written rules and administrative practices, combined with systems of data collection, enabling managers' performance to be evaluated objectively.

The trajectory of the ruling relations since the late nineteenth century, at least in North America, has been one that progressively expropriates locally developed forms of social organization embedded in particularized relationships, changing relations among women and men as well as among men. In his major study of the emergence of what he calls "the visible hand," Chandler (1977) directs attention to the progressive incorporation of the local organization of economic functions and their coordination through networks of market relations into the large-scale corporation. The unregulated processes of the market became integrated into the administration of the corporation. Problems of financing and credit that dogged systems of exchange based on sequences of transactions among small local businesses came to be regulated under the administrative umbrella of a corporation's managerial and accounting systems. Uncertainties in sources of supplies were resolved by vertical integration with manufacturing. For example, General Motors (Sloan 1964) first expanded in a process of vertical integration of independent craft firms that were suppliers of parts, in an attempt to secure a coordination of supplies with expanding production; a second kind of acquisition was of firms making automobiles occupying different market segments from General Motors but potentially in competition with it. Similarly, the expansion of mail-order retailing and department stores appropriated and displaced the local organization of jobbers, incorporating their functions into a single administrative system (Beniger 1986; Chandler 1977; Mills 1951, 25–26).

Complementing Chandler's account is Thorstein Veblen's (1954) earlier observation of the transformation of the country town with the expansion of what he calls "Big Business." He describes the country town as a "retail trading-station" in which townsmen competed to buy the product of farms or to sell to farmers the means of production (144). The coming of Big Business transformed this. Smaller retail and wholesale businesses became subordinated to the new, large-scale forms of organizing business:

> Increased facilities of transport and communication; increased size and combination of the business concerns engaged in the wholesale trade, as packers, jobbers, warehouse-concerns handling farm products; increased resort to package-goods, brands, and trade-marks, advertised on a liberal plan which runs over the heads of the retailers; increased employment of chain-store methods and agencies; increased depen-

dence of local bankers on the greater credit establishments of the financial centers. (154)

"The country town," Veblen writes, "is no longer what it once was," a local habitation in which a man might "bear his share in the control of affairs without being accountable to any master-concern 'higher up' in the hierarchy of business" (155; see also, Mills 1951).

The progressive appropriation of organization and control, the objectification of consciousness in Marx's sense of the term, is also an expropriation of the kinds of organization that developed among people as individuals. The changed organization of ownership and control of capital emerged in and may indeed have been promoted by changes of the same kind in other institutional areas. The governance of cities began to be transformed from forms of patronage to bureaucratic administrations. Public schooling came to be organized through the administrative apparatus of school districts and a professional educational staff of college- or university-trained teachers. Generally speaking, professions came into new prominence as a method of guaranteeing training, credentials, and standards of practice in the dispersed settings of professional practice (Collins 1979; Larson 1977; Noble 1977), a development of special importance in the geography of North America.[4]

An important dimension of the ruling relations is that identified by Michel Foucault (1970) in his conception of discourse. He used the term to pry thinking away from that of the traditional history of ideas that interpreted works in terms of the intentional thought of their authors. The concept of discourse located systems of knowledge and knowledge making independent of particular individuals. Rather than trace continuities and influences, he directed inquiry to discursive events—that is, spoken or written effective statements that happen and have happened (1972, 28)—and to the distinctive forms of power that discourse represents. He ascribed to discourse an order prior to any given moment of the making of a statement. The speaker's or writer's intention is never purely expressed. What can be said or written is subject to the regulation of the discourse within which it is framed.

Foucault's conception of discourse displaces the traditional basis of knowledge in individual perception and locates it externally to particular subjectivities as an order that imposes on and coerces them. In his account of the order of discourse (1972), he describes it as regulating how people's subjectivities are coordinated, what can be uttered, what must be excluded, what is simply not made present. What can be spoken or written and heard and understood by others is discursively determined (a term not to be misread as "caused"). As women learned in the women's movement, there are experiences that a discourse will not speak.

The development of new textual technologies radically expanded the sphere of public discourse: to the existing newspaper industry, radio was added and then television. These transformed public discourse profoundly. What we had ordinarily called "culture" was objectified: A massive cultural industry emerged. Instead of people making their own stories and songs, drawing or carving their own pictures, and acting their own dramas; instead of people passing on news from mouth to ear and waiting to hear about distant places from travelers, we watch television news, dramas, games, talk shows, and so on, which no one individual created and the sources of which are many.

In general, instead of being ruled directly by individuals whom we've known (and perhaps hated) for years and who were known before us by our parents, we are ruled by people who are at work in corporations, government, professional settings and organizations, universities, public schools, hospitals and clinics, and so on and so on. Though they are, of course, individuals, their capacities to act derive from the organizations and social relations that they both produce and are produced by. The relations and organization in which they are active are also those that organize our lives and in which we in various ways participate. Watching television, reading the newspaper, going to the grocery store, taking a child to school, taking on a mortgage for a home, walking down a city street, switching on a light, plugging in a computer—these daily acts articulate us into social relations of the order I have called *ruling* as well as those of the economy; what we pick up when we're out shopping will likely have been produced by people living far away from us whom we'll never know. And so on. These transactions aren't with people we know as particular individuals, such as family members or neighbors. It doesn't matter whether the taxman or the supermarket clerk is someone we have a personal relationship with; it's their job that is the basis on which we interact with them. It doesn't matter that we'll never know—except as screen images—the people who tell us news stories on CNN or CBC.[5] The functions of "knowledge, judgment, and will" have become built into a specialized complex of objectified forms of organization and consciousness that organize and coordinate people's everyday lives.

The progress of the ruling relations toward their present comprehensive extension into almost all aspects of our everyday lives created contradictions in women's situations, particularly for middle-class women. On the one hand, the gender divide that emerged among the white middle classes widened and deepened as the powers, technologies, and scope of the extralocal organization of the relations of the economy, the state, and public discourse increased from the late nineteenth century on. The domestic sphere of the middle classes became increasingly ancillary to the translocal organization of power, knowledge, and opportunity in which men were at work as subjects and agents, a period culminating in the gender relationships described in William H. Whyte's study (1956) of "organization man." This was the gender order of which Betty Friedan wrote her celebrated critique of suburban women's way of life (1963).

During the nineteenth century and into the twentieth, print and the consequent replication of texts provided the technological foundation of a reading public in which women participated both as writers and as readers. Though women were largely excluded from the public sphere as it has been specified by Habermas (1992), the consciousness of middle-class women was being transformed by the emergence of novels written by women and featuring women as the leading characters. New forms of subjectivity were made possible by the same basic technologies that expanded the arenas and powers in which men of the white middle classes were absorbed. Expanding railroads in North America expedited the distributions of news, literature, traveling speakers, and less formal kinds of news, creating new bases of organization among women. African American women, for example, in the late nineteenth century used the news media circulating in African American communities to mobilize opposition to lynching beyond the local communities in which it was used to enforce white dominance. In general, women's movements of the late nineteenth century were based on the reading circles, on pamphlets and other resources enabling organization that did not rely exclusively on networks of geographically localized connection. They were supplemented, as in the Women's Christian Temperance Movement, by traveling organizers and speakers.

Women, particularly middle-class women, were deeply engaged in the emerging educational system at all levels. They were successful in gaining at first marginal access to universities; they were active in establishing child development as a university offering; they were involved in the creation of a mothering discourse that mobilized the efforts and thought of middle-class women in North America across racial and ethnic boundaries to secure for their children the advantages of the public educational system (Dehli 1988; Griffith 1984; Griffith 1986; Griffith and D. E. Smith 1987; Griffith and D. E. Smith 2004; Rothman 1978; D. E. Smith 1997). A new form of middle-class family emerged in which the earnings of the husband/father enabled the wife/mother to specialize not just in housewifery (nothing new there) but in socializing the couple's children based on knowledge produced by experts and in supporting their children through the schooling process to secure for them the class status of their parents. And, after the Second World War, in the period of economic growth known sometimes as Fordism, working-class families too could begin to work with and through the public educational system to enable their children to move into higher education with the possibility of professional and managerial occupations. Though in the earlier period, middle-class white women's participation in higher education tended to focus in the fields traditionally associated with the domestic, they became, particularly after the Second World War, concentrated in the liberal arts. However, at all class levels and among whatever racial differences, women remained marginal within the ruling relations, playing the subordinate roles, lacking agency, producing their work for men's appropriation.

Locating Women's Standpoint in the Trajectory

In my life and in the lives of many women from those early years of the women's movement during the 1960s through the 1980s, the differentiated social relations and modes of subjectivity of the domestic sphere and those of the world of intellect, business, and politics coexisted. The gendered division laid down over the previous three or more centuries was being eroded through the very print-based media that had been the foundation of the ruling relations. The work of housewifery and the working consciousness of housewives must have been among the conditions that enabled men to avoid the distractions of thinking about the pragmatics of the working world so far as their personal needs were concerned. Indeed, Alfred Schutz (1962b) identifies as a necessary corollary of participation in that domain the exclusion from consciousness of the personal and pragmatics of the everyday world. These are precisely those encumberments of consciousness from which women could not divest themselves or from which they might divest themselves only by becoming unwomanly or going mad. Correlatively, the function of housewifery on which masculine freedom depended in order to engage in the extralocal relations of capitalism, the public sphere, and eventually the ruling relations required a consciousness continually attentive to the multiple, minute-by-minute demands that bring an orderly household into daily being. It is a mode of consciousness that is itself at odds with that of the domain of scientific theorizing as Schutz (1962b) has described it, and yet here, in my life and in the lives of other women like myself who were at work both in the home and in the academic world, these two modes of subjectivity and activity coexisted.

The women's movement made me aware of the disjuncture between my participation in the "masquerade of universality" (Landes 1996) of academic life and my everyday life with children and home as daily organization and reorganization of subjectivity. I became actively implicated in that masquerade when I went to the university as an undergraduate at the age of twenty-six. I thought I had entered a realm of mind in which I was no longer limited by my sex—fool that I was. It is hard to describe how deep the alienation of intellect and imagination had gone in me. I became aware of it only in what was at first the work of finding out how to resituate my self as an intellectual subject in my alienated being as a woman at home with her children. I discovered that I did not cease to be present and active in the everyday world when I went to work. Alfred Schutz's domain of the theoretical consciousness, stripped of local and biographical particularities, was also anchored in the specific locally created conditions (libraries, offices, and such) designed to insulate the subject's consciousness from particularity, enabling consciousness to be swallowed up in the universalities that texts make possible—including, of course, computer texts. Discovering these necessary anchors entailed by my bodily existence, I began to reconstruct how I connected with the world of intellect, which meant also reconstructing those aspects of it in which I was active, namely, the sociology I had been trained in, had taught, and, very occasionally, had written.

Once started, the process of unraveling the intellectual nets that trapped me could not be stopped. At the time, I thought of it as like being in labor. In childbirth, your body is taken over by a massive muscular activity, unwilled and uncontrollable; you can ride it, but you don't manage it. This deeply muscular period of transformation lasted, I think, for about three years. I worked with it by trying to be true to it and, beyond the period of major transformation, by continually engaging with the problem of how to tell the truth from where I was, whatever that meant, and how not to be afraid to do so. Above all, I had to avoid assenting to or re-creating the division between intellect and my being as a woman, a sexual and motherly being, anchored in her bodily being, in her everyday life and inside the society she meant to explore.

In taking up what I'm now calling "women's standpoint" in the local actualities of her everyday world, I learned that sociological discourse replicated the contours of the ruling relations that I was discovering. The issue wasn't sexism; it wasn't even the assumptions built into its theories or the lack of attention to women and women's issues and concerns. It was how its discursive practices created for knowers a universalized subject transcending the local actualities of people's lives. For the knower positioned as such, people become the *objects* of investigation and explanation (D. E. Smith 1987); we are not its subjects, its knowers.

Thus, the division I experienced in my working life was one that was replicated and reinforced in the sociology I practiced. I could not escape it; I could not find how to reassemble myself as a women without changing it. I had to find a sociological practice that could begin in the actualities of people's lives so that I could explore the social from there on, as it is brought into being in that same actuality.

My own experience was located at a distinctive moment in the historical trajectory of the expansion of the ruling relations and the changing technological bases of household organization, including the extensive labor of food preparation now provided, at least in Western industrialized societies, before purchase. The concept of women's standpoint that I work with has evolved from the conjuncture of the local and embodied work of mothering, immediate subsistence, and household care and the locally transcending work of participating in the extralocal relations of sociological discourse and the institutional regime of the university. I recognize the historical specificity of this intersection in the lives of women like myself. It locates a contradiction fundamental to our society between, on the one hand, forms of ruling (including discourse) mediated by texts and organized extra- or translocally in objectified modes of the ruling relations and, on the other, the traditional particularizations of both locale and relationships that still characterize family households.

It has been the exclusion of women as subjects from the objectified relations of discourse and ruling that situate my formulation of women's standpoint. We do not have to look for it in what women otherwise may or may not have in common. "I think, therefore I am" has been spoken by men; "I do sex, I give birth, I care for children, I clean house, I cook, therefore I am not" has been the unspoken of women since the emergence of these extraordinary new forms of ruling—at least until the women's movement began our work of eroding the barriers excluding us from agency within these forms of organization. What has been repugnant, dangerous to the purity of the world of enlightened intellect,[6] has been the presence of the mortal body that women's presence inserts, our breach of the divide that insulates mind's recognition that it has, dwells in, is not separable from, a body.

The concealed masculinity of the subject claiming the formal universality that is foundational to objectified forms of knowledge became visible in the women's movement somewhat indirectly. Perhaps it should have been obvious to us right off that when women claimed a subject position, it directly undermined the dichotomy of mind and discarded body on which universality depends. It wasn't just that subjects had bodies. Indeed phenomenology had been at work trying to ensure the cogency of a universal subject that was definitely embodied by bracketing embodiment. But women's claims to speak were not just as new members of the club; the starting point of the women's movement refused the separation of body and mind. Speaking from the experience of women, however diverse our experience and however refined and elaborated in feminist theory, was always and necessarily from sites of bodily being. Speaking from women's standpoint did not permit the constitutional separation between mind and body built into Western philosophy since Descartes and incorporated into sociology. Women's standpoint, as I've taken it up to remake sociology, does not permit that separation.

As feminist thinking has developed, theorists have moved toward developing a theorizing of the body that breaks with the Cartesian dichotomy, one reproduced in the everyday organization of my life. Here, for example, is Elizabeth Grosz (1995):

> For a number of years I have been involved in research on how to reconceive the body as socio-cultural artifact. I have been interested in trying to refine and transform traditional notions of corporeality so that the oppositions by which the body has usually been understood (mind and body, inside and outside, experience, and social context, subject and object, self and other—and underlying them, the opposition between male and female) can be problematized. Corporeality can be seen as the material condition of subjectivity, and the subordinated term in the opposition, can move to its rightful place in the very heart of the dominant term, mind. (103)

Grosz uses Derrida's analysis of the binary interdependence of two terms, one the dominant and the other its complement or supplement, often unrecognized but essential to the dominant. Her aim is to change the relation of these two so that the corporeal can be recognized as "in the very heart" of mind. Both Derrida's binary and Grosz's rearrangement of the two terms are, in my view, expressions of social relations underlying the text. The dominance of mind is more than conceptual; it is a local achievement of people who are active in the social relations that rule; these relations are also those of the gender regime that women of my generation inherited. The very notion of turning toward the body as a philosopher's move is one that relies on a deep and foundational division that people are bringing into being daily in their local practices.

The strategy of beginning from women's standpoint in the local actualities of the everyday/everynight world does not bridge this division. It collapses it. The embodied knower begins in her experience. Here she is an expert. I mean by this simply that when it comes to knowing her way around in it, how things get done, where the bus stop for the B-line bus is, at which supermarket she can pick up both organic vegetables and lactate-reduced milk, and all the unspecifiables of her daily doings and the local conditions on which she relies—when it comes to knowing these matters, she is an expert. It is another matter altogether when it comes to the forms of organization that authenticate the organic status of the vegetables; that brings the supermarket or the bus company into daily existence; or that constitute the responsibility of the municipal government for the state of the streets, the sidewalks, the standards of waste disposal, and so on. And going deeper into the complex of relations into which these locally visible and effective forms are tied are the social relations of the economy.

Such are the ordinary realities of our contemporary world in North America. There are people at work elsewhere whom we don't know and will never know whose doings are coordinated with ours, whether it's when we go to the corner store to pick up a laundry detergent after hours, or when we turn on the television to listen to the latest news on the catastrophic present, or when we pick up a book about the cumulation of sociological theory to connect with the work of others done at who knows what times and places. Social relations coordinating across time and distance are present but largely unseen within the everyday/everynight worlds of people's experience. A sociology from women's standpoint makes this reality a problematic, a project of research and discovery.

The project of inquiry from women's standpoint begins in the local actualities of people's lives. In a sense it reverses the traditional relationship between mind and body wherein mind may examine, explore, and reflect on what is of the body. Body isn't something to be looked at or even theorized. It is rather the site of consciousness, mind, thought, subjectivity, and agency as particular people's local doings. By pulling mind back into body, phenomena of mind and discourse—ideology, beliefs, concepts, theory, ideas and so on—are recognized as themselves the doings of actual people situated in particular local sites at particular times. They are no longer treated as if they were essentially inside people's heads. They become observable insofar as they are produced in language as talk and/or text. Discourse itself is among people's doings; it is of the actualities of people's lives; it organizes relations among people; and while it speaks of and from and in people's activities, it does not exhaust them.

Notes

1. Hartsock's concern is to reframe historical materialism so that women's experience and interests are fully integrated. Of particular importance to her is the adequate recognition of the forms of power that the women's movement has named "patriarchal." Women's marginal position, structured as it is around the work associated with reproduction and the direct production of subsistence, locates women distinctively in the mode of production in general. For her, taking a feminist standpoint introduces a dimension into historical materialism neglected by Marx and his successors. She designs a feminist standpoint that has a specifically political import. It might, I suppose, be criticized as essentialist, but, if we consider not just North America and not just white middle-class professional North America, it's hard to deny that Hartsock is characterizing a reality for women worldwide. In Canada a recent census report shows that while women's participation in the paid labor force has increased substantially over the past thirty years, "women remain more than twice as likely as men to do at least 30 hours a week of cooking and cleaning" (Andersen 2003, A7) and are more involved in child care than men, particularly care of younger children.

2. Rousseau's *Emile* (1966) designs an educational regime aimed at creating the autonomous male subject of civil society. His complement is a woman equally highly trained but not for autonomy; it's her role to sop up the bodily needs that are residual to the masculine project; she is never to appear for herself or as herself in the zone of civil society that is Emile's preserve.

3. Indeed Weber is one of the few sociologists who theorized organization to recognize the significance of texts and documents in bureaucracy.

4. Harold Perkin's study (1989) of the history of "professional society" in England from 1880 to the present is, I think, locating a parallel phenomenon to the emergence of what I am calling the "ruling relations" in the North American context. His study, however, adopts social class as its major framework, focusing largely on the emergence of a professional class, and it does not therefore focus on those aspects of the ruling relations that locate the objectification of organization and consciousness.

5. CBC stands for the Canadian Broadcasting Corporation, a national government-funded broadcaster of radio and television.

6. I am referring here to Mary Douglas's remarkable study, *Purity and Danger* (1966).

CHAPTER 2

Knowing the Social

An Alternative Design

Knowledge is socially organized (D. E. Smith 1990a); its characteristic textual forms bear and replicate social relations. The forms of knowledge we take for granted in social science have been created to simulate those of the natural sciences, external to our local actualities, standing over against us in a relation of dominance and authority. Lorraine Code (1995) is describing this social organization when she writes of

> a persistent professional and everyday conviction that knowledge is just knowledge; it does not matter whose it is, who has made it, who knows it. The facts, if factual they really are, will prevail. A long tradition of distinguishing between knowledge and "mere opinion" rests, in part, upon granting knowledge a status—and hence a generality, a universal scope—that enable it to transcend the specific experiences of particular knowers. (13)

Of course, the philosopher does not describe knowledge as social organized, but social organization is implicit in Code's account as she spells out the distinctive social grammar of the objectified representations that transcend knowers' experience. Later, in chapters 6 and 9, such objectified representations are examined as being the textual realities that are essential to the existence of institutions and of the ruling relations in general.[1] Here it is important only to note that how people become caught up in, and how our lives become organized by, the institutional foci of the ruling relations is mediated by institutionally designed realities that organize relations in the way in which Code describes. Representation in the mode of the ruling relations is objectified. The subject position assigned to reader, watcher, or listener by what is constituted as the real within the text is not articulated to his or her local actualities. Wherever watcher, listener, or reader is in her or his body, she or he is positioned as subject by the representations constructed in the text—written, printed, on screen or monitor. She or he is outside the events, the sites, the people, the stories, the things that are represented. The world in the texts of the ruling relations isn't seen from a standpoint in the everyday world that is part of the same world as the reader's. The textual real displaces even her or his own experience of an event of which she or he has been part.

Reorganizing the Social Relations of Objectivity

In the aforementioned passage cited from Code (1995), she describes objectification's power to displace what individuals know, believe, and experience as individuals. Code, of course, is criticizing positivism. But the forms of representation designed and practiced by sociology do not have to adhere formally to positivism to succeed in the same order of objectification. Most striking to me in the early days of my struggles with sociology was how inquiry from within the discourse committed the researcher or thinker to constructing people as the objects of her investigations or representation. Working as an activist, I and the feminist sociologists with whom I worked at the time wanted to make our skills as sociologists useful and relevant to women's organizations for change. In my role as supervisor of dissertation projects in my department, I'd find again and again that feminist students would want to take up topics that focused on, for example, the women's movement itself, adopting the discursive concept of "social movements" as a framework. Looking at the women's movement as a social movement transformed it into a sociological object. Imposing the social movement frame reconstructed as an object that of which we were part. We became conceptual outsiders. It seemed not possible to take up a topic sociologically without transforming people and people's doings into objects. It wasn't a matter of intention. Once the sociological frame was committed, inquiry and discovery *from within* the women's movement was precluded.

Sociology was not designed for exploring the institutional relations and organization from the standpoint of people, let alone of activists trying to bring about change. The discourse itself committed the working sociologist to the position of universal subject idealized in the notion of the

Archimedean point, the position outside the world from which it could be grasped objectively, such objectivity being sociology's holy grail. That the theory and research methods of mainstream sociology concealed positions of power became startlingly clear on an occasion when I'd set up a meeting of feminist sociologists with union women from the community with a view to finding out if there were ways we could work with and for them; they told us toward the end of our unsuccessful meeting that their experience of working with sociologists had been one of finding themselves becoming the objects of study. Sociology, I came to think, did not know how to do otherwise. Sociology seems to be stuck with this problem even when research is undertaken with a political intention that unites the researcher's interests with those of activists.[2]

The aim of the sociology we call "institutional ethnography" is to *reorganize the social relations of knowledge of the social* so that people can take that knowledge up as an extension of our ordinary knowledge of the local actualities of our lives. It is a method of inquiry into the social that proposes to enlarge the scope of what becomes visible from that site, mapping the relations that connect one local site to others. Like a map, it aims to be through and through indexical to the local sites of people's experience, making visible how we are connected into the extended social relations of ruling and economy and their intersections. And though some of the work of inquiry must be technical, as mapmaking is, its product should be ordinarily accessible and usable, just as a well-made map is, to those on the terrain it maps.

What Is Institutional Ethnography? Some Contrasts

To describe what it might be to work with institutional ethnography, I'm going to contrast it first with a study by Jean Anyon (1997) that proceeds according to a fairly conventional sociological procedure and then with Michael Burawoy and colleagues' extended case study method (Burawoy, Blum, et al. 2000; Burawoy, Burton, et al. 1991) that appears in some respects to be similar to institutional ethnography.

I emphasize that this is not a critique of Anyon's study of "ghetto schooling" (1997) in Newark, New Jersey. I want simply to use it to bring out what is distinctive of institutional ethnography by contrasting it with how she proceeds. Anyon participated in a staff development program at a K–8 school for approximately two years during a period of reform in the early 1990s, reforms that were subsequently abandoned, and thereafter for a year in other schools in the same district (xvii). Her study begins by providing background on the condition of urban schools and the reform movement that was influential during her fieldwork. She describes the level of poverty in the community served by the school in which she spent two years in the context of a general problem of poverty in urban, as contrasted with suburban, school districts. The school, the school classrooms, the children, teachers, and administrators, and their interactions are described.

A substantial part of the book is a historical study of education and educational reform in Newark and in the United States in general starting from 1860 and concluding with the most recent period of reforms ending in 1997. Anyon then returns to the school in which most of her participant observation was done to examine how the economic and political developments she had traced historically "contributed to the situation I encountered at Marcy School" (156). She summarizes the outcomes of the historical account in four major points:

1. "The social class and racial status of overall city and neighborhood population has been closely correlated with the level of the city's investment in education and with the district's success in educating its student population" (155).
2. "The contours and fortunes of Newark's schools in the twentieth century have also been intimately linked to the economic transformations of the city—and to federal and state policy as well as to local and national corporate decision making" (155–56).
3. "The political isolation of cities both before and after reapportionment in the [eighteen] sixties and seventies led to a century of tax and other financial policies that penalized cities—and therefore their schools" (156).
4. "In part because of the absence of sufficient economic resources (entry-level jobs, for example, and political representation in state and federal legislatures), for most of the last 100 years the city's schools have been enmeshed in local networks of corruption and patronage run by white ethnic—and more recently, African American—minorities" contributing to a staff less qualified than those in surrounding suburban districts (156).

The book goes on to discuss the various possibilities for change, politically and economically.

Anyon's strategy is typical for sociology. It interprets the everyday and local events in terms of a framework originating in sociological and political economic discourse. Its conceptual structure displaces people, displaces their activities, displaces the social relations and organization of their doings. Categories such as "sociocultural differences," "social class," and "racial status" become the subjects. The objectifications characteristic of its lexicon locate the reader externally to the everyday working lives of people, including the school administrators and teachers and the students and parents. Brief ethnographic glimpses are used as instances or expressions of pregiven categories. For example, a meeting involving two white volunteers who were retired executives and who came to the school to make their expertise available encountered a group over which the African American head of the Parent Corps presided. "The social gulf between the parents and reformers that to me seemed to impair communication and joint planning at this meeting was never breached" (Anyon 1997, 21). The signal failure of the meeting—together with other aspects of the school and community, such as the distinctive dialect of African Americans in that area—are used to illustrate the problems of sociocultural difference. The use of ethnographic observations or quotes from interviews with respondents as instances or expressions of the researcher's theoretical categories is a characteristic mode in which the potentially unruly (from the point of view of sociological discourse) actualities of people's everyday lives are selectively appropriated.

An institutional ethnography would proceed quite differently. It would begin in the actualities of the lives of some of those involved in the institutional process and focus on how those actualities were embedded in social relations, both those of ruling and those of the economy. It might, for example, start with the experience and concerns of the members of the Parent Corps, whose leader is also a leader in the neighborhood. From that standpoint, research would begin by building accounts of their situation and of what they, as parents of children in the school, and their children are experiencing both in school and in the community. But this is only the starting place. Their experience would begin to define for the ethnography the direction of the researchers' further steps. Here is where what institutional ethnographers call their "problematic" would become specified (Campbell and Gregor 2002). The institutional regime they confront would be explored from their perspective; their perspective and experience would organize the direction of the ethnographers' investigation. The social relations of schooling, administration, school board, administrative reform, municipal financing, and so on would be examined as and if they become relevant to the school experience of children and parents and particularly to the Parent Corps, the organization that represents them to the school and school board. Parent Corps members would, of course, already know a good deal about the workings of school and its administration, and research would aim to build on and expand that knowledge.

Though I cannot argue in the abstract that the knowledge produced would be useful and relevant to the Parent Corps, it has been our experience that institutional ethnographies produce a kind of knowledge that makes visible to activists or others directly involved the order they both participate in and confront. Because the research is ethnographic, it describes and analyzes just how that order is put together. Knowing how things work, how they're put together, is invaluable for those who often have to struggle in the dark. For example, knowing the implications for practice of changing the concepts and categories that operate in coordinating institutional processes can be very useful at the point where changes have not yet been settled and where there is room for maneuver. More generally, problematic institutional practices lying within practicable reach can be identified, creating possibilities of change from within (Pence 2001). These are in addition to the gains of knowledge that can be made from a method of inquiry aiming to discover just how our everyday worlds are being put together within social relations beyond the scope of our experience.

Institutional ethnography begins by locating a standpoint in an institutional order that provides the guiding perspective from which that order will be explored. It begins with some issues, concerns, or problems that are real for people and that are situated in their relationships to an institutional order. Their concerns are explicated by the researcher in talking with them and thus set the direction of inquiry. In a study that explored the relations of the work of mothering to schooling, Alison Griffith and I (Griffith and D. E. Smith 2004) began with our experiences as single parents (we talked to each other about these a lot). We decided that we wanted to understand why we had the kinds of problems with the schools our children attended, problems that we associated with being seen by educators as defective parents of actually or potentially defective children. Over the period of two or three years before we decided to undertake the research, we shared confidences, complaints, miseries, and guilt arising from our relationships to our children's schools. On long walks through the ravines of Toronto we shared the stories of our mothering work, of our children's struggles, of our fears about interfering, of pushing teachers too hard, of not pushing them hard enough. Our explorations opened up the social relations and organization of schooling as those in relation to which women's work as mothers is done.

On these walks, we also framed our collaborative research project on mothering for schooling. Alison had already laid the groundwork for our more systematic and sociological reflections on our experience by her research into the ideology of the single-parent family and its various uses by educational psychologists, educational administrators, and teachers (Griffith 1984). Now we thought we could find out more about what was so special so far as schools were concerned about the "Standard North American Family" (D. E. Smith 1999c) of a father/husband earning the income to support a wife/mother at home and children in school if we talked to mothers with children in elementary school about the work they were doing in relation to their children's schooling. Because our own experience had been as members of a "deviant" category of families vis-a-vis the school system, we were interested in learning more about the "normal" family against which our own had been seen as wanting.

We decided to work with a procedure that would first establish a particular standpoint located in women's everyday lives in the institutional context and hence in the ways they related to and participated in it. To establish a standpoint in the everyday of mothers' work, we decided that we would interview intensively a small number of women with children in elementary school. On the basis of our interviews with them, we could open up exploration from the side of the school and school board. An institutional order doesn't offer a "natural" focus. It is a complex of relations rather than a definite unitary form. Hence, in addition to whatever political interests the sociologist may have, locating a specific institutional standpoint organizes the direction of the sociological gaze and provides a framework of relevance.

We talked to the women we located about the work they did in relationship to their children's schooling. Our questions originated in "interviews" we had done with one another that brought into view for us the depth and detail of that work. Talking to women, we learned more of the range and variety of ways in which mothers' daily work in relation to schooling gets done. Some of the women we talked to had children in a school in a low-income district, others in a middle-class professional community. Their experiences of the specialized work that supplemented the educational work of the school varied and so did the availability of their time to do that work. Some women were employed full-time, and those simply had less time available to be involved in the educational work that contributed to their children's schools.

Exploration was not confined to the data from our research. We discovered, almost by accident, that our research assumptions had been deeply implicated in what we came to call the "mothering discourse," which, as I describe in the previous chapter, was established in North America in the early years of the twentieth century by educational professions and academics and promoted by a movement among white middle-class women concerned with reorganizing the practice of mothering in relation to the new public school system (Rothman 1978). The discourse mobilized women to take responsibility for the health and socialization of their children and more recently the supplementary educational work in the home that would contribute to their children's success in school (Arnup 1994). Their children's success in school has been increasingly important to middle-class families in ensuring access to positions in the professions, government, and management that sustain middle-class status (Collins 1979). The mothering discourse, continually renewed, modified, and sometimes radically rewritten by the educational intelligentsia, has been a key regulator coordinating mothers' work in the home with the work of teachers in schools (Griffith and D. E. Smith 2004).

Our library discoveries in these areas were made possible largely by the development of feminist historical research. We came to see the relationship between the organization of the model middle-class family, the "Standard North American Family" (D. E. Smith 1999c), as a piece of the organization of the middle class; we came to recognize the part played by the work of mothering in relation to the work of schooling in the reproduction of inequality as a normal feature of the operation of the public school system.

Here then is a distinction between institutional ethnography and the kind of study that Anyon's political economy of ghetto schooling represents. Institutional ethnography begins in the local actualities of the everyday world, with the concerns and perspectives of people located distinctively in the institutional process. From this perspective, an ethnographic exploration of those institutional processes is launched. What will be brought under ethnographic scrutiny unfolds as the research is pursued. From the beginning stages of inquiry, lines of further research emerge that are articulated to the first as research uncovers the social relations implicated in the local organization of the everyday. Each next step of investigation learns more from those involved of how their everyday work—and not just work as defined by employment (see chapter 7)—brings into being the institutional processes that are the focus of investigation. In principle, though there are necessary limitations to the practice, the ethnographic commitment to learn from those involved just how they go about doing things is preserved throughout. At the outset then, the institutional ethnographer may be unable to lay out precisely the parameters of the research, sometimes a source of difficulty with the ethical review processes of universities and with funding sources that require a clear account of who the "subjects" are and what kinds of questions they will be asked.[3] Yet the direction of inquiry is by no means random. Each next step builds from what has been discovered and invades more extended dimensions of the institutional regime. The mapping of social relations expands from and includes the original site so that the larger organization that enters into and shapes it becomes visible.

This research strategy might seem similar in some respects to the approach recommended by Michael Burawoy and colleagues (Burawoy, Blum, et al. 2000; Burawoy, Burton, et al. 1991) as the "extended case method." Yet it is also that which differentiates institutional ethnography most sharply from that approach. From my description, institutional ethnography could be seen as seeking "to uncover the macro foundations of a microsociology" (Burawoy, Burton, et al. 1991, 282) and to extend not only from micro to macro but also "from local to extralocal, from processes to forces" (Burawoy, Blum, et al. 2000, 29).

> [The extended case method] takes the social situation as the point of empirical examination and works with given general concepts and laws about states, economies, legal orders, and the like to understand how those micro situations are shaped by wider structures. (Burawoy, Burton, et al. 1991, 282)

On closer examination, however, the differences are significant. One key difference between the extended case method and institutional ethnography comes in the former's ontological shift as inquiry passes from micro to macro, from the "life world" to "the system." While at the "micro" level, the extended case method is ethnographic, using participant observation, at the macro, it is theory that is operative. Participant observation brings lives and work under scrutiny, and research analysis is "hermeneutic."

Once, however, investigation moves beyond the life worlds of people to discover "the properties of the system world," theory is in command and research becomes a "scientific" (Burawoy, Burton, et al. 1991, 284) exploration of forces acting at the global level (Burawoy, Blum, et al. 2000, 28). The theory that specifies system properties is refined and improved by its encounter with the ethnography; ethnography is framed by the theory.

> As observers who also stand outside the life worlds they study, scientists can gain insight into the properties of the system world, which integrates the intended and unintended consequences of instrumental action into relatively autonomous institutions. (Burawoy, Burton, et al. 1991, 284)

Combining the two modalities of research, the ethnographic investigation of particular cases with theories of objective forces operating globally, elucidates for each case "the way global domination is resisted, avoided, and negotiated" (Burawoy, Blum, et al. 2000, 28).

Institutional ethnography's program is one of inquiry and discovery. It has no prior interpretive commitment such as that which follows from concepts such as *global domination* and *resistance*. It means to find out just how people's doings in the everyday are articulated to and coordinated by extended social relations that are not visible from within any particular local setting and just how people are participating in those relations. Those relations are not assumed to be malign; indeed, institutional ethnography itself operates at the same level of organization, even though it is consciously directed toward introducing another form of organizing knowledge than those obliterating the presence of subjects as knowers situated in their own lives. As inquiry develops, the scope of the institutional ethnography pushes the boundaries of conventional divisions between micro and macro, sociology and political economy, without deserting its ethnographic commitment. The linked studies done by Alison Griffith, Ann Manicom (1988), and myself move from the local of women's work as mothers or teachers in relation to children's schooling into the institutional regime of public schooling, understanding progressively how people produce out of the particularities of their everyday living the standardizations and generalizations characteristic of institutions. The larger relations of class do not appear as external determinants but rather as social relations coordinating women's time and work in the home with the educational work of teachers and administrators in public schools. If a woman's husband earns enough to enable her to devote herself full-time to her children's education and if she lives in a community in which the majority are similarly situated, what is contributed to the educational work of a school enables it to function at a level that schools lacking such contributions cannot match. The work of schools in different socioeconomic environments get significantly different contributions of parental work.

In our research Alison and I discovered why, being single parents, we were defective as families in the eyes of the school. We were the kinds of family that did not have the resources needed to free women's time for the unpaid educational work that should be, from the point of view of the school, done in the home. We came to see that the educational work of middle-class parents in helping to reproduce their own employment status in their children is a piece of how class is organized intergenerationally through the public school system. Teachers' work in schools that cannot rely on substantial unpaid educational work on the part of parents have to put more classroom time into making up for what has not been done at home; they cannot, therefore, deliver the curriculum at the same level as in schools that can rely on extensive background educational work done in the home (Manicom 1988). Women's supplementary educational work done in the home contributes to the ability of schools in middle-class communities to maintain high standards of schooling without increasing staffing levels. As single parents, Alison and I were seen as unable to make those contributions.

Rather than insert theoretical connections that have an indeterminate relation to what has been discovered ethnographically, the connections of the locally discoverable with the extended social relations of which they are part are to be discovered in the articulations of people's everyday activities. Just how far the ethnographic project can be extended depends for the most part on matters of relevance to the research problematic as it has emerged from the ethnographer's and/or activists' concerns and out of the research process itself as well as on such contingencies as research funding.

A central difference between institutional ethnography and the extended case method is that an institutional ethnography opens up ethnographically that level of organization that Burawoy assigns to "the system." The connections of actual activities performed locally are coordinated translocally, contributing their organization to local practices. Carrying ethnography beyond the locally observable is made possible both by the approach to work organization through the work knowledges of participants (D. E. Smith 2003a; see chapter 7) and through innovative methods of incorporating the coordinating functions of text into ethnographic practice (D. E. Smith 2001a; see chapter 8 and 9). Translocal forms of coordinating people's work are explored as they are to be found in the actual ways in which coordination is locally accomplished.

Thus institutional ethnography is not focused on sites of "resistance" or of the avoidance of "domination" as these are explicated by "scientists" from a stance independent of the "life worlds" of people. That would be to overturn the project of a sociology written from people's standpoint, a project aimed at opening up to us how our everyday lives participate in and are embedded in relations that aren't visible from within them. Ethnography may start by exploring the experience of those directly involved in the institutional setting, but they are not the objects of investigation. It is the aspects of the institutions relevant to the people's experience, not the people themselves, that constitute the object of inquiry. The ethnographer's standpoint may be defined by her or his own experience or by what she or he has learned by talking with others.[4] However defined, it is people's experience which sets the problematic of the study, the first step in an inquiry that travels sequentially deeper into the institutional relations in which people's everyday lives are embedded.[5] Institutional ethnography does not have a pregiven theoretical destination; indeed, it doesn't have a theoretical destination at all. Those dimensions of "the system" that for Burawoy emerge at the level of the "wider structures" of "states, economies, legal orders, and the like" (Burawoy, Burton, et al. 1991, 282) are explored ethnographically rather than theoretically.

Experience and the Ethnographic Problematic

I have appropriated the term *problematic* from Louis Althusser (1971, 32) to locate the discursive organization of a field of investigation that is larger than a specific question or problem. Within such a field, questions and problems arise to be taken up, but they do not exhaust the direction of inquiry. The concept of the problematic makes it possible to differentiate clearly between, on the one hand, the actual properties of the everyday/ everynight worlds of our contemporary societies that are never self-subsisting but always tied in multiple ways to complexes of relations beyond them and, on the other, making that actual organization the problematic of an inquiry that tracks from people's experiences of the local actualities of their living into the relations present in and organizing but at best only partially visible within them.

The general problematic of institutional ethnography takes the everyday world as an unfinished arena of discovery in which the lines of social relations are present to be explored beyond it. Taking the everyday/everynight world as problematic does not, however, refer to the problems or issues that are the researcher's motivation to take up her or his work. It refers rather to the translation of an actual property of the social relations or organization of our/people's ordinary doings into a topic for ethnographic research. It locates the step that is taken from the ordinary doings and ordinary language that are the stuff of people's lives onto the terrain of a sociological discourse, the business of which is to examine how that stuff is hooked into a larger fabric not directly observable from within the everyday.

Susan Turner's study (2001, 2003) of the organization of municipal land-use planning started in 1986 when she found in her mailbox a notice inviting her to a meeting to introduce a development planned for a ravine in her neighborhood. The ravine had been an area of natural wilderness; local residents had taken it for granted. Now they mobilized to oppose the development. Turner became a leading figure in organizing opposition and became familiar with the municipal council proceedings and the process of development decision making. Here was an everyday world that was being subjected to transformation of a kind with which we are all too familiar. An orderly and familiar local world is suddenly disrupted by interventions that come from outside, that have no logic within the daily routines and the ordinariness of local life—the hole in the ground at the University of British Columbia that helped to awaken me to what it might mean to do a sociology starting in a standpoint in the everyday was one such intervention (see chapter 1). The relations that hooked up the local residents' settings and doings with the doings of others elsewhere had been only implicit presences, potentialities to take action of which residents were largely unaware. Susan was at that time a graduate student in sociology, studying in the field that was later to be identified as institutional ethnography. She took advantage of the discourse in which she was participating as a student to translate her everyday experience as an activist into an ethnographic investigation of just those relations and organization in which she was implicated. The sites of struggle were transposed into a *problematic* for investigation. She discovered and has described the sequences of texts and text-mediated work making up the course of a municipal land-use planning decision in which the voices of residents were hardly heard (Turner 2001).

The notion of the everyday world as problematic (D. E. Smith 1987) as the starting place for inquiry does not mean starting with people's *problems*. The problems and concerns that people are experiencing often motivate inquiry, but they do not define the direction of research. George Smith's (1988, 1990, 1995, 1998) research was motivated by his concerns about the kinds of harassment experienced by gay men; Turner's research originated in her commitment to environmental activism in the context of municipal development. Formulating a problematic out of such concerns and experiences means going beyond them to develop a project for inquiry which, while it may be oriented by such interests, must not be constrained by them or adopt their prejudgments. It means creating a project of exploration. Exploration may begin in talk with those concerned, learning from them sometimes more than they realize they knew about how they participate in an institutional process. From there the institutional ethnographer develops a project of research into those aspects of the institutional process that are relevant to the issues of concern *and* appear in how people talk of what is going on in their lives. Developing a problematic in institutional ethnography translates actualities of people's doings from forms of organization implicit in the everyday world into the forms of discursive representation in which they can be subjected to inquiry.

The everyday world is hooked up to complexities of relations and organization out of which such totally strange and apparently arbitrary interventions emerge, such as those experienced by gay men enjoying sex in a steambath when the police raid it (G. W. Smith 1988) or by the neighbors of the ravine to be developed (Turner 2003) or by nurses struggling with the new forms of management imposed on them (Campbell 1984; Rankin 1998, 2001, 2003). Such interventions are not happening all the time; they make visible what is ordinarily taken for granted, that the very organization of the everyday is permeated with connections that extend beyond it. The discourse of institutional ethnography constitutes what is implicit in the everyday as a problematic for investigation that has as its destination explicating the implicit social relations and organization.

But the social relations coordinating people's doings with those of others elsewhere and that hook them into the social relations of the economy and of ruling are not only those appearing as dramatically as the destruction of the natural beauty of a ravine in Turner's neighborhood. When Alison Griffith and I walked the ravines of a city other than

Turner's, obsessively concerned with how our children's schooling was shaped by the fact that we were single parents, we had very little understanding of how the schools worked, let alone what it was about our single parenthood that made us, in the school's eyes, defective as parents. Our experiential sharing created awareness of concerns we had in common. Those concerns were then developed, as described earlier, into the problematic of a series of studies, some by Alison alone (Griffith 1984, 1986, 1995), several involving Alison and myself (Griffith and D. E. Smith 1987, 1990a, 1990b, 2005), and one by Ann Manicom (1988), exploring how parental work with children in elementary school articulates to the everyday operation of the elementary schools to produce inequality.

The ethnographic problematic recognizes the real interpenetration of the present and immediate with the unknown elsewhere and elsewhen and the strange forms of power that are at once present and absent in the everyday. A problematic is a territory to be discovered, not a question that is concluded in its answer. Exploration opens up an institutional complex as it is relevant to the problematic. In opening up an institutional complex, it participates in institutional ethnography's more general discoveries of the workings of institutions and the ruling relations in contemporary Western societies.

Taking the everyday world as problematic (D. E. Smith 1987) to locate the starting point of inquiry anchors the ethnography in people's actual experience. It establishes for inquiry a subject position that remains open until it is filled by the subjectivity or subjectivities of those whose part is taken up as the starting point of inquiry: inquiry sets out from there; it explores with people their experience of what is happening to them and their doings and how those are hooked up with what is beyond their experience. Research is then projected beyond the local to discover the social organization that governs the local setting. In an institutional context, this is to discover the institutional order and its organization in those respects relevant to what has been and is happening to people.

Two things should be stressed:

1. The problematic isn't discursively constructed from what is particular to an individual; it may well start in an individual's experience, but as it moves to explore the social relations in which that experience is embedded, it necessarily brings under scrutiny relations that aren't peculiar to that individual. Rather, these relations are part of a complex of relations that reach beyond and coordinate what she or he is doing and

what others are doing in relationship to her or him that doesn't begin and end with individual experience.

2. Qualitative research is ordinarily treated as limited in its implications because any statements it might make are restricted in significance to the particular setting of the ethnography. This critique, however, neglects the contemporary realities of how the local is penetrated with the extra- or translocal relations that are generalized across particular settings. Indeed, it may well be that the current increasing interest in qualitative research is an effect of an invisible generalizability that is *in* the research because it is *in* the actuality that the research represents. Institutional ethnography addresses explicitly the character of institutions in contemporary society: that they are themselves forms of social organization that generalize and universalize across multiple local settings. While they may and do articulate differently in the particularities of local settings, their generalized and generalizing character is going to appear in any ethnography—indeed, it has to be there and should be there explicitly, even in an investigation that begins with the experience of one individual.

Such fundamentally political involvement is integral to how institutional ethnography proceeds. There are no "natural" boundaries to ethnographies other than those of the practicalities of research. Hence a major source of "control" over the natural expansions of ethnography into neighboring terrains is the political orientation and concerns of the researcher and those she or he is working with. It is this concern that regulates the researcher's focus of relevance. When sociology is imagined to rely on its objectivity and when that objectivity is in turn held to rely on the sociologist's indifference to the outcome of her or his research, then such political commitments are viewed as forms of bias that contaminate the research outcomes. But institutional ethnography is not an experimental approach; if it is to serve those whose standpoint it undertakes as its starting point, it must produce accurate and faithful representations of how things actually work; it must be truthful. Political commitment here enforces the researcher's responsibility to get it right. Others' decisions to act may draw on her or his findings; hence, the latter must be as good as she or he can make them if she or he or others are going to rely on them in action or organizing. The ethnographer's results aim at extending the knowledge of those she or he works with as well as the knowledge of others similarly situated in institutional regimes.

As soon as this problematic is adopted, the problem of the partiality and particularity of perspectives is transformed from a limitation to an essential dimension of inquiry. Any one individual's story necessarily implies the presence and doings of others caught up in and participating in relations that coordinate their doings. The relations that coordinate their doings are implicit in the particularities of their experiences. Each knows her or his own daily world as an expert and knows it from inside but participates in relations that connect and coordinate her or his work—in the sense in which we've learned to recognize housework as work—with what others' doings that aren't visible to him or her. The institutional ethnographer's research aims at discovering the different kinds of work from different sites as well as how they are coordinated to create just those institutional processes that the research problematic located for investigation.

Conclusion

This chapter has recognized objectivity as a distinctive form of that social organization of knowledge in which the presence of the subject is suspended or displaced and "knowledge" (the nominalized term in itself is indicative of this move—see chapter 5) is constituted as standing over against individual subjects and subjectivities, overriding the idiosyncrasies of experience, interest, and perspective. Institutional ethnography as a project proposes to realize an alternative form of knowledge of the social in which people's own knowledge of the world of their everyday practices is systematically extended to the social relations and institutional orders in which we participate. This approach has been further defined here by differentiating it, first, from a study that subsumes material assembled ethnographically under concepts and theories that formulate social concerns but do not explicate the social organization of the problems that people are encountering (Anyon's 1997 study of ghetto schooling) and, second, from an approach that deserts the ethnographic for theory at the point of entry into the macrosocial level of organization (Burawoy and colleagues' extended case method [Burawoy, Burton, et al. 1991; Burawoy, Blum, et al. 2000]). Institutional ethnography's commitment is to remain in the world of everyday experience and knowledge, to explore ethnographically the problematic that is implicit in it, extending the capacities of ethnography beyond the circumscriptions of our ordinary experience-based knowledge, to make observable social relations beyond and within it in which we and multiple others participate.

Institutional ethnography works from people's experiences in and of institutional forms of coordinating people's doings. How the research develops depends on the researcher, on his or her interests and skills, on how much time the researcher can give, which means, among other things, how it is funded. Some ethnographies focus on the experiences of those active in the institutional process. Others take the next step to locate investigation in the regulatory dimensions of institutions, exploring these also as people's work in particular local settings and explicating the distinctive institutional forms of coordination. As institutional ethnographic research builds up, it begins to be possible to reach beyond specific research into expanded dimensions of the social, informed by the research and discoveries of other institutional ethnographies.

In general, institutional ethnography works from the local of people's experience to discover how the ruling relations both rely on and determine their everyday activities. Its methods of research work with people's work knowledges of what they do, as these are collaboratively produced in the research process as well as with the texts that are essential to the production of the generalizability, generalization, and objectivity of institutional regimes. The regimes' objectification is explicated ethnographically rather than assumed. The methods of investigation that institutional ethnographers have developed, particularly those that bring the textual into ethnographic focus (see chapters 5, 8, and 9) as integral to coordinating local actions with others elsewhere and elsewhen, offer a potential for reaching much beyond the scope of ethnography as it's usually understood in sociology and into the forms of organizing power and agency that are characteristic of corporations, government, and international organization (D. E. Smith 1999c, 2001a).

Notes

1. See also, my *Conceptual Practices of Power* (D. E. Smith 1990a) for a more extended treatment of textual realities as socially organized.

2. Compare Leslie Salzinger's experience (1991). She concludes her study of immigrant domestic worker cooperatives in the Bay Area in the United States, using an approach called the "extended case method" (Burawoy, Burton, et al. 1991), with an afterword asking, "Ethnography for what?" She writes, "I began my project determined that my work be useful not only to other researchers, but to activists working within a particular political framework. For a long time, I was so focused on that framework that I was capable of seeing little else. It was only once my expectations had been repeatedly frustrated that I was able to see the au-

tonomous (and political) identities that were actually emerging before me. However, with the analysis behind me, a new set of issues arises. Now that I have come to understand processes that do not fit neatly into a preexisting political agenda, there are no longer obvious groups or institutions who could use the information I have gathered" (159–60). Salzinger sees "finding those who might want this piece of the puzzle [referring to her research findings] . . . a new and ongoing task" (160).

3. Ethical review processes in universities lag behind funding sources in this respect. Funders are more aware of innovations in sociological research strategies.

4. A number of institutional ethnographies have built the problematic of inquiry from their own experience. As I've described already, Alison and I (Griffith and D. E. Smith 2004) started with our concerns as single parents about our children's schooling and our relationships with our children's schools. Our experiences became our research problematic. Gerald de Montigny's study of social "work(ing)" (1995a) came out of his own experience as a man growing up in a working-class community who encountered the professional ideology of social work as a major contradiction with his experience and his allegiance. His ethnography explores both that ideology and the social relations and organization of social work practice. Roxana Ng's study (1986) of community organization and the state originated from her experience as an immigrant in Canada working in a voluntary organization dedicated to helping immigrant women find jobs and to acting as an advocate for them. Kamini Grahame (1999), also an immigrant to Canada, took up the standpoint of immigrant women in training programs in the United States in order to explore the organizational change tying the voluntary organizations delivering the programs into the interlocking policies of state and federal government. Janet Rankin (1998, 2001, 2003), a nursing instructor on Vancouver Island, has explored with hospital nurses their experience of the managerial restructuring of hospital and health care in the province of British Columbia. From Gillian Walker's experience (1990) of activism in the women's movement in relation to what came to be called "family violence" came an ethnography of the processes leading up to the governmental substitution of the concept of family violence for the concept of battered women per the definition of the women's movements. These are not the only ones originating in the ethnographer, as we shall see.

5. I recommend Marie Campbell and Frances Gregor's consideration (2002, 46–50) of how to define the research problematic for an institutional ethnographic project in their primer on doing institutional ethnography.

PART 2

An Ontology of the Social

CHAPTER 3

Designing an Ontology
for Institutional Ethnography

The problem addressed in this and the following chapter is how to design a sociology that aims at extending people's ordinary knowledge as practitioners of our everyday worlds into reaches of powers and relations that are beyond them. If the everyday world is to be taken as its problematic, then the approach must be one that works from and with people's experience. It cannot, however, be satisfied with the objectives and practices of much good sociological ethnography that remains within the scope of the observer's direct experience of a local site. Here ethnographic inquiry is to be developed that explores the translocal relations in which people's local doings participate and by which they are organized. As I pointed out, in contrasting Burawoy and colleagues' extended case method (1991) with institutional ethnography, the ethnographic inquiry pushes beyond the local settings of people's everyday experience, and it must do so by finding those extended relations that coordinate multiple settings translocally. I have stressed and will probably stress again that in institutional ethnography, the ethnographer explores and describes the same world as that in which the inquiry is done.

Institutional ethnography's project of inquiry and discovery rejects the dominance of theory. I have adopted the rather vague term *mainstream sociology* to locate what I view as general practices of sociology's order of discourse.[1] I realize that such a general term gathers a variety of sociological practices. I'm sure it would be possible to find exceptions, particularly in sociology's excellent ethnographic research, but the practices I refer to are general and are almost defining of sociology.[2] They are certainly a barrier to the approach to sociological inquiry recommended by institutional ethnography.

In general, mainstream sociology is amazingly cluttered with theory.[3] Research, it would seem, cannot proceed without theory; without it, what is discovered could not be recognized as sociology. Classical theory, according to Jeffrey Alexander (1989), is the only thing that makes communication among sociologists sustainable (27) in the absence (apparently irremediable) of determination by fact (21). Of course, institutional ethnography does not proceed without theory; indeed, I'm writing theory in this and the following chapter. Nor does it refrain from drawing on the theoretical thinking of predecessors—the thinking of Marx, Mead, and Bakhtin and to some extent Garfinkel have been important resources for me in my contribution to the making of institutional ethnography. But mainstream sociology clamps a conceptual framework over any project of inquiry; such a framework determines how the actual will be attended to, dominating and constraining selection and interpretation, setting up what Mikhail Bakhtin (1981) calls a "monologic" that suppresses and displaces the essential dialogic of the social (D. E. Smith 1999b). Further, mainstream sociological theory establishes the knower's discursive position as transcending the everyday worlds of people's experience.

In some ways the writing of an ontology for institutional ethnography is to write a resistance to such features of mainstream sociology. Institutional ethnography is proposed as an alternative sociology and not as a methodology. As it has become better known, I find that references to it in mainstream sociological literature turn up in texts or sections of texts on qualitative methods. I have referred to it as a method of inquiry, a designation that seems to support such allocations. But it is described as a method of inquiry because its findings are not already prejudged by a conceptual framework that regulates how data will be interpreted; rather, exploration and discovery are central to its project. Though we cannot avoid preconceptions, and we cannot avoid introducing concepts in capturing and analyzing data, the project exposes concepts to the discipline of the actualities with which the researcher is engaging. Actualities, of course, ultimately escape, but it is the ethnographer's business to sustain an engagement with them that enables her or him to check the conceptual against what she or he has learned and is learning. Commitment to learning from actualities as they are experienced and spoken or written by those actively involved in them is essential to the project. Indeed, research might be thought of as a dialogue in which, in classic hermeneutic terms

(Gadamer 1975), the researcher is changed. As described in the previous chapter, Alison Griffith and I (Griffith and D. E. Smith 2005) had just such an experience of being changed in the course of our research when we discovered what we came to call the "mothering discourse." That discourse had imposed on our thinking about ourselves and our research a model of mothers' responsibilities for their children's schooling that we had built into our research design and practice. The data collection was already done at that point, but we were able, so far as possible, to correct our analysis and interpretation.

The overall aim of institutional ethnography has a double character. One is to produce for people what might be called "maps" of the ruling relations and specifically the institutional complexes in which they participate in whatever fashion. People's knowledge of their everyday world is thereby expanded beyond the scope of what can be learned in the ordinary ways we go about our daily activities. Research projects working from problematics located in people's everyday experience have this as their objective. Like the map of the underground mall, with its arrow pointing to a particular spot accompanied by the words YOU ARE HERE! institutional ethnographies are designed to enable people to relate the locus of their experience to where they may want to go.

The second aim is to build knowledge and methods of discovering the institutions and, more generally, the ruling relations of contemporary Western society. Institutional ethnographers had not expected, when we started out, that studies in widely different institutional settings would provide resources for an interchange among us from which we were learning about institutional processes in general and how institutions are put together. This has been a piece-by-piece learning process, but it has certainly enlarged the scope of what is now possible. We were also discovering that the individual studies were more than case studies, that entering into the regions of the ruling relations meant an ethnographic exploration of processes and relations that generalize beyond the particular instance. That indeed is an aspect of how institutions operate.

An Ontology of the Social

The problematic of the everyday establishes a general orientation; the problematic of a particular study orients its focus and direction; the questions of what to look at and where to look remain. Institutional ethnography's impetus is inquiry into and discovery of the social in people's lives and doings. But what does that mean? Paradoxically, having eschewed theory of one kind, I turn to another that I am calling an "ontology." An ontology is a theory of reality. This chapter and the next write a theory of how the social is real. That's what I mean by an ontology of the social. As developed in this chapter, it is intended as a guide to what might be observed and recorded and become data for the ethnographer. The term appears abstruse and esoteric. It is associated with the intense labors of reading and understanding such grandmasters of philosophy as Hegel or Heidegger, who were concerned with the most general and difficult problems of being, existence, what is reality. The ontology I'm writing here is modest. I want a theory of how the social exists of such a kind that it will help us see what we might be observing, listening for, recording, and analyzing. I emphasize that I am not concerned with epistemological issues, as was, for example, ethnomethodology, at least in its earlier days.[4]

Problems of how we can know the social, the objectivity, or the status of institutional ethnography's findings vis-a-vis "reality" are largely irrelevant to a project of inquiry that does not claim to transcend indexicality, that is, the actualities from which its findings are extracted and to which the latter refer back. Its findings are in and of the same world that it investigates. Its discoveries and analyses depend, as maps do, on the actuality in which they originated—they make no sense without it and are intended to extend rather than displace people's expert knowledge as local practitioners of their everyday worlds. There are, of course, issues of accuracy, rigor, the adequacy of analyses to explicate the social at particular sites, and so on. However, the design of an ontology as a theory of the being of the social is intended to provide a guide to the aspects or dimensions of actual ongoing social processes, in time and in place, that institutional ethnography's project of inquiry can appropriate. It does make the claim, as an ontology, to provide a conceptual framework for selective attention to actualities such that the project of inquiry can proceed as discovery of and learning from actualities. Returning to the metaphor of a map, it proposes cartographic principles for what might be incorporated into the mapping of the social in its institutional forms.

In working through the design of an ontology for institutional ethnography, we confront, as a problem, the strange disappearance of people from mainstream sociological discourse and the strange detachment from actualities to which sociology's discursive practices commit its practitioners. Institutional ethnography's design, by contrast, must ensure that people remain the subjects, the knowers, or potential knowers of what institutional ethnography discovers. Mainstream sociology imposes theoretical organization interpreting what people are actually doing and saying in a fashion that situates the knower outside the account and represents people as objects. When actor and action are theorized, both are abstracted from the ongoing historical process of the moment and what people are doing and bringing into being, and both are resituated in a discourse fully under sociological control.

> "Action" is not a combination of "acts"; "acts" are constituted only by a discursive moment of attention to the durée of lived-through experience. Nor can "action" be discussed in separation from the body, its mediations with the surrounding world and the coherence of an acting self. What I call a stratification model of the acting self involves treating the reflexive monitoring, rationalization and motivation of action as embedded sets of processes. The rationalization of action, referring to "intentionality" as process, is, like the other two dimensions, a routine characteristic of human conduct. (Giddens 1984, 3–4)

But, of course, the very theorizing of "action" and "acts," let alone attaching them to "the body," performs the very separation that Giddens's theorizing proposes to undo.

Giddens, of course, is a canny theoretical operator and isn't going to be caught by obvious problems such as ascribing any reality to "acts" or anything as brutal as dismissing actors' "lived-through experience." I look up from my reading of Giddens, sitting on a bus in Victoria, British Columbia, to see an old man walking by on the sidewalk. To fit him to this theoretical frame, I must skip my own presence—one of the major virtues of sociological theory according to Jeffrey Alexander (1995). I must find out what it might mean to recognize the old man as "actor" and his walk on the sidewalk as "action." Actors are no longer actual people—an old woman sitting on a bus reading sociological theory and looking up to see an old man on the sidewalk—they become scripted personages in a theoretical drama. "I" becomes "she" no longer sitting in the bus but on an Archimedean point (hardly comfortable). "She" is the sociologist who disappears in the very act of doing sociology—the very alienation the women's movement taught me to escape. The old man's walk along the sidewalk (seeing the bus passing?), reconstructed as action, entails his monitoring what he's doing, rationalizing it, and having a motive for his walk. The conceptual transportation into sociological discourse displaces the actualities of my experience and the old man's walking on the sidewalk, which we will never learn about as he experienced it; magically, the sociologist disappears altogether and the old man becomes merely an expression or instance of a theoretical category. His discursive appropriation is also her/my textual absence. Objectivity appears as the stylistics of a discourse rather than as generated by a research methodology.[5]

Actual Activities of Actual People

There is an alternative: Marx and Engels (1976), in their critique of those they describe as the German ideologists, propose to ground social science in the activities of actual individuals and the material conditions thereof. They write an ontology for social science. History and society exist only in people's activities and in the forms of "cooperation" that have evolved among them. They criticize the ideological reasoning of the German ideologists because it replaces the actual with the conceptual. The critique is more than one simply against an idealism that treats historical change as generated by ideas. It is a critique of a method of reasoning about society and history that treats concepts as if they were agents.[6]

This, I suggest, is precisely the problem of mainstream sociology. Concepts are substituted for or displace the actual in which, by whatever indirect means, they originate: the actual becomes selectively represented as it conforms to the conceptual; the conceptual becomes the dominant mode of interpreting the resulting selection.[7] Conceptions of social system and social structure are theoretical constructs that can be assigned a determining role in human behavior without claiming an empirical reference. When I was working on my doctoral thesis, I remember sitting in the cafeteria of the state mental hospital in which I was doing my fieldwork and asking myself "But where *is* social structure? How do I find it?" I think I remember that moment in the cafeteria because it became a question that nagged in my mind for many years. Accounts such as Giddens's (1984) of social structure as "rules" simply translates one abstract noun into another, equally short of determinate reference. The social appears to have a reality that can be encompassed only in theory and is not, as such, to be found in the local actualities of people's lives and doings. The positivism of such epistemologists as Carl Hempel (1966), among others, served to establish in sociology an acceptance of notions of theory as formal statements from which hypotheses could be deduced and tested against people's behavior in groups or as collections of individuals. No notion here of learning from observing their doings or discovering the social in how they went about their lives. Concepts such as social structure come into play for mainstream sociology in their imputed effects on people and their doings, but how they exist is not seriously problematized.

Institutional ethnography stands in direct opposition to mainstream sociological discourse's perpetuation of conceptual distance from the local actualities of people's lives. Distinctive stylistic practices create what Charles Bazerman (1988) has called an "underdetermination" of meaning—contrasting sociological writing with that of the natural sciences. Sociological terms don't have decisively specified referents on which all participants in the discourse agree. Hubert Blalock (1969) identifies the problem of the underdetermination of sociological theories in his project of translating them into formal mathematics. In his view, "verbal theories" are too vague, too complex, and contain too many variables; they would have to be radically reworked before they could be subjected to mathematical scrutiny and testing (27). Jeffrey Alexander (1989) takes as central to sociology that "there is no clear, indisputable reference for the elements which compose social science" (21) and that "the conditions of social science make consistent agreement about the precise nature of empirical knowledge—let alone agreement about explanatory covering laws—highly unlikely" (19). Underdetermination of meaning is in sharp contrast with what institutional ethnography aims at; its conceptual practices are intended to *explicate* the social in people's actual doings, and they have to be modified or discarded as further discoveries display problems or inadequacies.

Embedded in sociology are practices of constructing entities attributed to the world that have the following distinct properties:

1. They are words that are in some way or another derived from verbs of action and have been converted into nominal forms in which the subject/agent has already disappeared. These are such terms as *organization, institution, meaning, order, conflict,* and *power,* which get to function as agents in sociological sentences.
2. They are terms such as *role, rule, norm,* and so on, which isolate aspects of the social, are derived from them, and are treated as existing out there in the real world.
3. They are concepts taken over from the writings of sociologists and detached from their original contexts to contribute to the inventory of staple sociological entities. A concept such as *bureaucracy,* which came to sociology through the late-nineteenth/early-twentieth-century work

of Max Weber can be used, as it is in Charles Perrow's *Complex Organizations* (1986), as if there were no change in how large-scale organizations are governed from Weber's time to our own.

4. Finally, sociology relies extensively on metaphors such as *social structure* (with its implicit reference to architecture), used extensively and in a variety of minimally defined ways, or *cultural capital*, as used by Pierre Bourdieu (1973) to express the kinds of advantages and opportunities that education or other privileged access to a culture valued in a society create for individuals.

Such stylistic devices constitute what might be described as a "blob-ontology"; that is, for every such concept, there is taken to be a something out there corresponding to it. The disappearance of people and activities is striking once we attend to it. Agency is assigned to conceptually constructed entities that lack determinate referents. It is left to readers to fill in for an absence of specified referent or clearly defined meaning.[8]

Though institutional ethnography is indeed committed to an ethnographic enterprise and not to the investigation and theorizing of historical process, it has learned from Marx's own theoretical and conceptual practices. In moving from the ontological principals for social science laid down in *The German Ideology* to a theory of the workings of a capitalist mode of production, Marx does not desert these principles.[9] It's not, of course, that he is without theory, but it is important to recognize its distinctive character, namely that theoretical concepts are held to express actual social relations (D. E. Smith 2004). The concepts themselves are founded in an actuality of people's activities as these are organized in the social relations—the forms of cooperation characteristic of a given stage of development of a mode of production. Marx is careful to show how theory is subtended by the historical actualities of people's doings and relations.[10] The emergence of an "economy" as a distinct phenomenon is a differentiation of distinctively abstract relations in which people are exchanging money for commodities and in which those relations take on a dynamic independent of individual intention. Note that the "abstract" property of these relations is not, in the first place, conceptual; rather, it is an effect of the way in which, in the real world, relations of exchange between money and commodities accomplish the disappearance of the concrete particularities of things and their uses to people.

Concepts such as capital are spelled out as distinctive relational sequences in which money is exchanged to produce commodities that will be exchanged for a value of money greater than the amount used to produce them. These social relations are also shown to be grounded in the emerging relations between a bourgeoisie owning property and a large class of people who are not able to produce their own subsistence but must depend on employment and getting paid a wage to work on materials and with the plant and technology owned by the capitalist to produce the commodities that go into the sequence of capital briefly described earlier. That care to underpin theory and the abstract social relations with a concrete historical ground is characteristic of how Marx proceeds, but it is not at all a characteristic of sociology.

Institutional ethnography does not attempt to take up Marx's project; it is, after all, committed to ethnography. It does, however, take seriously Marx's scrupulous attention to the ontological grounding of the concepts and theories of social science. For Marx, the concepts of political economy are not to be taken as the givens of a social science. They express the social relations that have emerged historically, and it is these social relations that should be the object of investigation (D. E. Smith 2004). Thus, theories or concepts explicate actual social relations rather than occlude or impose on them. The ethnographic practices of institutional ethnographies are directed toward an inquiry engaging with the actualities of the social. They create an essentially dialogic relation between concepts and the actual social relations and organization in which the adequacy of the former to explicate the latter is subject to test. Of course, there can be no guarantees that preconceptions will be exposed and disrupted or that the implicit grounding of concepts in social relations will be uncovered, but there is a commitment to the actual rather than the conceptual. Learning from actualities means treating them as existing beyond what the researcher already knows how to think and utter.

The Social Understood as How Activities Are Coordinated

The actualities of people's activities are not adequate to specify the phenomenal object of institutional ethnography. Yes, we can go after people's practices, their work, their activities of all and any kinds, but there is a missing sociological piece. Basing ethnography in people's activities individuates action and those who act. This is a perennial problem in sociological thinking.

Individuating the subject is also a problem for institutional ethnography's proposal to reach beyond the local particularities of people's everyday lives and into the regions of the relations that organize them. Exploration into institutional relations and, more generally, the ruling relations runs into problems when individual action is the exclusive ontological ground of inquiry. For the most part, issues of ontology, of how the social or society exists, do not, as I've suggested, arise for sociology. Questions of how the social exists may be dissolved into reifications of society. For Georg Simmel (1950), while society inheres in the individual, "it develops its own vehicles and organs by whose claims and commands the individual is confronted as by an alien party" (58). Èmile Durkheim (1966), writing a constitution for sociology as a science, posits "social facts" that exist outside the individual. They are "a category of facts with very distinctive characteristics; it consists of ways of acting, thinking, and feeling, external to the individual, and endowed with a power of coercion, by reason of which they control him" (3). Anthony Giddens (1984) modifies earlier conceptions to permit the agency of individuals to participate in the creation of structure, a process he calls "structuration," an interplay between individual action and structure in which structure shapes individual behavior and in which the actions of individuals affect structure. Appealing as this may be, it preserves the original practice of imagining the social as some kind of entity existing externally to individuals. He is quite properly cautious about attributing anything decisive to rules—they are merely "implicated in the reproduction of social systems" (185). Nonetheless, the land of blob-ontology is reinstated. Perhaps following Chomksy's model of a generative grammar, which may be theorized but never observed, the concept of social structure remains at a convenient level of theorizing where my question of long ago in the state mental hospital cafeteria about the whereabouts of social structure seems irrelevant, even stupid.

Where the reifications of the social in an externalized society or social system are rejected, theorists have resorted to founding the social in the individuated subject. Weber (1978), for example, derives the social from individual consciousness:

> Action is social insofar as, by virtue of the subjective meaning attached to it by the acting individual (or individuals), it takes account of the behavior of others and is thereby oriented in its course. (88)

Phenomenological sociology suffers similarly from its philosophical foundations in a theory of consciousness that is deeply committed to an individuation that it has struggled in various ways to overcome (Gurwitsch 1964; Schutz 1962a). More recently Pierre Bourdieu's concept of habitus (1990) installs the reproduction of the social in the learning and experience of individuals:

> [Habitus] produces individual and collective practices . . . in accordance with the schemes generated by history. It ensures the active presence of past experiences, which, deposited in each organism in the form of schemes of perception, thought and action, tend to guarantee the 'correctness' of practices and their consistency over time, more reliably than all formal rules and explicit norms. (54)

The assumption of the individuated subject is deeply embedded in sociology. We can, indeed, see Parsons's conception of norms and values, Giddens's of structuration, and Schutz's of intersubjectivity as designed to overcome the problem created by a foundation in the individuated subject.

Institutional ethnography needs a solution that neither dispenses with individual subjects, their activities, and experience nor adopts the alternative reification of the social as system or structure or some ingenious combination of the two. For institutional ethnography, the social as the focus for study is to be located in how people's activities or practices are *coordinated*. Individuals are there; they are in their bodies; they are active; and what they're doing is coordinated with the doings of others. That is the four-part package that is foundational to the institutional ethnographic project. Coordination isn't isolated as a phenomenon that can be differentiated from people's activities; it is not reified as "social structure" nor as "rules"; it is not conceived to be a specialized form of action in itself. For institutional ethnography, the social, as the focus of sociological inquiry, is specified as people's activities as they are coordinated with those of others. This is what is meant by "the social" in this context. It is not a phenomenon distinct in itself but an aspect of what people do to be explored and explicated.[11] The focus of research is never the individual, but the individual does not disappear; indeed, she or he is an essential presence.[12] Her or his doings, however, are to be taken up relationally.

An ontology of the social as the coordinating of people's activities creates the possibility of ontological coherence among sociologies exploring different levels or different aspects of the social. Much sociology can be tied back into such a conception. George Herbert Mead (1962), for example, has examined and formulated the symbolic modes that coordinate people's activities in interaction and, indeed, has explicated the symbolic itself as a definite form of coordinating people's actions (more about this in chapter 4).[13] Ethnomethodology's conversational analysis can be understood as investigating how people's ordinary talk is coordinated. I remember a film shown at an ethnomethodological meeting in Boston many years ago.[14] If I remember it correctly, it showed this simple sequence: a receptionist in a physician's office gets up and goes over to speak to a woman waiting in a chair. The sequence is in slow motion and there is no sound. As you watch, you see how the bodily movements of the two, one approaching, the other recognizing and orienting, coordinate with one another. It is like a dance and clearly operating at a level well below consciousness.

At a very different level of the coordinating of people's activities is Marx's conception of the economy and the relations of exchange. In contrast to much of the theorizing that has adopted Marx's original writing, Marx's actual theory is careful to provide for the transition from actual people to relations in which people no longer appear to one another directly. Concepts such as "commodity" and "commodity fetishism" play a key theoretical role in this respect. There is no concept that is not a relational term. It is this that ties them into the marvellously coherent complex of abstract concepts that make up the theory explicated in *Capital*.

Short of such general possibilities of a conception of the social as a focus on the coordinating of actual people's activities, institutional ethnography's modest proposal is to work from what people are doing or what they can tell us about what they and others do and to find out how the forms of coordinating their activities "produce" institutional processes, as they actually work.

Difference and the Social

Theories that posit patterns or structure also require that actors share the norms or rules that produce them. Once, however, attention shifts from such reifications to the ongoing coordinating of people's doings, it becomes apparent that social processes themselves generate differences in perspective, concerns, and experience. Take a very ordinary example of two people maneuvering a dining room table up a rather narrow stair into a second-floor apartment. Each is positioned differently in relation to the other; each experiences the process differently; the man at the top can see the next stage and is trying to figure out how to make the turn at the top of the stairs to enter the apartment; the woman at the bottom can't see the top, but she's familiar with this kind of situation—she's done this before; she is the expert. The stair, its width, the curve, the table size, shape, and weight, and so on are the common conditions of the movers' work. The two talk back and forth, the man at the top giving information—"It's sticking at the corner"—the woman at the bottom proposing ways of shifting the table, "Boost it up a bit and lean it over." The coordination of the doings of each is in language, but it is also in what each does in shifting the table—each move changes the distribution of weight and the shape of the table in their hands and arms and how it is aligned in the stairwell; it changes how the two can move their bodies in the relatively confined space, and so on. They have the work, the staircase, the table in common. But these also produce differences in their experience out of the diverging perspectives and actions that enter into the successful performance of the job; it produces the irritation in the voice of the woman at the bottom, who is making suggestions that she's sure the guy at the top isn't listening to. Their experiences are also projected into the future in a process that we may think of as dialogic, where what they have learned in the episode—of each other, of the particular settings, of moving an awkward piece of furniture—enters dialogically into the next moment of their relationship as well as the next time they move furniture.

The social coordinates differences and generates differences. Institutional ethnography takes for granted that each person is unique; each has a biography and experience that is her or his own; each is positioned differently from the others; each therefore sees things from a different perspective, feels things differently, has different needs and desires, different interests. What people are isn't the institutional ethnographer's business in this sense: she or he does not aim at explaining people's doings in terms of a theoretical system in which they must be accorded proper theoretical value. Rather, she or he is concerned with learning from their experience and with tracing how their everyday lives and doings are caught up in social relations and organization concerting the doings of others, although they are not discoverable from within the local experience of anyone.

The diverging perspectives and interests of the two at work shifting a table up the stairs are a paradigm of social organization at all levels of the social. The social, as the concerting of people's doings, builds on and generates divergence of perspective and interest. Large-scale organizations and institutions, though their objectives may be defined as shared, generate and indeed rely on differences. The abstract social relations of capital theorized by Marx are, as he makes clear, grounded in differences between bourgeoisie and proletariat that had been specifically developed and promoted actively and repressively by the bourgeoisie. Underlying the apparently perspectiveless relations of exchange is the relationship between a working class and a bourgeoisie established historically in the course of what he calls "so-called primitive accumulation" (Marx 1976). The institutions of Western European imperialism subordinated peoples who could be distinguished from Europeans by physical traits. That subordination has translated historically into the racism of postcolonial society.

Social relations and social organization generate differences in experience and perspective, whether at the macro- or microlevels. We participate in the ongoing historical commitments of the social relations organizing racism in our everyday lives, and how we know each other arises from and builds upon a past that is coming into being in the present and projects into the future. Diverging experiences arise in the most ordinary ways whether generated at the macrolevel or in microsequences of organization such as that of the people hefting a table up the stairs. The deep epistemological problems for sociology posed by the women's movement originated historically in a division between men's and women's work in Europe and North America that assigned women to the domestic sphere and excluded them from the male-dominated sphere of intellect, science, and rationality (see chapter 1). A gendered perspective and experience is built into what we call the Enlightenment in Western society. The theories of postmodernism have theoretically formalized the diverging perspectives and interests that have been created historically from the institutions of imperialism as well as those of gender. The social coordinating of people's doings creates differences in experience among individuals and takes its distinctive local character out of differences, both those that preexist and those it generates.

Since it rejects such a knower from the outset, institutional ethnography does not claim universality. It does not aim to produce a single unified representation that supersedes diverging perspectives and experiences. As mentioned earlier, Bakhtin calls such unifying languages "monologic." Michael Gardiner (1992) writes,

> Monologism, for Bakhtin, describes a condition wherein the matrix of ideological values, signifying practices, and creative impulses which constitute the living reality of language are subordinated to the hegemony of a single, unified consciousness or perspective. Whatever cannot be subsumed under this transcendent consciousness is regarded as extraneous or superfluous. (26)

Take the account of two people hefting a table up the stairs. A strategy aimed at a unified account would try to produce from the diverging stories of what went on a single objectified account, its meaning, perhaps. Exploring the coordinating of people's activities would, by contrast, learn from differences of experience and perspective in the same overall process and look for how the actions (including talk) that went into it were being concerted. The ethnographer is not looking for agreement among different informants but for the intersections and complementarities of their different accounts in the relations that coordinate their work. Indeed, in institutional settings, difference in perspective and experience are central to discovering how people are active in producing institutional forms of coordinating.

Research aims to take advantage of the different ways in which people participate in social relations and in which what they do and experience is organized by how others' doings are coordinated with theirs. Ellen Pence's investigations (2001) of the organization of the judicial processes dealing with domestic abuse in Duluth, Minnesota, began with her experience as an activist in a group providing support and advocacy for women whose partners were charged with this offense. The group of advocates learned directly from the women about problems of safety and protection from their partners that the judicial process did not recognize and indeed sometimes intensified. Pence studied just how the process was organized, beginning with the 911 calls, the dispatch of a police patrol car, the writing of the police report, and the processing of cases all the way through to sentencing. The method of research was observational, through interviews, and through the analysis of texts. Police talked to her about their work, how reports were constructed; she talked to detectives, probation officers, city attorneys, and she learned from them how they went about their work and so on. Each had a different story to tell, a different knowledge of the process.

The ethnography describes just how these work processes are put together. Different viewpoints are not displaced by the ethnographer's interpretations, as they are (1) in the grounded theory approach as described by Charmaz and Mitchell (2001), which proceeds inductively to arrive at a theory that is to be refined and evaluated as an interpretation of data over the course of the study; (2) in approaches such as those recommended by Hammersley and Atkinson (1995), according to which ethnographic research design should begin with a problem or a specific focus or with the aim of producing descriptions and explanations of particular phenomena; or (3) with developing theories (Hammersley and Atkinson 1995, 25). In Pence's study (2001), the overall orientation that establishes the general relevance originates in the concerns and experience of women who were involved in the judicial process through the involvement of their partners. That orientation does not displace the experiential knowledge of people working in different positions in the judicial process. The account produced relies on assembling the process as it is known by those who bring it into being. Their experiential knowledge is not subdued or subjected to an overriding interpretation. Rather it is put in a place created by the complementary accounts of others also involved (more about this in chapter 7).

Recognizing the Social as Happening

Whereas for institutional ethnography the coordinating of people's doings is seen as an ongoing and active process, mainstream sociology has worked with notions of order and pattern and in general with concepts that reify the social as distinct states or determinants. Talcott Parsons in his study of *The Structure of Social Action* (1937) argued that the central problematic of sociological theory was the problem of order. Social order could not, in his view, be extrapolated from the interaction of multiple individual purposive acts, leaving a problem of order originally conceptualized by Hobbes in his carefully reasoned analysis of the implications of a society without regulation and of the war of all against all. But rather than go Hobbes's route to finding a solution in the political dominance of one individual over all, Parsons argued that the very existence of society depends on shared norms and values that override the built-in unruliness of purposive action. In the same tradition is Giddens's conception of social structure (referred to earlier) "as rules and resources . . . recursively implicated in the reproduction of social systems" where structure "is understood as referring to the institutionalized features . . . of societies" (1984, 185). Such rules, he writes cautiously, are "implicated in the reproduction of social systems" (185). Interestingly, Herbert Blumer (1969), presumably influenced by the mainstream current of his time, reconstructed George Herbert Mead's social in motion into a theory of shared interpretations as a condition for the existence of patterns of group life.

From Parsons on, the problem of the orderliness of the social is resolved by introducing theoretical entities such as norms, shared interpretations, roles, or rules that reproduce the underdetermination of meaning discussed earlier (Bazerman 1988).[15] While the patterning or orderliness that is held to constitute society is a product of norms or rules and so on, norms or rules cannot be found other than as inferences from observed patterning or orderliness. In conceiving of order, structure, or pattern as generated by rules or norms, mainstream sociology imposes synchrony on what is essentially in motion.[16]

Bakhtin (1981, 1986) offers an alternative model that rejects the theorizing of structure as independent and determining of particular occasions of people's doings and how they are coordinated with others. Bakhtin is, of course, writing a literary theory. He is taking on de Saussure's distinction between *langue* and *parole,* between language as a system of signs and of speech as people actually speak language. For de Saussure, the two are independent focuses of study. The meanings and properties of signs are determined by the system of signs; language is theorized as structure or system. Speech is distinct as a phenomenon and can be studied in separation from the system of signs generated within language. Bakhtin's alternative is to treat the relationship between language and utterance (speech or writing) as dialogic. Language is an ongoing and developing complex within which people's intentions are realized in utterances; at the same time, each utterance both reproduces and elaborates language.

> An utterance is never in itself originary; an utterance is always an answer. It is always an answer to another utterance that precedes it, and is therefore always conditioned by, and in turn qualifies, the prior utterance to a greater or lesser degree. (Holquist 1990, 60)

The notion of structure is dissolved into the continuities of a historical process in which every moment of utterance is embedded and hence constrained by the past and at the same time projects into the future its idiosyncrasies.

Rather than look for the impalpables of social structure as generating particular "patterns" of action, we might adopt something like Bakhtin's model. Dialogue is a form of coordinating in language. Moving to the more inclusive conception of coordination, the social might be conceived as an ongoing historical process in which people's doings are caught up and responsive to what others are doing; what they are doing is responsive to and given by what has been going on; every next act, as it is concerted with those of others, picks up and projects forward into the future.

For example, much of the orderliness of driving a car is just such a local historical process. If you are from North America and you travel in Australia or Britain (or vice versa), you are required to follow a rule that tells you to drive on the other side of the road than that to which you're accustomed. Such a rule doesn't exist in an abstract conceptual space that can be conceived as determining action. It is legislated and available in material forms in instructional manuals and the like. Though you know there is a rule in Australia (or Britain) about driving on the left side of the road, you discover how much more is involved in driving following a rule than just following a rule. For example, it's much easier to drive in traffic than on an empty road. In the former case, you have to coordinate your car in relation to others; in a sense, they guide you. In the latter, you've no such guidance, and it's easy to find yourself automatically drifting over to driving on the wrong side of the road. It's here that "rule" may kick in again, with a bit of luck, as you remind yourself that you should be driving on the left or the right depending on where you are.

Coordinating the movement of your own car with that of others may at certain points involve hooking into a rule, but much of the time coordinating is in and of the ongoing local historical process of driving in traffic. Traffic volumes and flows differ at different times of the day and in different areas. Ongoing coordinating is always a local historical development. Rather than system, pattern, or structure emerging, there is process that is historically committed. By "historically" here I don't mean that it is in the past; I mean rather that the shape it takes for a driver has been developed in how she or he and others have been driving and is being projected into the future in which she or he participates. There is no point where it becomes fixed and objective and frozen in time. Rather, as in Bakhtin's model, each next act is "dialogically" engaged with a past that is not concluded.

But, of course, there *are* rules; there *is* regulation. But these are not separable as determinants of the ongoing historical process; they are integrated with it. Institutional ethnography follows the model and recommendation of the ethnomethodologist Lawrence Wieder (1974), who started out in his study of the convict code by assuming that the code shaped the social life of convicts. In the course of his ethnography, however, he came to see the code not as an external order governing inmate behavior but as it was spoken by inmates to each other and the staff. "Rules," Wieder saw, are people's local practices. A young driver sweeps through the stop sign when my grandson and I are about to embark on crossing the street; I let out a yell: "That was a stop sign!" Ineffectual, of course, but I am expressing a rule. I've "read" the rule from the stop sign itself and the bold white line that stretches half way across the street. And somewhere back there then, I read the traffic regulations. The rule entitles me to protest; my advanced age gives me the freedom to shout—I don't care any more what people think. My shout coordinates with the driver's failure to stop. I want her to hear me and to think next time. I want her to recognize what I recognize, a rule that says something like "Where there's a sign saying 'stop,' stop and check to make sure there's no car or person crossing." But driving a car in a city can't be reduced to a knowledge of rules. Though police enforcement controls the vagaries of drivers, it cannot prescribe the ways people adjust to traffic's ongoing flow. Similarly local practices of legally prescripted legislation are integral to the sequences of judicial action described by Pence (2001; see chapter 9) in her ethnography of the processing of domestic abuse cases. At each stage the law requires that this or that be done, and the validity of the steps taken depends on conformity. But the prescriptions of the law do not exist in an abstract theoretical space; they are locally incorporated into people's work and the coordinating of their work as a sequence of action.

Isolating and individuating the subject objectifies the historical commitment of the ongoing process. The concept of social structure hypostatizes what is external to the individual subject active in it. Though ethnomethodology does not reify order, understanding it as being produced by the methodical practices through which members accomplish sense and accountability, its methodology cuts out pieces of the social for scrutiny and analysis. The latter are allowed an internal temporality, though one that disconnects them from past and future as well as from the ongoing social processes in which the originals were necessarily embedded. In isolating stretches of talk for investigation and analysis, ethnomethodology and, more specifically conversational analysis, differentiates talk from what becomes its context, relegating the latter to a region that its methods do not embrace. In the original, of course, that separation does not exist and hence theoretical debates go on concerned with whether and how properties attributed to social structure such as gender can be admitted to analyses of talk (Schegloff 1987, 1991; Wilson 1991; Zimmerman and Boden 1991). These debates address a problem created by removing talk[17] as an object of investigation from the ongoing process of which the originals were part.[18]

By adopting Bakhtin's dialogic conception of an ongoing historical process in which each moment of interchange, of people's doings, of our use of language, and of our work is embedded in and contributes to the movement of the present from the past into the future, institutional ethnography avoids extracting the particularities of people's everyday lives and doings to construct abstractions that isolate them conceptually. Social structure is dissolved into an ongoing historically committed interplay of people's doings. The constraints of the past-in-the-present are recognized but not reified as structure or order. Rather institutional ethnography attends to people's actual activities in relation to how they are coordinated with others within the historically committed process. The institutional, in this sense, is to be discovered in motion; its distinctive modes of generalizing coordination are themselves seen as being brought into being in people's local doings in particular sites and at particular times.

Institutions, Language, and Texts

I have suggested that we recognize institutions as functional complexes within the ruling relations. By "functional complexes" is meant nothing more than the observables of complexes of organizations and discourses that are focused on functions such as education, science, law, health care, government, corporate profitability, and so on. They do not become, in institutional ethnography, objects of investigation as such. Rather, they come into view only partially as they are explored from the standpoint of people who in one way or another are involved in them. Indeed inquiry may reach into intersections or interconnections of more than one functional complex or of the more inclusive ruling relations. Characteristically, any such exploration will not conform to the conventional circumscriptions that define a particular entity. Actuality isn't bounded by institutional categories; in the real world, the social relations that are significant in organizing people's ordinary participation do not conform to what can be represented institutionally. The researcher does not know in advance where her or his investigation will go. Directions come from the original problematic as it was brought forward in the experiences of those with whom the researcher was working at the inception of her or his study.

Exploration into the ruling relations, into institutional complexes, from the standpoint of experience in lived actuality, opens into a world that is organized in language and is based in texts of various technological orders (see chapter 1). The ruling relations confront the researcher with phenomena that the foundational ontology set in place by Marx and Engels in *The German Ideology* will not encompass. Although Marx and Engels insist that consciousness must be recognized as always in and of individual people, they do not provide for us a way of understanding or analyzing those social relations—forms of coordination—that have emerged largely since their work was completed. In the nineteenth century, consciousness, thought, ideas, knowledge, reason, and so on could be assimilated to what was going on in people's heads. The developments with which we are so familiar were beyond conceptualization at that time. The institutions of individually owned capitalist enterprises were foundational to their account of the two classes that confront one another in the capitalist mode of production. What was not visible to them nor recognized in their thinking was the shift to corporate forms of capitalist enterprise. Max Weber's later sociological observations could register such changes, at least in the context of government, though his conceptualization of the major changes that were beginning at the time of his writing relied largely on the abstract notion of "rationality."

The notion of the ruling relations, however, recognizes a major transformation in the organization of society in which "consciousness," "mind," "rationality," "organization," and so on become reconstructed in objectified forms external to particular individuals. This is the region into which inquiry ventures as it moves from the experiences of people into the ruling relations. I have not envisaged this move as one that reverts to an idealism that substitutes ideas, beliefs, and so on for "material forces." Institutional ethnography attends to those phenomena of consciousness, thought, culture, and the like as they have become objectified in the translocal organization of people's work and as a product of that work. They are people's activities; they are actual; they are material; they are ongoing. Therefore, language is central to these forms of organization, and language must be brought into the scope of institutional ethnography's ontology so that it and the variety of what gets done in language can be incorporated into ethnographic investigation just as any other local practices. This topic will be developed in the following chapter.

Conclusion

This chapter has written a conceptual design for institutional ethnography as an ontology, an account of how the social exists as the object of inquiry. That design works from the actualities of people's doings with a focus on the social as the coordinating of those doings. The conceptual design has been based both on previous theoretical work by institutional ethnographers but also, and perhaps more importantly, on how the development and refinement of concepts have come out of institutional ethnographic research. It also comes in my own work and that of others out of the necessary explication of what is at first known intuitively for the purpose of teaching it. Inquiry is given primacy over theory, subordinating theory or concepts to the explication of just how people's ongoing activities are coordinated. In marking and explicating the difference between institutional ethnography and the mainstream of sociology, I have identified these major aspects of the social as the object of inquiry.

1. The first and most important step is establishing institutional ethnography's ontological ground in actual people's doings under definite material conditions.
2. But the social isn't yet quite there if we're left with that. Add in then the idea of how people's doings are coordinated. The social as definer of institutional ethnography's focus is on actual people, actual activities under definite material conditions explored for how those activities are coordinated.
3. Starting with actual people means that you start with individuals who are unique, each of whom has a perspective of her or his own. In the very process of coordinating people's doings, divergence of perspective and experience is being created. Thus the social itself generates diverging perspectives, experiences, interests, and know-how.
4. The world of people's activities and how they are coordinated among individuals is always in motion. Each moment of action is conditioned by what is historically given and reshapes the already given in moving into the future.
5. The last point is promissory. It introduces phenomena of language as integral to the investigation of the social with special significance to an ethnographic practice that reaches beyond the local into the institutional forms in which those whose standpoint establishes the takeoff point for research—its problematic—are engaged.

Institutional ethnographers take for granted that people's doings happen, that there is an actuality, and that there is the possibility of establishing agreement or, equally important, recognizing disagreements about that actuality. Hence inquiry goes forward on the basis that it is possible to correct misapprehensions, to use notions of accuracy without metaphor, and to arrive, among institutional ethnographers at least, at a developing knowledge of how to explore institutional regimes from people's standpoint. The project is to discover how institutional relations are put together so that we can talk and write reasonably about how they work and so that we can share our findings with each other, with other sociologists, and with those who participate in the institutional regimes under study. The product of such an inquiry is an ethnography that should stand up to examination from other sociologists and from those whose everyday lives are implicated and active in producing the institutional processes on which the research has focused.

Notes

1. The concept of the order of discourse is Michel Foucault's (1981). It refers to procedures by which discourses are controlled and delimited.

2. Notable exceptions, in my view, are the ethnographic studies of Charles Goodwin and Marjorie Harness Goodwin; ethnomethodology is another exception, particularly conversational analysis.

3. While other sciences accumulate knowledge, or at least findings, sociology, it seems, "cumulates" theory—see Jonathan Turner's "assessing theory cumulation" (1989).

4. See, for example, many of the essays in Button (1991).

5. Stylistics defines "the particular use of linguistic structures to create facsimiles, models or distortions of the real world" (Bradford 1997, xii).

6. The critique first formulated in *The German Ideology* is carried over into a critical treatment of how political economists treat the concepts of political economy as if they were the reality itself (Smith 2004).

7. For a full explication of Marx's ideological critique as it applies to sociology, see my chapter, "The Ideological Practice of Sociology," in *The Conceptual Practices of Power: A Feminist Sociology of Knowledge* (D. E. Smith 1990a).

8. A problem pointed out by Harold Garfinkel (1967) in his critique of standard sociological practice.

9. Later versions of Marxist theory, such as Louis Althusser's (1969, 1970, 1971) structuralist or the dogmatic forms that Jean-François Lyotard (1984) deserted and then repudiated in his *The Postmodern Condition*, have failed to take this commitment as seriously as Marx did.

10. This was an aspect of Marx's thinking that Althusser wanted to junk; see his *Reading Capital* (1970).

11. It is important here to note that conceiving of the social as a focus on people's activities as they are coordinated does not mean excluding violent forms of

dominance. Physical violence is used by men to assert dominance over their partners; it is used by police to preserve the orderliness of the streets as well as to enforce the law and is an aspect of the work and work organization of policing; parents' physical power over their children, however benignly exercised (and it is not always so), is equally a medium of coordinating doings. These and other modes of domination coordinate the activities of the dominated with those desired by the dominators.

12. What is known as *activity theory* might be expected to be congenial to institutional ethnography. It derives from the very same ontological declarations that Marx and Engels make in the first part of *The German Ideology*. It has been developed on the basis of the psychological thinking of Lev Vygotsky, who founded an exceptional tradition of psychology in the Soviet Union that incorporated the social environment into its conceptions of the psyche and, most notably, in its theorizing of psychological development. It has been more recently re-created as a sociology, notably in the work of A. N. Leont'ev (1978, 1981) and, more recently still, by Yrjö Engeström (1987; Engeström, Miettinen, et al. 1999). The problem with developing the linkages between institutional ethnography and activity theory as a theory of the social is that the latter is deeply informed by its psychological origins. Leont'ev (1981), for example, introduces the notion of a division of labor as a property of the collective—not so very different in its conceptual logic from the individual–society dichotomy that haunts mainstream sociology. Engeström's move is somewhat different but perhaps more resistant to institutional ethnography in extrapolating from the individual to systems. Activity systems are built from individual activity according to certain formal rules, and the results can be used to analyze actual work organization. Although the models are constructed from ethnographies of actual work organizations, the commitment to formal models preempts institutional ethnography's commitment to inquiry into and discovery of people's activities and how they are actually being coordinated in given institutional settings.

13. Mead's method was one of making theoretical formulations based on carefully observed interactions among humans and animals, a method singularly congenial to institutional ethnography.

14. As I remember it, it had been made by Al Robillard.

15. With the notable exception of Harold Garfinkel's investigations of order (1967).

16. Ethnomethodology has created a signal departure from the generally taken-for-granted relationship between norms and the patterning of social action: "A fundamental insight of ethnomethodology is that the primordial site of social order is found in members' use of methodical practices to produce, make sense of, and thereby render accountable, features of their local circumstances. In so doing, they constitute these circumstances as a real-world setting of practical activity" (Zimmerman and Boden 1991, 6).

17. Isolating a stretch of talk from ongoing processes is also technologically achieved. Audio recordings and the technical transcription procedures used by conversational analysis perform a fairly radical editing, both by selecting a stretch of talk for recording and producing by artifice a temporally isolated sequence and by separating what is in language from other dimensions of communication that rely on copresence.

18. Alessandro Duranti and Charles Goodwin (1992) have raised this problem as a more general one for research into language as an interactive phenomenon: "In our view the fundamental asymmetry of the figure ground relationship of focal event and its context has had enormous consequences on how these phenomena have been studied. First, differences in salience are accompanied by corresponding differences in structural clarity. The effect of this is that the focal event, with its far more clearly articulated structure, receives the lion's share of analytic attention while methods for analyzing, or even describing, the more amorphous background of context are not given anywhere near the same amount of emphasis. Thus linguists have taken the segmental structure of language as the key focal phenomenon that is relevant to the production and organization of talk. One result of this is a vast disparity between the incredible amount of work that has been done within formal linguistics on language structure, and the very small amount of research that has focused explicitly on the organization of context" (10).

CHAPTER 4

Language as Coordinating Subjectivities

The ontology of the social developed in the previous chapter extends to thought, ideas, concepts, mind, theories, and so on that are generally assumed to occupy an ontological realm distinct from people's doings, if indeed they are accorded any kind of ontological status at all. Issues arise about how they may influence, affect, and determine what people do, but they aren't seen as active or as forms of action in themselves. The separation of mind and body for which Descartes wrote the constitutional conventions is perpetuated in a separation of the regions of thought and mind from people's doings and, most strikingly, from the social. With the notable exceptions of George Herbert Mead, V. I. Vološinov, and the tradition of psychological theory descending from Lev Vygotsky to Alexander R. Luria, the lexicons of consciousness and subjectivity give us no sense of the social; not only are consciousness and subjectivity represented as if they existed outside time and place, but they also appear as if they were not implicated in how people's doings are coordinated. Traditions of scholarly investigation of phenomena of language trace the same boundary, while language and mind, language and cognition, language and thought are the preoccupations; the social is no more than an afterthought. Few—M. A. K. Halliday is one—treat the social as integral to the investigation of language.[1] Here is Marjorie Goodwin's critique of the major tradition originating in the work of Ferdinand de Saussure (1966):

> The processes of interaction within which talk is characteristically embedded were systematically excluded from study *within* linguistics by the way in which Saussure formulated the langue/parole distinction. In

his quest to define language as a "self-contained whole," he located the social character of language in a shared grammatical system . . . rather than in interaction between speakers and hearers (and indeed from his perspective, speaking is not a social act but an individual one). For Saussure the great virtue of defining the social character of language in this way was precisely that the linguist did not have to be concerned with phenomena such as social interaction: "Language, unlike speaking, is something that we can study separately." (Goodwin 1990, 2)

To annul the ordinary sociological divorce between action on the one hand and ideas, thought, concepts, meanings, and so forth on the other, the latter have to be brought out of a transcendence that has elevated them above action. One move is to insist that ideas and so forth are also doings in that they happen at actual times and in particular local settings and are performed by particular people. They must therefore be taken on as phenomena in language, particularly since it is in language that people's ideas, concepts, theories, beliefs, and so on become integral to the ongoing coordinating of people's doings. Hence bringing phenomena of mind into the action requires also an account of language that does not reproduce the separation. To bring phenomena of language and in language within the scope of the social as I have specified it in the previous chapter means shifting focus from what is within the psyche or within language as a phenomenon in and of itself to what is going on among people. This chapter addresses this issue in two ways: first, drawing on Vološinov's, Mead's, and Luria's thinking, it develops an account of language as coordinator of people's consciousnesses or subjectivities; second, it addresses some of the differences between the experiential and the text based in the constitution of what Vološinov called *interindividual territory.*

Reconceptualizing Language as Social

The first step is to take up the problem of conceptualizing language—talk and text—as among people's activities or practices and as the primary coordinator of people's consciousnesses/subjectivities. Language is par excellence the medium in which people's doings are coordinated at the level of subjectivity or consciousness. The notion of language as coordinating individual subjectivities and, as we shall see in later chapters, of discourse as a regulator of coordinating languages provides us with a way to avoid using concepts that hide the active thought, concepts, ideas, ideology, and so forth in people's heads. I don't mean that people don't think, have ideas, conceptualize and so on. I am concerned rather with what enters into the social and hence with (a) ethnographically practical ways of finding concepts, ideas, and so on in people's local activities (in this case in language) and (b) bringing such phenomena within the social as I've defined it in the previous chapter, where they can be recognized as people's doings in particular actual settings, as in time and as in connecting or coordinating with others' doings, whether in language or otherwise.

To explore language as coordinator of consciousnesses, I'm appropriating Vološinov's (1973) concept of language as creating an *interindividual territory*. Vološinov's theorizing is in many ways congenial to that of Mead, whose concept of the significant symbol will be taken up a little further on. Vološinov views a word as a "two-sided act" that is "the product of the reciprocal relationship between speaker and hearer" (86).[2] The relation between subjects that the two-sided act of the word or utterance constitutes is *between* them; it is interindividual.

Vološinov's notion of interindividual territory should not be confused with the phenomenological notion of *intersubjectivity* particularly associated with the thinking of Alfred Schutz (1962a). Interindividual territory is *in* language and is always coming into being. Intersubjectivity, by contrast, is designed to overcome the problem deep in phenomenological approaches in sociology of a starting point in individual subjectivity (discussed in chapter 3) that creates the mystery of the other's subjectivity. As Vaitkus (2000) tells us, at the simplest level, intersubjectivity is considered "as a 'mundane problem' which simply assumes the existence of the Other as our natural attitude in the everyday life-world" (280). The term is, however, projected further as foundational to "the meaningful and manifold articulations of interesubjectivity within the higher reflective spheres or domains of the world" (280). Vološinov's (1973) conception of interindividual territory differs radically because it arises out of the two-sidedness of the word in the interchange between speaker and hearer; it comes into being for them as their consciousnesses are coordinated in language.

We, as a species, share—given differences in age and special disabilities—a world known through our senses and in how our bodies are in constant interaction with what we call, not altogether appropriately, our environment. The interindividual territories of language are built into this sensory community. Language, as Mead argues, does "not simply symbolize a situation or object which is already there in advance" but makes "possible the existence or the appearance of that situation or object" (Mead 1962, 78). At the experiential level, language organizes our sensory communities as interindividual territories; that is, it organizes a reciprocal relation between speaker and hearer (and, I would add, between writer and reader) in which their differentiated experiences and perspectives intersect in a world known and named in common.

Here is an example of how language constitutes that world in common as a reciprocal relation. Made blind and deaf by an illness early in her childhood, Helen Keller (1955) was unable to communicate other than in gestures (signs) that expressed her needs. Her teacher, Anne Mansfield Sullivan, taught her to extend the range of this form of communication by spelling out the letters of words on her hand. At first spelling words on the palms of hands merely extended Keller's range of gesture as ways of expressing her needs. Sullivan describes her difficulties with getting Keller past this use of spellings (Sullivan, quoted in Keller 1909, 312) to the interindividual territory that language builds. Keller was, in a sense, alone with her desires; "nouns" signed on the palms of her teacher's or others' hands were merely expressions of a consciousness lonely in its own desire. One day, however, when her teacher ran water from the pump over her hand at the same time spelling out the letters W A T E R on her palm, Keller's consciousness was transformed. Here was the moment at which she entered, with Anne Sullivan, the interindividual territory of the symbolic process and into a world in which there were other subjects and in which she herself became, reciprocally, a subject. Before that moment in the well-house, Keller tells us, she was a "Phantom" (Keller 1955, 37) "What happened at the well-house was that the nothingness vanished" (42).

The role of what Mead calls *the significant symbol* in the organization of an interindividual territory in the relation between Keller and Sullivan is made vivid in Keller's story. Before that moment, "signs" were for her no more than expressions of need; they did not constitute a symbolically organized and organizing relation among subjects. Though Helen Keller's discovery founded for her the very capacity to participate in the symbolic, analogous discoveries were made in the early days of the second phase of the women's movement (described in chapter 1). As women, we came together to talk, knowing only that we had something to talk about, much to talk about; but what we would talk about was, at the outset, without a name. Betty Friedan's first chapter of her *Feminine Mystique* (1963) is titled "The Problem That Has No Name." For all the words, she tells us, that were written about us, for us, and to instruct us, our own strange sense of dissatisfaction was never named. Within the consciousness raising we practiced in various forms—sometimes simply as talking among other women, sometimes as something more organized—the transformative step became naming our experiences and constituting thus an interindividual territory among us as subjects who could now speak our experiences; our spoken or written experiences could thus become the bases of political organization and activity. We became subjects for each other in a new way.

A notion such as "interindividual territory" must not be reified and turned into just another blob. A way of seeing language is needed that recognizes it as activities organizing other activities and as inseparable from the more general coordinating of people's doings that I have identified in the previous chapter as the *social* and that are inseparable from those doings. In engaging with the various fields and theories of linguistics, the institutional ethnographer encounters a field of investigation that is deeply resistant—as the aforementioned quote from Goodwin suggests—to incorporating the social (as specified in the previous chapter) as in any way integral to the phenomena with which it is concerned in all their diversity. Linguistic theory in general is built on the paradigmatic foundation of an individuated subject,[3] deeply embedded in the intellectual traditions of Western Europe since Descartes wrote its constitution. The phenomena of language that theory brings into focus are assumed to be generated in or by individuals, as processes, practices, or properties of brain, mind, psyche, cognition, and so on. Noam Chomsky's (1968) theory of a universal grammar as an innate attribute of mind realized in all languages is notable in the total absence of any notion of language as social. The issue isn't whether or not the disposition to learn the grammatical forms of the language in which a child is growing up is innate. It is rather that grammar and syntax are represented as if the sequencing of words has nothing to do with organizing how people coordinate in language.[4] In general, syntax is represented as if it were an autonomous system. Actual utterances made by people in particular situations may deviate from the model, but the deviations are held to occur at the surface while underlying that surface is a "deep structure" in which the theoretical perfection of the model remains intact. If included at all in linguistic theory, the social appears only as a secondary function of language or as communication. For Ray Jackendoff (2002), for example, the social only appears as a special region of the relation of language and thought: "The understanding of the social world" includes "the identification of persons, their social roles with respect to each other . . . [and] the characterization of their beliefs and motivations" (274–75).

A rather different kind of problem is presented by M. A. K. Halliday, one of the leaders in the field of what he calls "social-semiotics." In isolating the phenomena of language for investigation, Halliday works with the notion of the text. His usage is not at all the same as that which is developed for institutional ethnography later in this book (particularly chapters 8 and 9), where it denotes words or images in some material form that gives it existence beyond the moment of speech or event. Halliday's concept of text refers to utterance in general. For Halliday (1994), "any instance of living language that is playing some part in a context of situation, we shall call a text. It may be either spoken or written, or indeed in any other medium of expression that we like to think of" (10).[5] Text, a semantic entity, isolates the phenomena with which the researcher is concerned. Having extracted language from social action, Halliday then reconnects it to what he calls, following Malinowski, *the context of situation.* From thence further connections can be made to social structure, considered "as one aspect of the social system" (4). Whatever the merits of this approach, language has already been lifted away from people's activities and their coordinating into a specialized phenomenal region of its own. Hence, Halliday's approach will not work for institutional ethnography. For institutional ethnography, the social *is* people coordinating activity; language is part of that. Hence the account of language that institutional ethnography needs is one that recognizes it both as an activity and as coordinating those dimensions of activity that are ordinarily described as consciousness or subjectivity.

Language as Coordinating Subjectivities

Mead's theory of the significant symbol complements and extends Vološinov's theory of the word as a two-sided act. It provides an escape from theories of language that place it somehow or other outside the social. His conception of the significant symbol builds the social into the very foundation of the phenomena of language and meaning; it bypasses the traditional problems of the relationship of word or signifier and signified, concept, object, or referent. Language, according to Mead, comes into being only as there is a conventionalized vocal gesture that activates in speaker and hearer the same response or assembly of responses. A vocal gesture or word activates responses stored from people's experience; experience is thus organized socially.

Mead's theory is complicated for us because he's arguing with a previous tradition of interpreting gestures and interaction. He's rejecting a model of gesture put forward by Charles Darwin, who argued that the gestures of animals express emotions—first emotion, then gesture expressing it.[6] Mead's counterargument is that gestures arise in interaction among animals, that the movement of one animal to, say, attack another, as in a dog fight, is responded to by another before it has been fully developed. The act that is cut off by the other's response becomes a gesture; a gesture is a truncated act.

The difference between the gesture in this sense and the significant symbol is that the vocal gesture, the conventionalized sound we call a *word*, is heard, understood, and responded to by both speaker and hearer. The gesture is in a sense defined by how it is responded to; by contrast, the word or vocal gesture is defined as it is responded to by both speaker and hearer (and presumably writer and reader) as having the same meaning. The meaning of a gesture is the other's response. It has no meaning otherwise, since until it's cut short by the other's response, it's just the beginning of what the actor was about to do. The word, however, means the same response to both speaker and hearer. The speaker hears and responds to what she or he has said as does the hearer.

Mead's theory of the significant symbol is one that views it as integral to the social act. It projects into and organizes what comes next as it controls the responses of both parties to what has been and is being said. The significant symbol is thus specified in terms of a coordinating of subjectivities. It is a concept in radical contrast with the traditional concept of how words mean. Saussure's influential formulation sets up the signifier corresponding to Mead's "vocal gesture" on the one hand and the signified or conceptual meaning of the signifier on the other. For Mead the significant symbol comes into being only in the social act in which consciousnesses are coordinated through a vocal gesture for which the responses are the same for those participating.

You can anticipate and you can participate in the organizing of the social act because your own awareness of the meaning of what you said is also an awareness of how the other has heard it. This does not mean that there's no room for misinterpretations and misunderstandings. It means just that the significant symbol is defined by its capacity in the social act to evoke the same responses in speaker and hearer. The very notion of misinterpretation presupposes that the speaker knows what the hearer should have heard. The social act is entered thereby into a different dimension of coordination, one in which participants can structure their own and others' responses, projecting responses onto what is to come rather than responding minute by minute to cues as they appear—the difference between guiding a car in response to others' movements and reading a traffic sign that is there for any driver on that stretch of road.

I was taught as a young driver not only to signal but also to start moving the car in the direction in which I intended to go. The idea was to double the information provided to other drivers by both signaling and making a tentative move in the direction indicated. The latter movement is what Mead calls a *gesture*. We can quarrel some other time and place about whether the blinking lights on one side of the car should really be called a gesture, but right here the point is to get clear about Mead's distinction between gesture and significant symbol. A gesture is an action cut short by another's response. When, on the highway, a lane comes in from one side, the incoming cars insert themselves into the ongoing traffic. I see a car edging into my lane, and I slow down to let it through. But I could have equally well speeded up and left the driver to find a place after I've gone by. Those kinds of interchanges are what Mead means by gestures: one begins to act, the other responds, the first responds to that response, and so on.

Language or, to use Mead's term, the *significant symbol*, creates a new dimension of organization in the social process. People aren't just waiting for cues from another or others and responding. Rather they introduce into the social act an utterance, a conventionalized sound or script to which both speaker and hearer respond in the same way. That is the defining property of a significant symbol. On the highway, a sign appears on a massive board across the highway. It reads COLLECTOR LANES MOVING SLOWLY PAST THE 427 EXIT. The written message is the same for all its readers, but at the same time it is taken up into different courses of action—depending on where the driver is going and what her or his options are. That's what is meant by "reading" it in the setting of Toronto's 401 highway. Each driver can take into account that others have read what she or he has read. Each coordinates her or his own driving decisions with the message, all the while remaining responsive to the ongoing traffic around her or him and taking the local traffic pressure, including what she or he can see ahead, into account in deciding how to interpret it. We count on the messages being read by other drivers as we are reading them. This is how a significant symbol is defined: a speaker speaks, and both hearer and speaker respond to what has been said as meaning the same thing; the utterance means the same to both.

The Interindividual as an Organization of Experience

A. R. Luria (1961, 1976; Luria and Yudovich 1971), following and developing the thinking of Lev Vygotsky (1962, 1978), focused, in some of his major studies, on the development of language in children in its role in controlling and organizing both the child's actions and his or her interaction with instructors, the experimenters. Luria's interests were primarily on the intersection of the psychological and the social. He introduces the notion of a *verbal generalization system* (1961) that organizes how the person orients to what he or she's doing, what's going on, what is there. Words abstract and systematize, suppressing attention to the particularities of what they focus on and subordinating them to verbal generalization.

We can get a clearer idea of what Luria is getting at from the story of the language learning in the *Wild Boy of Aveyron* (Ingram 1993). In the early nineteenth century, a small boy was found near a village in the district of Aveyron in France. He had been seen two or three times over a period of a few years and had once or twice been captured, clothed, and fed. But for the most part he had lived in the wild. When he was captured, it was found that he could not speak. He was sent to Paris to an institute for deaf-mutes where a physician there, Dr. Jean-Marc Itard, took him over when others had lost interest. Itard was never successful in teaching Victor to speak, but he did teach him to associate written words with objects.[7]

Itard persisted and finally, after months and months of intensive one-on-one training, Victor was able to associate some printed words with the objects they represented. Dr Itard would place a few common objects like a book, a key and a knife in his study, then move to another room with Victor. Itard would point to the names of these objects and ask Victor to go to the study and get them. Victor had no problems with this test, until one day when Itard locked the study door. Victor returned empty-handed, and Itard then pretended he couldn't find the key, and asked Victor to find the same objects around him. The particular objects Victor was to retrieve that day were a stick, bellows, brush, glass and knife, examples of all of which were in plain view in the room. If Victor recognized that these were the same kinds of things as the objects behind the locked study door, it would demonstrate that he understood that the word "stick" meant all sticks, not just the one he had been trained with. But he couldn't do it, even when Itard suggested—by gestures—that he look around and see if there weren't objects around him just like the ones he was supposed to be retrieving. The wild child was seeing differences instead of similarities—apparently every knife looked slightly different to him, so it didn't make sense to choose one when he knew the other wasn't the same. (Ingram 1993, 204)

Victor, at least as he is reported, never acquired language as a verbal generalizing system. It is this generalizing capacity of language that makes it possible for us to recognize lots of different kinds of dogs when the word *dog* is used or to bring to mind a variety of dog experiences. As Mead (1962) says,

> If one asked what the idea of a dog is and tried to find that idea in the central nervous system, one would find a whole group of responses which are more or less connected together by definite paths so that when one uses the term "dog" he does tend to call out this group of responses. A dog is a possible playmate, a possible enemy, one's own property or somebody else's. There is a whole series of possible responses. There are certain types of these responses which are in all of us, and there are others which vary with the individuals, but there is always an organization of the responses which can be called out by the term "dog." So if one is speaking of a dog to another person he is arousing in himself this set of responses which he is arousing in the other individual. (71)

What Mead and Luria offer is the idea of words as assembling and organizing the sensory world as interindividual territory so that the particularities of objects—which for Victor differentiate them—are disregarded in favor of what enables them to be treated as the same. A language-generated organization captures identity and disregards differentiating particulars as a word comes into play in the course of the social act. A word referring to an object is also an organization of perception.

> The mother's very first words, when she shows her child different objects and names them with a certain word, have an indiscernible but decisively important influence on the formation of his mental processes. The word, connected with direct perception of the object, isolates its essential features; to name the perceived object "a glass," adding its functional role "for drinking," isolates the essential and inhibits the less essential properties of the object (such as its weight or external shape); to

indicate with the word "glass" any glass, regardless of its shape, makes perception of this object permanent and generalized. (Luria and Yudovich 1971, 23)

Thus the word that, according to Vološinov, is a two-sided product of speaker and hearer also organizes the perceptions articulated to interindividual territory. This is not a flight into nominalism—that objects are no more than their names. Of course the objects that words refer to are "really there," but their existence *as objects*—and hence as referents of the words that denote them—is an accomplishment of language. We are not stuck with the dilemma Williams Hanks (1996) has formulated in his discussion of the theories of Charles Peirce and Saussure, who treat the word as referring to a concept rather than an object:

So the object of "table" would be an idea, something like "piece of furniture made of rigid material, with flat surface raised from the ground by means of legs or some other device." In this view the sign stands for an intensional object, a conceptual entity defined within the system [of language]. The problem here is . . . How do we ever connect with things in the world . . . which are material objects and not only concepts? (Hanks 1996, 41–42)

Luria and Mead propose a very different understanding of the relation between words that refer and the objects they refer to than the established word–meaning nexus in whatever form. Both work with the idea of words as *organizing*—in Luria's case perceptions of objects and in Mead's the responses of participants within the social act. Luria's account (1961) of how the development of language in children organizes their perceptual practices in the course of practical activities emphasizes how "the word" for an object focuses the child on the generalized features that make it identifiable as such. The particulars that differentiate it from instances of the same object are neglected to locate what can be treated as the same. Word and objects are in this account not independent of one another. The object perceived is already organized as such, that is, as an object, by the word that refers to it. Of course there's a real thing there, but how it becomes an object for us is, according to Luria, already organized perceptually by the referring word.

The perceptual standardization organized by a word means also that people differently positioned in relation to a named object can see it as the same. Hence diverging perspectives that are the necessary outcome of being in bodies and starting from each individual's own center of co-ordinates (Schutz 1962a) can be concerted in words that organize perceptual generalization. This is where language failed for Victor; it would not organize the world for him so that particularities could be disregarded. Victor cannot participate in words for how they *organize* the object, and hence he cannot assimilate to the interindividual territory of language that Keller discovered.

Luria gives us words as generalizing organizers that build a world spoken and heard as in common through time as well as among people. Mead, on the other hand, focuses on how the significant symbol organizes the what-comes-next of a social act. To repeat and reemphasize a quotation from Mead (1962) that I cited early in this chapter, language does "not simply symbolize a situation or object which is already there in advance" but makes "possible the existence or the appearance of that situation or object" (78) for those active in a given social act.

Experiential and Text-Based Territories

As I argue in chapter 1, institutions and the ruling relations in general are mediated by texts, not texts in Halliday's sense, but materially replicable words or images. The technologies that make the replication of words and images independent of particular local settings are foundational to the generalized forms in which the ruling relations exist. In this section I want to take up the difference between interindividual territories building on communities of experience not identical but coinciding and those that are built on texts in the material sense that I'm using the term here.

Bakhtin (1986) has introduced the concept of speech genres to embrace the heteroglossia of societies, the multiplicities of different ways of talking and writing within a given language: "Each separate utterance is individual, of course, but each sphere in which language is used develops its own relatively stable types of these utterances. These we may call speech genres" (60). He makes a distinction, which is useful here, between primary and secondary speech genres. Primary speech genres correspond to those that operate at the level of direct experience. "Artistic, scientific, sociopolitical" genres are secondary; mostly they are "written" and include "novels, dramas, all kinds of scientific research, major genres of commentary, and so forth" (62); that is, they are based on texts. This is the distinction that this section pursues with some modification to be addressed further on. While, in a sense, the experiential is never displaced, the ground on which interindividual territories are built differ radically in the move from primary to secondary speech genres.

For the most part, the interindividual territories on which linguists and philosophers rely implicate the sense-mediated world of experience—dogs, tables, trees, and so on. Of course, the sense-mediated world is one of action, and it is already social. Object table, word table connect to this organization of what Mead would call "responses"; what we do, what we say, what we write, is already organized as Luria's concept of a *verbal generalization system* proposes. Ernst von Glasersfeld (1995) takes us further into an exploration of how words do their coordinative work. He suggests that word and object emerge originally for a child in a complex of socially organized activities: "The child's concept of cup often includes for quite some time the activity of drinking and sometimes even the milk that happened to be in the cup" (141). Over time as the sound "cup" is heard and used by a child in multiple actual social acts, the word comes to differentiate the generalized object. At the same time, neither word nor object loses its connection with the socially organized activities that constitute the relation we call "reference."

Von Glasersfeld's observations complement Mead's account of how the word *dog* elicits a number of possible dog connections by indicating how the differentiation of the object to correspond to a word is embedded in the experiencing of its uses in multiple socially organized activities. Everyday talk among people relies on such experientially grounded forms of symbolic coordinating in our local activities and relationships. In what follows, the word *table* is used to illustrate the activating of experience-based interindividual territory.

When Hanks (1996) specifies *table* as a concept, he describes it as "a piece of furniture made of rigid material, with flat surface raised from the ground by means of legs or some other device" (41). However, objects are not so simple when we rediscover them in the context of people's activities. The word hooks up a range of socially organized and organizing responses—just as Mead illustrates with the idea *dog*: Tables separate floor and foot level from actions on a surface apt for the upper part of the body. A table as a mere physical form stripped of its social organization can be imagined if we think of a small child peeing on a table surface or if we remember how a table appears to children from the underside. When my granddaughter, Calla, crawls across the table and her father calls out, "Calla, get off the table!" she's learning that whole bodies aren't welcome on the dining room table.[8] Mealtimes at the table are times for what is done with the upper part of the body. Tables may be places for writing letters on or for reading a book. For talking heads, tables enable a discreet suppression of legs and genitals. In public settings, tables organize distances among people; they establish discrete territories for temporary appropriation in cafés and restaurants and so on. The socially organized practices that respond to the term *table* can be applied when there is no "piece of furniture made of rigid material" and so on. Someone moving into a new living space has a friend coming to dinner; she finds a sturdy packing box, spreads a cloth on it, and, as a final touch, puts a water glass with a flower in the center, arranging pillows around it to sit on. When her family sits down to meals, Calla is learning how *table* organizes relationships among people—she enjoys choosing who is to sit next to her. She learns daily at family meals that the table surface also serves to differentiate the tools for eating that are on the table from those that have fallen to the floor and must be picked up and dumped in the sink rather than reused. She is learning there that at mealtimes, too, only certain parts of her body are acceptable on the table surface.

To make the distinction between experience-based and text-based interindividual territories,[9] I am misappropriating two conversations by researchers working in the tradition of ethnomethodology's conversational analysis. One is taken from Goodwin's study (1990) of the talk of black children in Philadelphia. Goodwin observed and recorded the conversation of children interacting on the street without adult presence (other than her own nonobtrusive presence). She tells us that she "chose to closely document the activities of a particular natural group which formed as children on one city block played with one another" (20). This is an example of experience-based talk. My contrasting example is from Deirdre Boden's study (1994) of conversations in business settings. It illustrates talk based on a text. Both of these examples are, in a sense, being misused since the conversational analyses of both Goodwin and Boden are disregarded. I am appropriating them to make available to the reader the difference between what I'm calling the experience versus the text bases for building interindividual territories.[10]

Here is an extract from Goodwin (1990, 253).[11] Chopper is telling a story that represents Tony as a coward.

95	Chopper	'Member that time, (0.5) Lemme see we
96		got about-where we were playin'
97		basketball at? (1.2) And you had

98→	Tony	Where *who* w'playin' basketball at
99	Chopper	You know, where we were playin'
100		basketball? And you wasn't even waitin'
101		for us, you was up there runnin',
102		Until you got way around the
103		corner.' Them boys said, those boys kep,
104		those boys kep on (*I* said,) "Hey, Tony
105		what you runnin for." He said "*I* ain't
106		runnin." Them boys woulda come next to
107		*me* I (h) woul(hh)da, ((*snicker*))*hKkh I woulda
108		kicked their *ass*. And / / Tony was
109		all the way ar(h)round the corner.

I hardly need to point out here the way in which his story depends on a community of experience as his story weaves its interindividual territory. Chopper begins this sequence by telling Tony and the others to remember. He's connecting them to his experience of an event that took place, as he tells it, in a local basketball site. The story is about Tony and is told to Tony as well as to other friends. The uses of deixes such as "we," "them boys," and "those boys" impose Chopper's experience as "ours"—at least as to be recognized as shared by Chopper and Tony. Contrast this with the following sequence from Boden (1994, 134) of a recorded phone call from a research project director, Vic, to Alan, a participant in the project:

1	Vic	The *primary* reason I'm calling . h is-
2	→	uhm- (0.3) . hh : You will recall that when we
3		submitted our earlier budget? That we
4		deliberately pulled out? (0.4) a series of
5		three subheadings, and said we would bracket
6		those- uhm, for the time being? But that we
7		would bring 'em forward into c- the coming
8		year?
9	Alan	Ri[ght]
10	Vic →	[Well,] it's now ready for that?
11		Now- ((khnn)) there- there are several ways
12		we can go- go at it. And they're very
13		complicated an'tied in with the
14		nature of the accounting procedures, mm-
15	Alan	Yeah.

16		_on the one hand, and the *computing*
17		environment (0.2) on the other?
18	Alan	Hmhmm?
19	Vic	So what I want to suggest is . . .

Here are the deixes "we" and "our," as in Goodwin's little group, but Vic is orienting Alan to a text rather than a local basketball site, and the "we" is not just inclusive of a group of friends, or at least of Chopper and Tony, present to one another, but of those participating in and at some level responsible for the project. It draws in Alan plus those indefinite others also involved. Vic's instruction to recall/remember does not direct the hearer to a shared experience but to changes made in a text or document that Alan has presumably read or even partially written. Coincidence of time and place is not implicated in the interindividual territory created as it is in Chopper's story.

Each of the central speakers, Chopper and Vic, has a world-in-common with his conversants and so relies on it as a base of reference. Chopper speaks from and organizes for others from a position that Alfred Schutz (1962a) would call the *null point*:

> The place which my body occupies within the world, my actual Here, is the starting point from which I take my bearing in space. It is, so to speak, the center O of my system of coordinates. Relative to my body I group the elements of my surroundings under categories of right and left, before and behind, above and below, near and far, and so on. And in a similar way my actual Now is the original of all time perspectives under which I organize the events within the world such as the categories of fore and after, past and future, simultaneity and succession, etc. (222–23)

Chopper's story takes for granted that Tony is located bodily in the same space and at the same time as he is. His story imposes on Tony an experience of fear that he, Chopper, does not share; the difference orients to what was present to both, "them boys" who did not in fact stop but kept on. Everyday talk among people relies on just such experientially grounded forms of symbolic coordinating in our local activities and relationships. A husband in the kitchen asks his wife whether the day's newspaper has arrived; she is in the next room. She relies on her own and on his positioning to tell him it's on the table (Hanks 1996, 1). Each speaks from the coordinates organized around her or his "center O." The wife relies on this positioning of her husband in telling how to find the newspaper (it's right in front of him). Contrast that story with how Vic and Alan, speaking on the phone, talk about a text: it positions them outside their own bodily sites; their positions are not differentiated in relation to the text; it is in that sense objectifying. Differences in perspective and views might arise as participants go to work to revise and resubmit the proposal, but as it is, it has already entered textual time (D. E. Smith 1990a), external to both of them.

We must be careful not to confuse the distinction between experientially based speech and text-based speech with the distinction between oral and written speech. Here we shift away from Bakhtin's distinction between primary and secondary, which equates the latter with speech genres that are written. In this context the focus is on the mode in which interindividual territories emerge. We have had an example above of text-based talk, and we are familiar with the expression of experience in writing. Writing that expresses experience relies on and presupposes the reader's capacity to bring his or her resources of experience to bear in finding its sense. The distinction between experience-based and text-based interindividualities is between the resources that the hearer/reader brings to making sense of what is heard or read. Texts that express or describe experience constitute, as the reader activates them, experientially based interindividuality:

> A reader or hearer who, as we say, "follows" the actions of the characters, engages in an active process of interpretation. Since the teller of a story can never give an utterly complete account of what happened, the reader, in "making sense" of the story, must "fill in" her own sense of how people are and how things work, into what the text gives. . . . She has no choice but to be reminded of her own experience. Thus, to follow a story is to orient both to the experience related, and to one's own experience, as that is used in interpreting what is related. Part of the attraction of stories is that while they allow one to live through things with their characters, at the same time they pull out one's own sense of experience. The reader's experience mingles with that of the characters. (Darville 1995, 252–53)

There are, of course, other kinds of stories that rely on creating a text-based, rather than experientially based, interindividuality. News media, for example, create a textual ground on the basis of which people may build into interindividual territories. A world of objects and persons in common is accumulated that constitutes its own internal storehouse of referents. Expanded by other textual realities, such as geography, the conventional parameters of national history, and so on, it can be generalized to participants in the public sphere. These are textual realities and are connected only indirectly with the everyday actualities of the experientially grounded forms of symbolic coordinating, whether talk or text. The reader becomes familiar with what the newscaster is talking about or what appears in newspapers. She or he builds a resource of in-text identified people, events, objects, and institutional presences (government, police, and so on) that connect or can be connected when she or he watches or reads the news.

We're lucky to have an ethnographic account of making intratextual connections on which the coordination of reader/watcher/listener and news media relies. Alec McHoul (1982) did an ethnography of reading a news item in an Australian newspaper. He describes a very different kind of procedure than that which appears to characterize experiential symbolic coordinating. The headline of the story he decides to read is "Key areas 'safe.'" It doesn't mean much to McHoul. The "Meadian" process in which what is spoken gets the same response from speaker and hearer or writer and reader has partially broken down here. McHoul can't bring his response into line with what is written though, as we shall see, he does know how to look for what will make sense. Under the rules he's set for himself in writing this ethnography, he carefully avoids what he would ordinarily do, namely, rapidly skip ahead to discover what the headline "means." In reading in orderly sequence, he now finds a sentence that helps him: "Key areas in the Public Service would not be affected by the reductions in the number of public servants." According to McHoul,

> So far I've found what the mysterious "key areas" are. Or rather, what the "areas" are: they are areas of the public service. But which such areas are "key"? I've found some of the sense in which they (whatever they are) are "safe," why "safe" was in quotes in the headline. It was a statement: said to be "safe" not are (definitely) safe. . . .
>
> I ask myself: What reductions in the number of public servants? The article seems to take it that I will know about them already. That "the" appears so sure. . . . I begin to think back to about that time but nothing occurs. So I go outside the guidelines I've set myself for this reading and check some other, earlier papers. Then the controversy comes to mind, as I see the budget had just been handed down prior to this. (119)

His ethnography makes visible the work he had to do to align his responses with those of the text: "The article seems to take it that I will know about [the reduction in the number of public servants] already." It's the breakdown of the normal spontaneously produced responses that motivates McHoul to search into back issues of the paper. This is a very different referential procedure from my pointing out to my grandson an osprey above the cliffs, coasting upward on an updraft—he turns and looks in the direction I'm pointing. We can, so to speak, bring our systems of coordinates (see earlier Schutz reference) into alignment. McHoul's recourse is very different. He tracks back through the pile of old papers in the corner of his room from which he'd picked the one in which he found the story he worked with. The universe of things, events, and people that the story relies on are to be found "in the news." The action of looking for earlier news stories substitutes for the spontaneous response, that is, just knowing what the news story is about. Once the in-text referent is found, the "just knowing" kicks in; "the controversy comes to mind."

Hanks (1996), in rejecting the Saussurean commitment to associating meaning with speech in favor of his "practice" framework, stresses the importance of "printed language":

> Print mediation is a mode of distribution, implying the possibility for widespread, displaced reception. When the newspaper arrives in 100,000 homes, it actualizes a network of reception. Most of the agents of reception never meet face-to-face, and they need not know just the same language in order to participate in a public. Their community is interpretive, and their unity is largely imagined. (235)

News media, however, may and often do become occasions for talk among people, sometimes among those who otherwise have few occasions for such engagement. I'm familiar with the experience of getting into a taxi with one or other of my sons to find them in no time talking with the driver—if it's a man—about the latest scores of whatever team playing whatever sport has recently been on television, radio, or in the sports pages. They have allegiances and interests, but the texts themselves on which their talk is based are stable and unchanged by what they say; it is independent of the perspectives of participants in the talk. I hear a female shopper in my local Safeway store talking to the pharmacist (also a woman). They were doing media talk. On the previous night, there had been what the news headlines called a "riot" in downtown Vancouver. A

New York team had beaten the local team in a hockey game, and crowds had rioted in the streets thereafter. Or so the newspapers and, presumably television, informed us. The shopper and the pharmacist were talking about the riot: "How dangerous things are becoming!" they were telling one another. And yet, there we were (I voyeur as well as the two women talking), in the calm, well-to-do area of Vancouver known as West Point Grey. It is rarely disturbed even by local teenagers; it is relatively wealthy, always well kept. No experience here of public violence or riots. Though the news stories seemed to reference the same world that the shopper and the pharmacist shared, they were referencing a text, just as were Vic and Alan in the interchange recorded by Boden. They could not have found what the stories told in their own experience.

Like McHoul, they relied on the textual medium for the shared resources activated by the terms of their conversation about the riot. Unlike the term *dog* that elicits, in Mead's example, experiences of dogs as playmates, enemies, and so on, the term *riot* elicits television images of streets filled with shouts, lurid lights, smoke, charging police dressed like aliens from another planet and smashing people's heads with batons, and the wounded or dead lying on the ground in the wake of fleeing crowds of people.[12] The term *riot* activates fears of danger in the streets. The news stories assemble a textual reality, claiming to exist in the same world that the two speakers did. They could recall for each other what each had seen on the television news the night before. Danger was transmitted like an infection, from news media to the everyday world to supersede what might be available to them on the basis of their experience.

Conclusion

This chapter has introduced a theory of language as the medium in which thoughts, ideas, ideologies, and so on are lifted out of the regions of people's heads and into the social understood as the coordinating of people's doings. For institutional ethnography, language is of central importance because the distinctive forms of coordination that constitute institutions are *in* language. Institutional ethnography needs a theorizing of language that enables examination of its role in coordinating—making social—people's consciousnesses or subjectivities. The standard approaches of linguists adopt a radical disciplinary separation of phenomena of language from the social. Such approaches, however, do not provide what is needed. Hence, here we have had recourse to a line of thinking on language as essentially social that is provided by Vološinov (1973), Mead (1962), and Luria (1961, 1976, Luria and Yudovich 1971). The emphasis then is on language as *organizing* what Vološinov calls "interindividual territory."

Bakhtin distinguishes between speech genres that are based on direct experience and those that are written or, as institutional ethnographers would say, mediated by texts. This distinction is pursued and elaborated using a variety of examples that suggest some of the differences in the ways in which language coordinates people's doings—that is, whether what people are doing is on interindividual territory anchored in a shared, experiential world or whether the interindividual is a territory anchored in texts. The contrast between the two is highlighted by drawing on recorded conversations, one from an interchange among a group of children, one of whom is telling a story based on his experience, shared at least in part with others in the group; the second, a piece of a phone conversation between two men in which a text grounds the building of the interindividual. Other examples expanded on the distinctive character of text-based interindividual territories by relying on shared intertextual bases rather than on the experiencing of a senses-based world in common. The two combined themes—that is, language as organizing the social and the difference between the building of interindividual territory based on experience and that based on texts—will recur as we move into the next phase of this journey, that of laying out a general framework for institutional ethnography as a practice.

Notes

1. See, in particular, his book with Ruqaiya Hasan (1989), *Language, Context, and Text: Aspects of Language in a Social-Semiotic Perspective.*

2. See also, Mikhail Bakhtin's formulation (1981) of language as lying "on the borderline between oneself and the other. The word in language is half someone else's" (293).

3. See my essay on "telling the truth after postmodernism" (D. E. Smith 1999d). The problem of the individuated subject deeply invades what might otherwise seem a congenial theory. The concept of speech acts, as developed by John Searle (1969), is confined to a conception of act as performed by individuals. The problem of the essentially social character of speech, indeed of language, is bypassed by introducing *rules* that govern speech acts, simultaneously producing and concealing the social. Searle's work originated in the thinking of J. L. Austin (1962), whose work—modest, unassuming, and revolutionary—introduces the

notion of a performative, overcoming the problem of the essentially social character of ordinary language by describing a class of utterances as performing an act that is more than what the utterance says. So "I do" performs a marriage; "I promise such and such" performs a promise. The performative is a function of an individual's utterance. The problem of the missing social is overcome by introducing concepts—"illocutionary" and so on—that claim while ignoring it.

4. From a secondary account of Chomsky, I read the following passage from Dowling (1999):

> Consider the following situation: a mother who knows that the family has to leave for a party in twenty minutes, and who suspects that her young daughter, a notorious dawdler, is dawdling again, comes into the child's room, points a finger, and says "Dress!" The point of the generative grammarian in such cases will be that "Dress!" is the sort of thing an adequate syntactic theory must account for by positing ellipsis. To use the term favored by Chomsky in his earliest and most influential work, the utterance "Dress!" merely gives us the surface structure of the utterance. At the level of deep structure—that is, at precisely the "invisible" or "unseen" level that Wittgenstein wants to show is nonexistent—the imperative form contains an "unrealized" second-person subject.
>
> . . . The way in which Chomskyan theory demonstrates that there is an "invisible" second-person subject at the level of deep structure is to show by examples that denying its existence would in a sense involve throwing out our entire grammatical competence as English speakers. So, for instance, the linguist will show that any raising of the "invisible" subject to visibility only produces a sentence that any native speaker will accept as being identical in sense to the elliptical utterance: "You dress!" "You dress yourself!" "You dress yourself, you!" If, on the other hand, one tries to put a third-person subject in either pronoun position, one immediately "hears" that something has gone grammatically awry: *"Dress itself!" *"Dress themselves!" etc. (I observe the usual convention of putting an asterisk before ill-formed utterances.) (31)

If, however, we start with grammar as essentially a coordinator of the social, then the theoretical imposition (and it is a theoretical imposition—there's no observational evidence) of underlying syntactic forms generating the surface (observable) structure makes no sense in this instance. For the participants, the "second-person subject" is unambiguously present. The form of the utterance is not elliptical. It is the mediation of the text and the entextualized phrase that produces the illusion of a surface structure. It is the text's magic to disconnect words from the actualities in which they are spoken. Maybe Wittgenstein gets it right, and the unseen and invisible lurking behind do not exist. If we take syntax not as an innately evolving structure of the individual mind that governs language but as being integral to language conceived as coordinating subjectivities, we might begin to think of sequencing procedures of syntax as having something to do with the practical logic of speaking intelligibly to others—for instance, how the noun phrase announces the topic or focus and the verb phrase declares the action or event. In this story, the noun-phrase phase is not needed. The mother is right there shouting to her daughter. The verb phrase is inserted into a sequence of action. What the noun phrase in other contexts substitutes for is *in the room and the social act* and not in the words. What is underlying the surface, for the analyst, is the co-presence of mother and daughter. How is it that Chomskyan amendments produce sentences that would be almost unsayable in that context of "You dress yourself" and "You dress yourself, you"? They'd also mean something quite different if spoken in that setting.

5. Halliday appears to use the term *text* to identify "any instances of living language" that become the data of linguistic analysis. He does not attend to that ambiguous transition between what was actually said (and, of course, it is always in the past by then) into the recorded and perhaps transcribed form in which it is scrutinized. In my view, this is a crucial moment, since it isolates the spoken from the social act and setting in which it was originally embedded.

6. Note that Mead's rejection of Darwin's model also applies to Saussure's (1966) account of "communication" as a sequence: a concept in the mind of one individual *unlocks* a sound image; the brain then sends that image off to become a sound; the sound then travels from one's mouth to another's ears and brain, where the reverse sequence takes place (27–28). Saussure's model is analogous to the Darwinian view of gestures originating inside the organism and moving from emotion to its expression, a view from which Mead's theory specifically dissents.

7. The moment when Helen Keller entered the interindividual territory of significant symbols was never to come for Victor. The words he learned to use were used to name particular things.

> Itard not only was never able to teach Victor to speak, he never even came close. Early on in their relationship Itard was delighted when Victor said the word *"lait"* when presented with a glass of milk. But, as Itard later realized, it's not enough to have the word and the glass at the same time. Victor could have been using the word *"lait!"* (which Itard had been trying to teach him) simply as an expression of delight. He almost never said the word *before* getting the glass, as he would have had to if he were asking for the milk. He never used the word when the milk wasn't right in front of him, nor did he ever make it clear that he understood what *"lait"* meant. (Ingram 1993, 202)

8. Though, I was suspicious after I wrote this that she knew exactly what she was doing and did it to get a rise out of her dad.

9. Note that experience-based interindividuality may also be generated in writing. Richard Darville (1995) points out that "readers of a story must use their own experience in following it and seeing its significance" (253).

10. The difference marked here is between experientially based versus textually based interindividual territories. No reference is intended to the differences in

styles of talk that appear to trace differences in social class speech as in Basil Bernstein's contrast (1966) of restricted and elaborated codes: While the working-class
students he observed tended to speak exclusively in a fashion (later described by
Bernstein as a *restricted code*) that relied on shared experiences of a local environment and people, the middle-class students made use of an elaborated code of
more abstract concepts and took into account that what was referred to was not
necessarily shared by the reader or hearer. While middle-class students com-
manded both restricted and elaborated codes, working-class students tended to
be at home only in the former. Similarly Schatzmann and Strauss (1966), in their
study of a Midwestern city struck by a tornado, noticed in the interviews that had
been collected a significant difference in how stories were told between working-
and middle-class respondents. Of course, there was overlap, but the differences
could be traced clearly and at the extremes were very marked. Middle-class respondents tended to tell the story from the standpoint of the city in general. Their
stories emphasized the city institutions, the fire department, the Red Cross, the
mayor's office, the police, and so on. Working-class respondents were more likely
to tell the story from their own points of view, describing what happened to them
and to those close to them. It could not be said that one way of telling the story
was better than the other. Some of the stories told of the tornado as it was experienced were vivid and powerful, but others were disjointed and hard to follow. The
stories told by the middle-class respondents were, however, easier for the sociologist to follow because they were told from the perspective of the city; they were
in a sense already processed in a form that could be directly incorporated into the
sociological account.

   11. Note that I have preserved, as best I could, Goodwin's notation, originally
developed for conversational analysis by Gail Jefferson (Sacks, Schegloff, and Jefferson 1974).

   12. I don't suppose that media-designated *riots* are accurately represented in
such images. Television has to go for what is a visibly warped representation in
the process.

PART 3

Making Institutions
Ethnographically Accessible

CHAPTER 5

Texts, Text–Reader Conversations, and Institutional Discourse

This chapter introduces part 3 of this book's account of institutional ethnography. This and the following five chapters all focus on how institutions can be made ethnographically accessible. In this, the first chapter of the part, I introduce the key role of texts and the problem of how to incorporate them into an ethnography based on the ontology formulated in the previous two chapters. Institutions exist in that strange magical realm in which social relations based on texts transform the local particularities of people, place, and time into standardized, generalized, and, especially, translocal forms of coordinating people's activities. Texts perform at that key juncture between the local settings of people's everyday worlds and the ruling relations. They come before us as something to read, watch, or listen to.

While I'm writing this at my desk, my attention goes from noticing my son and daughter-in-law's large and excessively loving golden retriever wandering about outside the window, to rereading what I've just written, to the radio in the background announcing a renewed threat of forest fires in the interior of British Columbia (I don't understand how the presumably living people who are our politicians aren't registering the already experienceable effects of climate change). Noticing the dog and the weather (it's very hot for this time of year in Vancouver) are entirely encompassed within the everyday local world. But writing and reading this and listening to the radio both enter me into the interindividual territories described in the previous chapter as textually based. I am connected through these various texts into relations elsewhere, with those who may read this book, its publishers, and so on and with others who are listening to the news and are or are not concerned about the environment and the whole organization and economy of a radio station that delivers it to my ear.

The problem with introducing texts into ethnography is their ordinary "inertia." Somehow we don't recognize them as located in the same temporal and local world in which we exist as bodies. We construct them, I suppose, as a world that isn't present in our lived spaces and thus don't recognize texts as being "active" in coordinating what we are doing with another or others. When we are reading, watching, or listening, somehow or another we treat texts as given; we are responding to their internal temporal organization, the shape of a song or a concerto, or the page, the chapter, what's on the monitor, but not to their *occurrence* in time and place. The words or images that will always come again as long as a material thing that presents them exists have a kind of stasis under our eye. Things may be changing around us; the book that we were reading on an airplane isn't finished when the plane lands but we know that when we return to it, it will be the same. The power of the sacred text to remain across seas and generations is a condition of its holiness and its capacity to be read again, rediscovered, reinterpreted in the ever changing local actualities of people's lives and doings.

The stasis, the local *thereness* of the text haunts those who have been working to incorporate the text into ethnographic practice or into social research more generally. Lindsay Prior (2003) has developed a conceptualization of "documents in action" that aims to knit documents into people's activities. Examples of documents in organizational settings show "how documents can be recruited into alliances of interests so as to develop and underpin particular visions of the world and the things and events within the world" (67). His examples include

> examin[ing] how the identities of "patients," "clients," and the criminally insane are structured through documentation, how forms of documentation can be used as warrants for action or as props in interaction, and how "organization" is made evident "performed"—through the written record. (Prior 2003: 67)

Prior's approach is in many ways congenial, but from the point of view of institutional ethnography it presents some problems. For one thing, people have disappeared and documents become the focus of research. "The task of the researcher" writes Prior, "should . . . be to follow a document in use" (68): How is a document "enrolled" in routine activity, what is its function and how does it differ in different contexts, or what is its role in constituting a phenomenon (68)? The researcher produces then an account that both detaches document and its uses, functions, or role (Prior uses all three terms) from local settings and sequences of action and leaves people out. Action is ascribed to documents, but just how people are implicated in that action is not a focus of research attention.

Rod Watson (1997) has developed for ethnomethodology a research approach to texts that both preserves their "active" character and situates them in people's local courses of action. He proposes analyses of the text in terms of its implications, looking thus for those aspects of a text that orient themselves to what is to come. In analyzing the data that he and John Lee collected in the course of doing fieldwork in street settings, he observed a group of people waiting for a bus. He noticed how, as a bus approached, its number led to some standing back and others moving forward in line. Different numbers sorted the group into those who wanted and those who did not want the bus route that the number identified. He introduces the notion of the "duplex-action" of the text of the bus number:

> The first "moment" of this is parties' monitoring of the sign(s), and the second "moment" is the incorporation of the sign into "further" action. (93)

Watson's observations and proposed method of analysis are promising in terms of how to explore ethnographically (or ethnomethodologically) how texts are taken up locally. The method does not, however, respond to the extralocal dimension of textually mediated forms of coordination that are called for in ethnographic explorations of institutions or of the ruling relations in general. Institutional relations are present in the everyday, but the translocal connections cannot be tracked using the traditional observational approaches of much ethnography and ethnomethodolgy. Texts have this capacity for a dialogic or dual coordination, one as they enter into how the course of action in which they *occur* is coordinated and the other in how the text coordinates a local and particular course of action with social relations extending both temporally and spatially beyond the moment of the text's occurrence. Just take the number 16 on the front of Lee's and Watson's bus. Reading a bus number as information about the route it travels presupposes organization beyond the text itself. Watson's analysis shows us the local practices of reading and action of those waiting for the bus; it does not, however, open up another kind of connection, namely, the bus company's design of bus routes and how that is organized in relation to the layout of the city, passenger flows, and peak times; the work of bus drivers, mechanics, and others who get the bus to the bus stop on time; and beyond that, the organization of the bus company, including clerical workers, managers, and so on. That goes beyond observation at any one site.

I have to remind myself at this point that, unlike ethnomethodology, an institutional ethnography is oriented by a problematic, namely, the everyday experience of people active in an institutional context. John Lee and Rod Watson are, by contrast, making observations; the work of observation for the purposes of description produces an objectified account. Their interest is in what people are doing in urban settings as they can be observed and recorded. The standpoint implicit in the description is that of the academic discourses in which the observers participate and for which the descriptions are produced. Institutional ethnography, however, works from a standpoint within the institutional relations from which the research problematic has been created. It is concerned with discovering dimensions of institutional relations that are at work in the local setting. Institutional relations are, as emphasized in chapter 1, essentially text mediated—hence the need for an ethnographic strategy that recognizes texts as actual presences in people's activities and in how activities are coordinated both as local sequences of action and institutionally.

The remainder of this chapter addresses two topics. First the notion of a *text-reader conversation* is introduced. Earlier in this chapter I suggested that texts might be seen as occurring in courses of people's activity. The *text-reader conversation* expands the idea of a text *occurring* so that the reader's and the reader's active engagement with the text's inertia can be made visible. As a reader activates a text, she or he engages with its language and is also responding to it. That is the text-reader conversation. Second the notion of *institutional discourse* will be explored to identify its distinctive features and describe its characteristic text–reader conversations.

The Text–Reader Conversation

In a face-to-face conversation or in talking on the phone, you would not think that there was only one party to the conversation. You would not think that the conversation did not take place in time. You would not imagine that there was no interchange, even though one party is talking rather a lot and the other only gets to say, "Uh huh," "Yeah," and so on.

> Well, of course, texts are written—or spoken. No one denies that. But texts have to be read in order to be understood. Textuality is a scene in which readers respond to the texts they encounter. If one locates the reader at the center of textuality, it is because the text is passive and silent, because it needs the reader's activity to infuse it with meaning, to bring it back to life. (McGann 1993, 4)

Reading a text is a special kind of conversation in which the reader plays both parts.[1] She or he "activates" the text (McCoy 1995)—though probably never quite as its maker intended—and at the same time, she or he is responding to it or taking it up in some way. Its activation by a reader inserts the text's message into the local setting and the sequence of action into which it is read. Notice that the concept of activating the text differs from Watson's "monitoring" stage of reading. For Watson, the text is still external to its reader. The concept of a text–reader conversation, however, brings the text into action *in* the readers who activate it. It also, and equally important, anchors the text in the local actualities in which people are at work.

In institutional settings, text–reader conversations are integral to the ways in which institutional discourses regulate people's local activities. We can explore the text–reader conversation as a process that translates the actual into the institutional (a topic to be developed further in chapter 9) and, conversely, the distinctive ways in which institutional discourse subsumes and renders "institutional" the particularities of everyday experience. The latter is a focus of the observational exhibits discussed later in this chapter.

The text–reader conversation is active, but it is also peculiar and unlike conversation in that the text remains the same no matter how many times it is read. Spoken conversations take shape as each speaker responds to the other, whereas in text–reader conversations, one side is fixed, predetermined, and remains unchanged by the history of its reading (though, of course, a reader's reading of it may change). One "party" to the conversation is fixed and nonresponsive to the other; the other party takes on the text, in a sense becoming its voice—even, as we shall see, its "agent" (D. E. Smith 1990b, 1999d)—and at the same time, responds to, interprets, and acts from it.

Many, if not most, text–reader conversations are not observable. Watson's observations at the bus stop are not actually of people reading a text but of a text that people are responding to in a way that allows the observer to infer the reading he attributes them. The work of reading the bus number is missing.[2] A long time ago I reviewed for a publisher an anonymous draft of a book that made the work of reading bus numbers visible. It was an ethnography of people who could not read and of how they managed their everyday lives. It described reading bus numbers as one example of a problem they routinely encountered. The nonreaders used various ingenious methods of getting others to read bus numbers for them without disclosing that they could not read. They wanted to avoid being labeled *illiterates*. The reading stand-in's reading of the bus number became observable because he or she was reading aloud. The study made observable the complexities of a text–reader conversation that could be observed only because it had to be mediated by a third party. We can find the traces of text–reader conversations. For example, library books are sometimes highlighted or contain marginal comments that impose the traces of one reader's conversation with the text on the later reader. There are also instances, though few, of a sociologist's observations of her or his own text–reader conversation. As we saw in the previous chapter, McHoul (1982) provides that rare study, an ethnography of one's own reading—in this case, an item in a newspaper—that follows closely the actual process of reading. I adopt a rather different approach in analyzing the procedures of reading the text of an interview describing someone becoming mentally ill in which I show how my reading follows instructions provided in the text for how it should be read (D. E. Smith 1990d). In her study of activating the text of wedding photographs, Liza McCoy (1995) invented a method of making text–reader conversation observable by getting three people together (she was one of the group) to talk about the photographs of the wedding of one of them. Though the conversation was instigated by McCoy, she did not control it. She shows how the character of the photographs organized the conversation that developed among the three. She describes practices of reading that both activate and respond to the photographs as representations of the wedding of one of the participants. The idealization of the wedding in the photographs is "read through" (D. E. Smith 1990a) to the real occasion in which they originated. The bride is a resource for details of the original occasion. For example, the photographs show the wedding cake being cut, but this, according to the bride, was actually a pose for the camera; the bride and groom never actually cut the cake.

In the conversation, the photographic text is a visual presence before all three parties to the conversation. The talk treats the photographic text as referencing an event beyond the text that the conversation can address directly. That referential procedure for reading photographs is also characteristic of how factual accounts are read. The reader doesn't treat the text in and for itself but rather as a medium through which the reader can connect with what actually happened or was there (D. E. Smith 1990a). The actual events may be contrasted with its representation. On one occasion, the woman who was the bride, in describing the colors of the bridesmaids' dresses, says, "Unfortunately in the photograph it [the color of the dresses] looks black." In this instance of a text–reader conversation, we can find these features:

1. The text's presence as "the same" for any reader is attested in how each speaker takes for granted that she can reference the same image as others.
2. In activating the text, the readers recognize it as a representation of the wedding of one of those present.
3. The text–reader conversation is, in this instance, made visible as an ongoing situated activity.
4. The interpretive aspect of the text–reader conversation articulates the words or images of the text to the situation and sequence of action in which reading is embedded.
5. The readers make use of the distinctive interpretive procedure that applies to factual or veridical texts; namely, the texts are read "through" to what is taken to be an actuality on the other side that can be used to check on its textual representation.

That the text does not change in response to the reader's responses and that it is the same to any reader seems obvious. Some theorists, such as Julia Kristeva (1986), have put forward the view that the text becomes what it is *in* the reader and therefore that there is no final text on which the analyst can found her or his claim to the true interpretation. Introducing the notion of the text–reader conversation does away with this kind of difficulty. Of course, a given text may be read differently at different times and by different people and in different sequences of action. Indeed, the very possibility of different interpretations or readings of a single text presupposes the constancy of the text—that is, that it is the same text interpreted differently.

The constancy of the text is essential to the role it plays in organizations and institutions (D. E. Smith 2001a). Indeed, institutional texts may be designed to be read differently in different settings of action. The constancy of the text is also key to the effect of institutional standardization across multiple local sites of people's work. It produces for any institutional participant reading the text a standardizing vocabulary, subject–object structure, entities, subjects and their interrelations, and so forth. They are the same for all readers, and as readers talk or otherwise act to coordinate across situations in relation to the text, it regulates the discourse effective among them. Sure, they may use other speech genres, some of which resist the institutional, but even resistance adopts the standardizing agenda, if only as a foil.

The Course of Reading

It is the reader who activates the text. When the text is written, she or he takes on the role of the text's agent, taking up in the social act of the conversation the attitudes it puts into place as procedures for anticipating, recognizing, and then assembling coherences. In exploring how readers activate the text, we go back first to Mead's analysis (1962). The reader cannot discover what the text means without evoking responses associated with the words known to himself or herself. Those responses become her or his own. Most of the instances Mead uses and most of his thinking are based on face-to-face interactions and the spoken word. In these respects, the written word does not operate differently as a symbolic organization from the spoken. In reading, in activating the text, the reader's consciousness is coordinated with the words of the text. Of course, activation may be selective; perhaps, it often is. The difference comes in how the actual conversation and the text–reader conversation are inserted into the social act. In the actual, talk is part of an ongoing historical process, embedded in the process, responding to it, and controlling its direction. In the text, the reading that forms the conversation is in itself a social act, but that act may be entered into and may form an integral part of varied ongoing historical processes.

Within the text–reader conversation, however, the text exerts significant control. It is a control exercised through how its words and sentences activate the reader's responses. In being activated, the reader becomes, in a sense, the text's agent. For example, the text based on an interview with someone describing her experience of discovering that a friend was becoming mentally ill starts with the discovery as the topic (D. E. Smith 1990d). Discovering that someone is becoming mentally ill, as an intro-duction, sets up something like instructions for reading what follows. In taking up these instructions as a procedure for reading, the reader be-comes the text's agent. With those instructions, my reading looked for and found how to take up the text's descriptions of the individual's behavior as indications of mental illness or of a process of her becoming mentally ill.

Here is another and analogous example from my own experience of what I mean by becoming the text's agent as the reader takes on the re-sponses it sets up.

I was reading a mystery novel by Val McDermid (2002) during the same period as I was reading a passage in Mieke Bal's *Narratology* (1997), in which she analyzes how Evelyn Fox Keller deploys the concept of "se-cret" to examine the traditional gender order of the natural sciences.[3] Go-ing from Bal to McDermid's mystery and having had my attention focused by Bal's analysis, I began to track just how I worked the concept of "secret" in my reading. Here are summaries of a sequence of passages that follow the introduction of the term *secret*. The barge skipper's grand-father is found drowned near the barge; the barge skipper has secrets. The term *secret* operates as a set of instructions for finding those items that can be fitted to the concept, very much as the topic of someone becoming mentally ill instructed my reading of the interview referred to earlier (D. E. Smith 1990d)—that is, I knew what to look for. McDermid presents the following sequence to be fitted to the concept of *secret*.

1. The barge skipper "had never forgotten the liberation of the old man's accident" (32). The old man was his grandfather who had brought him up and mistreated him.
2. The crew members "had [not] known about [the old man's death] till morning" (32). When the "old man" doesn't turn up in the morning, the crew members look for him.
3. The skipper goes about his work as usual but conceals the fact that he killed his grandfather.
4. Crew members find the "old man's" body "jammed between the boat and the pilings of the wharf" (33). It is thought that "the old man had had too much to drink and tripped over one of the hawsers that held the barge fast against the wharf" (33).
5. The official finding is that the death was accidental. "Nobody doubted it for a minute" (33).

This is not a face-to-face conversation. There is no speaker, no hearer. The reader plays both parts, activating the text and "operating" it. What we might describe as a socially organizing grammar is activated by the word *secret*. The reader adopts and "operates" the concept. For example, I notice that it is only the crew members who did not know about the old man's death until the next morning. The concept "secret" picks out for the reader the relevant elements, which it also orders and arranges, particularly the differentiation between those who are in the know and those who are not. You, reading my text and the sequence of items from McDermid's story, will probably have also read them using the term *secret* as among your organizing instructions. Thus a course of reading gets put together as the reader assembles what is given in the text: she or he is told that the skipper has secrets and so looks to learn what others do not know; that the barge skipper hated his grandfather becomes a clue; reading on, the reader discovers that the others who do not know are the crew of the barge; only at this point is the reader told what it is that is hidden from them and what it is that she or he has been waiting to discover, that the barge skipper has killed his grandfather. That waiting itself is an attitude inserted by introducing the term *secret*. In the original, I remember that the structure of anticipation created a tension in the passage, an effect of "looking for" what is to be disclosed. First the reader learns that the barge skipper hated his grandfather. Then that the grandfather is missing, and so on. That tension, of course, is the writer's art in deploying the grammar of "secret" to organize a sequence in which, bit by bit, the secret is revealed. In reading, understood as a course of action, the concept of "secret" orients the reader to items that can be plugged into its grammar. There are insiders and outsiders to a secret; a structure of opposition is created between those who know and those who are excluded. And over all is the position of the voyeuristic reader who knows the skipper's secret.

This organization is traceable in sequences of interaction, whether talk or text. Young children use the grammar of "secret" to organize bonding and exclusions in elementary school classrooms. Though its sequential operation won't always be the same, its grammar is, I suggest, built into how "secret" means, using still a Meadian understanding of meaning as a dynamic of "responses" among parties that *controls* or organizes interaction, including that between text and reader. Once the term *secret* is launched, either what follows is organized by the grammar of the sequence, or a previous sequence is "claimed" as an expression of the same grammar. The reader is oriented to finding that the protagonist has something to conceal from others, that there are others who would want to know but who do not know what she or he knows.

In a sense, this process of becoming agent of the text in activating it is unavoidable. It is intrinsic to knowing what the words mean. Of course, this doesn't mean agreement or automatic implementation. But it does mean that resistance, repudiation, disagreement, and rejection work with and from the text's agenda.

The Text–Reader Conversations of Institutional Discourse

Institutional discourses are central to the coordinating of the work that people do in bringing into being every day the institutional complexes embedded in the ruling relations. Here I'm going to suggest that the text–reader conversations that are foundational to institutional discourses involve distinctive procedures. What follows is based on observations, my own and others', but as is every other empirical example, my general notion of how institutional text–reader conversations proceed is open to question and elaboration with further observation.

In the previous chapter, we looked at an instance of naming an object that showed the intimacy of the referential moment in the language of everyday experience: Ann Sullivan writes the letters W A T E R on Helen Keller's hand as she splashes water from the pump. The referential terms used by Mead—and, indeed, quite generally by philosophers and linguists—are of everyday objects—"dogs," "tables," and so on. But when we encounter what I am calling institutional discourses, we find that this intimacy of reference between word and experience is dissolved.

Janet Giltrow (1998), investigating management discourse, discovered a characteristic feature. She found that nominalizations[4] predominate in the discourse (much as they do in mainstream sociology) and, following the example set by M. A. K. Halliday and James Martin (1993), she sought to "unpack" them. Many, if not most, such nominalizations originated in verbs of action. Nominalizing suppressed the presence of subjects/agents. Things are getting done, but no one is present to do them. "Unpacking" means resolving such nominals into an active verbal form: someone or something does something or is supposed to do something. Halliday shows how scientific nominalizations can be unpacked. He uses an example from Isaac Newton's scientific writing. Newton uses the nominal "refraction" but also unpacks it, as in "The light is refracted"

(Halliday and Martin 1993, 7).[5] Giltrow (1998) runs into a problem when she applies this method to the nominalizations of management discourse.

> Modelling my analysis on Halliday and Martin's "unpacking," I worked on the nominals of management studies, anticipating that, in the complexities and resources of the nominal phrase, I might find the kind of disciplinary traces that appear in scientific nominals. Are management nominals like scientific nominals in representing a particular experience of the world and enabling a particular kind of thinking? Or are they as illegitimate as Halliday claims? (341)

She finds that the nominalizations of management discourse were finally ambiguous: "Agents [tended] to be recursively deleted" (341). Their absence is not just a matter of being unable to identify who those involved might be but about the continuities of agents across different elements of the unpacked nominalization. It turns out that, once unpacked, the agents are not necessarily the same person. Take a phrase such as "the creation and implementation of institutional arrangements" (341), and unpack it into its underlying active statements. Now agency is visible. Some actual individual, w, creates, and another, x, implements; or, w creates and yet another, e, implements. But a fundamental ambiguity remains: "We can't be sure if it's a single actor or set of actors linked in a chain of action: are w, x and y the same entities or different ones?" (341–42).

Giltrow's analysis suggests that institutional discourse might present a problem when it comes into play in actual sequences of action in which a text–reader conversation plays a part. Readers of institutional texts encounter not just the discourse's nominalizations but categories of persons and events that are not specified in terms of individuals. The reader can't go from a given institutional text to find what it refers to. In a strict sense, it does not function descriptively. Yet it seems to do so.

There is a type of noun that lacks specific content—for example, *thing, fact, case, reason,* and so on (Schmid 2000). Schmid calls them "shells." They do not stand alone but remain to be filled with substance by clauses that usually follow directly or are part of the same text—"The reason I was late for dinner was that my car ran out of gas" where *reason* is the shell term. Linguists in general adhere to the stasis of the text, and readers are generally absent in this analysis.[6] Sequence is recognized, but it is internal to the text and doesn't happen in time. The linguistic treatment is, of course, highly technical. In this context, I am adopting the concept of words or utterances that function as shells in the text–reader conversations of institutional discourse. The utterances contain "gaps" (Schmid 2000) waiting for the reader to fill them with substance extracted from the local actualities of her or his work. This supplies a model for the workings of the text–reader conversations of institutional discourse. Giltrow's findings (1998) suggest that those text–reader conversations that participate in sequences of institutional action would run into the problem of discovering how to trace their conceptual contours over the everyday actualities of people's work. How do you translate institutional discourse into something that has to be done by someone? Institutions happen in everyday actualities; people produce them in the course of their everyday doings. How are the texts that accomplish the distinctive standardizing and generalizing essential to what we mean by institutions entered into the local actualities in which institutions exist? How are the shells of institutional discourse filled?

Harold Garfinkel's treatment (1967) of the everyday work of the Suicide Prevention Center staff, of jurors, and of the sociological coding of data from a psychiatric clinic suggests an alternative formulation to the one that is modeled on the straightforwardly referential. Staff are engaged in "the concerted work of making evident from fragments . . . how a person died in society, or by what criteria patients were selected for psychiatric treatment, or which among the alternative verdicts was correct" (10). Garfinkel rejects the paradigm that treats the "patterning" or "typicality" or "repetitiveness" of social activities as an effect of conforming to norms or rules. He turns around the implicit temporal sequence from rule to act, proposing rather that what people do is *aimed* at producing what participants can *recognize* as rational and objective. The rationality of the inquiries done by those at work in such settings should not therefore be treated as a direct property of their activities. Rather, the "*recognizably* rational properties of their common sense inquiries . . . are *somehow* attainments of members' concerted activities" (10).

So rather than view institutional discourses as prescribing actions, we might see them as providing the terms under which what people do becomes institutionally accountable. They are distinctive in that they displace and subdue the presence of agents and subjects other than as institutional categories: they lack perspective; they subsume the particularities of everyday lived experience.[7] This, then, is how we can begin to frame the distinctive properties of institutional text–reader conversations. Somehow or another, the text–reader conversations of institutional discourse involve procedures for treating actualities as their instances or expressions.

Here is an observation of my own that makes these properties of institutional text–reader conversations visible as local practices. Some while back I did an analysis of two texts, both describing the same event, a conflict between people on the street and the police in Berkeley, California, in the late 1960s (D. E. Smith 1990d). One text told the story from the point of view of a witness to the events; the other was a report on the same event from the chief of police, embedded in a report by the mayor of Berkeley addressed to the public at large. I stress my presence and my engagement in text–reader conversations, indeed many of them, because I want to draw on that experience of reading. As I read them at first, the accounts were very different, the second contradicting the first's accusation that the conflict had been staged by the police. I started, as this suggests, by reading them as two different factual accounts. On closer reading, however, the accounts did not appear as different in substance as they did upon first reading, yet they were still contradictory.

Finally I recognized in analyzing them that the two texts were historically a sequence: first, a statement accusing the police of improper behaviour told originally from the point of view of one of those present, and, second, an official response. The official version of the events was part of a larger document, which provided some "instructions" for "reading" the sequence. I am usng the term *instructions* here to identify the kind of guide to how to read what follows that is often presented in the introductory paragraph of a text. Remember, we are thinking in terms of a course or a sequence of reading in a text–reader conversation. I described earlier an analysis (D. E. Smith 1990d) of how the phrase "becoming mentally ill" operated as instructions to the reader of an interview to find out how to take the various descriptions of the young woman's behavior as instances and evidences of her becoming mentally ill. I drew on that as a model for how to read a passage from McDermid's mystery story as instructed by the concept of secret. In the Berkeley case, my original reading of the two texts did not attend to the instructions for reading the sequence of the two provided by the official account. When I did, I found I became an agent of the second account, the institutional text, in rereading the first according to the reading procedures that the second supplied. Here are the instructions provided by the official account:

It is obvious that in an era of instant, capsule news there is an urgency that the public becomes more sophisticated in its viewpoint toward the news, an urgency that the young be educated to get the full story before reaching conclusions, an urgency that the difficulties of law enforcement in a permissive society be recognized. (quoted in D. E. Smith 1990d, 158)

The "unsophisticated" reader takes the original "alternative press" story as veridical. The sophisticated, however, proceeds differently. She or he will look for "the full story," and looking for the full story meant, I found, reading the two accounts in a sequence in which the official version substituted for or, more powerfully, *subsumed*[8] the account written by the witness. Whereas the first story provided descriptions of events witnessed by the writer that seemed to be instances of grossly improper behavior on the part of the police, the second reconstructed those descriptions so that they could be read as instances of properly mandated police behavior misinterpreted by the original witness.

Once I took up the frame of the institutional version as a method of reading, I could see how the events as described in the original had been retooled to fit the institutional frame of properly mandated police action. Here is one episode as described by the original witness:

I was standing just below the corner of Haste and Telegraph opposite Cody's and I saw a boy, 16 or 17 years old, walking up Haste and past two policemen.

Suddenly a young policeman . . . with a cigar he had just lit in his mouth grabbed this young man, rudely spun him around, pinned him against his patrol car, tore at his clothes and pockets as though searching for something, without so much as saying one word of explanation. Then he pushed him roughly up the street yelling at him to get moving.

In the version presented in the police report, we can see clearly the operation of a discourse that subsumes the original.

The first [incident] concerned a young man who was frisked and who appeared to be then released. In fact this man was a juvenile who was arrested and charged with being a minor in possession of alcoholic beverages. He pleaded guilty and the court suspended judgment. This young man was one of those involved in the event which precipitated the subsequent events.

The original account, no doubt consciously, strips the young policeman of his institutional status. He has just lit a cigar, is physically rough with the young man, and searches him without speaking to him. In this account, such details specifically displace the institutional. The police chief's version restores it. As I read the witness's version, using the official version as an interpretive frame, I, as reader, could see how the use of institutional categories enabled the original account to be treated as instances of the institutional. In a sense, the official account established a shell that could be filled from the original account. Spinning the young man around, pinning him against the patrol car, tearing at his clothes and pockets as though searching for something—all these become merely instances of properly mandated police behavior. The report that the young man was later arrested and charged is a retrospective validation of the search. It is also noticeable that the difference between the witness's account and the police account is precisely on the latter issue. The police account adds material that contradicts the witness's account. The witness describes the "boy" as being pushed roughly up the street after being searched. In the police account, the young man is "in fact" arrested. It is material that reconstructs the "frisking" of the young man to fit an institutional procedure.

I want to emphasize the intervention of the text–reader conversation here, indeed more than one, and my active part in going from the police version to that of the original witness and in being able to find how to treat the particularities of the latter as expressions or instances of the institutional. The institutional version set up directions for reading the witness's particularized description. Subsuming was a course of action. It involved activating the set of "responses" evoked by the police report and, taking on its agency, being able to find the fit between the witnessed event and the institutional. It would not work the other way round.

The institutional discourse installs its own temporality. In the police version of the "frisking" of the young man, the event is located as a moment in an extended sequence of institutional action that lies outside the immediacy of the witnessed events. The use of the institutional categories of "juvenile" and "a minor in possession of alcoholic beverages" inserts the boy of the witness's story into institutional relations beyond the immediacy of the events that anyone who was present might have seen. Events described by the original witness to the events in his letter to the newspaper are articulated in the mayor's version to an "administrative" knowledge that locates those events in sequences of organizational action extending before and after the events. The institutional categories locate the subjects of institutional courses of action, not as particular individuals, but as a class of persons. As Giltrow (1998) indicates, agents have no constancy: individual police officers are substitutable as agents; they have no constancy across incidents. In the text–reader conversation, the institutional narrative of being charged, pleading guilty, and receiving from the court a suspended judgment subsumes the original description of a boy or young man who had been walking up the street and was stopped and searched by a police officer. As the reader goes to work as agent of the institutional text, she or he cannot find the perspective of actual people. Their experience, the reader's experience, must be subsumed or set aside.[9] Giltrow's "experiencers" "discreetly retire" (342). Agency is assigned to institutional categories. Someone who can't be subsumed under the institutional categories assigning agency has no agency.

Stephan Dobson (2001), an elected representative of a trade union in his university department, describes bringing a grievance on behalf of a teaching assistant. The first step is, of course, filling in a complaint form, and then there's a sequence that moves the text forward until it arrives at the point where the union takes it up with the university's human resource department. The complaint was finally successful, but Dobson comments on the process as follows:

> We can see here a whole series of actions concerted and coordinated by texts, beginning with the Problem Report form which required us as union officials to activate a sequence of standardized events. But we also begin to see people disappear; just as in standard sociological accounts, my prior acquaintance and friendship to Sarah is irrelevant to both my "role" as problem recorder and my "position" within the local's hierarchy, so (and worse) we watch as Sarah begins to disappear *as a person* as the bureaucratic process is actualized by our procedural actions. While I could have recorded her emotional state and her complaints that her rent cheque had bounced on the Problem Form, or reported them to the head of Human Relations, her experience was not relevant to the case and so it was neither recorded nor mentioned, even though it was her desperation which forced her to come forward (while other workers in the department kept silent throughout the grievance, until she "won," at which point more came forward). Sarah became an objectified notation in an institutional sequence partly beyond her control (unless she wished to stop the grievance), and so disappears as a living subject from the institutional procedure. And it is exactly in the progress of such juridical procedures that experiences of race, class and gender often disappear. (151–52)

Texts as Institutional Coordinators

Institutional texts are designed; they are, as we will see in chapter 9, interlocking (rather than intertextual); setting their categories, concepts, and frames is highly politicized, not only in those settings ordinarily thought of as political. Texts are key to institutional coordinating, regulating the concerting of people's work in institutional settings in the ways they impose an accountability to the terms they establish. Gillian Walker (1990) explores the struggles in the early days of the women's movement in Canada, both within the movement and between the movement and the government over how to conceptualize and make institutionally actionable (more on this topic in chapter 9) the violence inflicted on women by their male partners. She examines the texts of a series of reports produced over a seven-year period "as moments in a conceptual process, bringing into being a 'social problem'" (65). She traces the processes through which women's experiences of violence were translated into the formalized terms that made possible political struggle (Walker 1990) and how political struggle transformed movement activists and the character of the movement in this area:

> In order to be heard women served on committees and task forces, shaped funding proposals to fit governmental imperatives; and scrambled to prepare briefs for professional bodies and for various government hearings and conferences. Working in this way reorganized our work into a more professional mode as pressure and lobbying groups or as service providers. (Walker 1995, 77)

The process that Walker (1990, 1995) traces eventually arrives at the highly ambiguous concept of *family violence* as the concept used to determine governmental mandate. This concept further marginalized issues specific to women by defining the governmental mandate to act to include child and elder abuse (1990). Walker's accounts of the political process, negotiating/struggling over the concepts vested in texts, make visible the centrality of texts and the concepts they establish and standardize across local settings in the formation of institutional regimes and the ongoing coordinating of people's work within them.[10]

Institutional discourse is set in texts, though, of course, in the ongoing coordinating of people's doings, there is both talk and text. In an account of the experience of residents protesting a planned development in their neighborhood, Turner (2001) writes of the interrelations of text and talk in the institutional setting as follows:

> In the dialogic organization of people's activities, a public governing institution is produced; a public knowledge is produced and so are concrete outcomes on the land. Residents are drawn into the legally required text-based processes via standardized texts embedded in those processes. The texts operate to shape residents' strategies. People meet and talk, producing and inserting texts into "conversation." There is an extended inter-textual exchange, and the outcome is a powerful public knowledge and administrative "regime." (300)

As one of those residents, Turner found that in the course of making the protest, "the texts that came to hand immediately provided the frame for how to speak about the project and our concerns" (300). Though this discursive move was needed if the activists were to be effective within the institutional process, it was also consequential for what could be voiced, whether in text or talk. As they became competent as intervenors in the processes of municipal government, they were also captured by the institutional discourse. Institutional capture (DeVault and McCoy 2002; D. E. Smith 2003b) is that discursive practice, regulated by the institutional procedures of text–reader conversations, through which institutional discourse overrides and reconstructs experiential talk and writing. It is, as we'll see in chapter 7, a problem for institutional ethnographic practice.

Conclusion

This chapter proposes a conceptual strategy enabling texts to register ethnographically in the exploration of institutions. The difficulty is to get texts out of the stasis that is given in the everyday experience of those of us whose work lives are intimately engaged in and with them. The text is there before its reading, and it is there afterward. Reading does not seem to be an act. It may often be work and may be experienced as such, but somehow the text just sits there before us, waiting. It doesn't move. It resists an ethnography that engages with the concerting of people's practices, their doings.

Yet texts are of central importance to institutional ethnography because they create this essential connection between the local of our (and others') bodily being and the translocal organization of the ruling relations.

Somehow they have to be brought into the same dimension as that of people's everyday doings. They have to be seen to "occur," to happen, to be active, to be integral to the organization of institutional relations.

To get texts going, I've introduced the notion of a text–reader conversation. It does three things for us:

1. It enables us to recognize the reading of a particular text as something that is being done in a particular local setting by a particular person.
2. It proposes that the reader, engaged in a text–reader conversation, plays two parts: first, she or he activates the text and, in activating it, becomes the text's agent; second, she or he responds to it in whatever way is relevant to her or his work.
3. It makes it possible for us to see the text, activated by a reader, as participating and playing a part in organizing definite sequences of action. This latter aspect has not been very fully developed here, but it returns again later in the book (chapter 8).

Text–reader conversations are, of course, multifarious. Reading the number on a bus approaching a bus stop (Watson 1997) is different from looking up a name in a telephone directory, let alone on the Internet, and both are different from reading a novel or looking at wedding photographs with some friends. What they are and how they work are always empirical questions. But our focus is on institutions and hence on the distinctive features of the text–reader conversations of institutional discourse.

Institutional discourses shift from the perspectives of individuals to a view from nowhere; institutional discourses objectify. Nominalizations that depersonalize the act are a favored device in such discourse. As Giltrow (1998) points out, its nominalizations cannot be unpacked to find corresponding references to an actuality. If people are present at all, they are as categories of persons. Using the interpretive instructions of the institutional frame provided by the official report from the police to read a witness's story made visible a discursive procedure that *subsumes* the particularities of witnessable actualities; the latter become merely instances or expressions of the institutional.

Finally the significance of institutional discourse, both text and talk, for the coordinating of people's work in institutional settings has been brought into view. Institutional discourse is designed, and the processes of design are essentially political; that is, they concern the forms of power that emerge in institutional regimes. These aspects of institutional discourse as local practices of talk, reading, and writing texts will be revisited down the line as we move further into discovering how institutional ethnography makes the actualities of institutional relations accessible. As we will see, institutional discourse is also the context within which institutional ethnographers practice, and within which we are exposed, to capture how such discourse subsumes and displaces other forms of knowledge.

Notes

1. Most of the textual phenomena with which institutional ethnography has been concerned are written (including, in this term, printed or computerized texts)—hence the emphasis on reading. The concept of a text–reader conversation can, however, be adapted to other kinds of texts, including images. See, for example, Liza McCoy's study (1995) of activating a photographic text.

2. In part, the reason is that ethnomethodological conventions preclude the direct introduction of the ethnographer's experiential knowledge.

3. Here's the passage from Bal (1997):

> I want to focus on the metaphor in that word "secret," which sounds so common and ordinary. Whereas the word "secret" in combination with "life" or "nature" has indeed become quite usual, the word is here a substitute for something else, not a single term but, I will argue, a narrative. What is unknown, as the negating prefix suggests, can be known. The subject of knowing is the researcher. What is secret can also be known. But here, the subject is not quite the researcher. The world "secret" implies an action, hence a subject of withholding. If there is a secret, then somebody is keeping it. This fits into the network of gendered language in which nature and life are made feminine. And this implicitly tells a story in which secrecy is an act. "Secret" as metaphor for the unknown establishes an opposition between two subjects, the researcher who wants to know the secret and "woman" who withholds it. The opposition is easily turned into hostility, as the well-known metaphor of Francis Bacon shows, who wanted to put nature on the rack to torture "her" secrets out of "her."
>
> But the gendering of the unknown comes with a second aspect of the word "secret" which is of an altogether different nature. A secret that must be found out implies a process in which that finding out takes place. The series of events involved in that process can be considered a fabula. That narrative is "told" by the user of the metaphor, the male scientist's spokesman is the narrator. The narration is subjective in the precise sense of emanating from a subject. The word tells the narrative in the version of—from the perspective of—the subject of unknowing; who feels excluded by the lack of knowledge and experiences it as an action by an "insider," the subject of knowing and withholding. That subject is the narrator's opponent. (35).

4. See also, Richard Darville's account of what he calls *organizational texts* (Darville 1995, 256).

5. My own reading of Halliday suggests that there's more to tracking back through scientific nominalizations than a lexical exercise:

> M. A. K. Halliday (Halliday and Martin 1993, 7) has identified in Isaac Newton's scientific writing . . . a textual procedure that goes from statements in an active verbal form such as "the light is refracted" to a corresponding nominalized term, in this case "refraction." A process is thus reconstituted as an "entity." Once constituted the entity can be treated as active causally in relation to the other events or processes with which Newton is concerned.
>
> , Halliday treats Newton's nominalizations as strictly lexical innovations (he and Martin are critical of social scientific nominalizations). He does not refer to Newton's experimental work or its possible significance for creating the conditions under which it makes sense to replace statements based on observations to a nominal form. I suggest that this shift is grounded in Newton's ability, with the technology at his disposal, to isolate a process, recreate it, observe it again, and recognize it as the same. (D. E. Smith 2001b)

6. In Winter's analysis (1992) there are traces of a dialogic process.

7. Again, see Darville (1995, 256) for a description of the "agentless" character of organizational discourse.

8. Compare Darville (1995): "In organizational literacy, in bureaucratic, administrative, legal, and professional language . . . what counts is how matters can be *written up* (to enter them into an organizational process), not how they can be *written down* (to relate experience or to aid memory)" (254).

9. Compaire David Buckholdt and Jaber Gubrium's account (1983) of the work of professional staff in human service organizations and what they do to fit their patients or clients into the institutional categories that enable the subsequent funding of services.

10. George W. Smith (1995) introduced the concept of an institutional regime to institutional ethnography as a mechanism for facilitating an investigation and description of how ruling is organized and managed by political and administrative forms of organization (25).

CHAPTER 6

Experience as Dialogue and Data

The previous chapter introduces institutional discourse and the textual practices that transform the local particularities of people's experience into perspectiveless representations in which people disappear as subjects and agents. In a world of multiple perspectives and speech genres, the ruling relations impose monologic objectified perspectives operating in a particular discourse or speech genre to subdue diversities of viewpoint among participants—Bakhtin's monology (Bakhtin 1981; Holquist 1990; see chapter 3). The local actualities of people's doings appear, if at all, only selectively and as instances, examples, illustrations, or expressions of institutionally constituted virtual realities. By contrast, speaking from experience is always from someone's perspective and, whether this is made explicit or not, is always from a particular time and place.[1] Institutional ethnography relies on people's capacity to tell their experience. It is the essential resource for a project that proposes to return inquiry to the everyday world that is shared both by the researcher and by the informants she or he consults, and it preserves in its data the diversity of perspectives from which they came.

A central problem for the institutional ethnographer is to escape from the objectifications of the ruling relations and the monologies of institutional discourse and find her or his way back to the actualities that are always there, always going on, and always ultimately more than can be spoken. When George Smith and I talked in terms of making an ontological shift (see chapter 1), we meant that we'd found a way of thinking and exploring outside the monologies of, in his case, philosophy (his original field of specialization), and in mine, sociology. Our practices had shifted into the ontology I spell out in chapters 3 and 4. The object of our investigations was conceived to be in the same everyday world as that in which we lived. In any actual project of inquiry, the institutional ethnographer's fundamental resource is people's experience, both the researcher's and that of her or his informants.

I am unmoved by Judith Butler's and Joan Scott's dismissal of the importance of experiential stories (Butler and Scott 1992; Scott 1992). It is true, of course, that the experiential can't be directly translated into the factual. The social organization of the factual is one that suspends perspective and subjectivity. At the same time, experience is spoken or written directly from the actualities of a person's life. Speaking or writing experientially has been central in how women have been able to go beyond and outside established discourses as well as to disrupt what seemed at one time the consolidated forms of masculine dominance of intellectual, political, cultural, and domestic life. In this context, giving voice to experience remains a rich source of understanding women's lives, people's lives, inserting knowledges that rupture those subject to the monologies of institutional discourse and ideology, including the monologies of sociology.

Experience as Dialogue: The Problem

The critique made by Butler and Scott (1992) focuses on the constructed or dialogic character of experience that prohibits treating it as a simple source of knowledge. Scott (1992) is critical of historians who take for granted the representational validity of experiential accounts and neglect the problem of their constructed character:

> When experience is taken as the origin of knowledge, the vision of the individual subject (the person who had the experience or the historian who recounts it) becomes the bedrock of evidence upon which explanation is built. Questions about the constructed nature of experience, about how one's vision is structured—about language (or discourse) and history— are left aside. (25).

For Scott, recognizing experience as constructed means that experiential accounts can't be taken at face value. The speaking or writing of experience is always in language or discourse and hence always subject to structuring effects beyond the speaker's or writer's intentions. The constraints and exclusions, the ordering, the logic of categories and distinctions of a discourse are all at work in the production of an experiential account; or, as Paula Moya (2000, 81) argues from a somewhat different viewpoint, experience is always ideologically or theoretically mediated.

I am in general agreement with the view of these theorists that experience arises only at the point where what is remembered comes into speech or writing in particular settings among particular people and hence is never a pure representation of some original. The institutional ethnographer encounters the problem formulated by Scott. She or he depends on the experiential resources of informants, on her or his own experience, or on experiences doing observational work in a field setting. Whether in an interview or in the experience of participant observation, ethnographers rely on people's experience. The experience that is produced as data may be our own; it may be gained through participation in a workplace, or it may rely entirely on interviews. Dialogue is involved in its production, even when the experience is the researcher's. There is no alternative. Dialogue is the language factory that produces out of the actual the experiential knowledge that can then be further processed into ethnography. Experiential accounts cannot give direct and unsullied access to an actuality; actuality is always more and other than is spoken, written, or pictured. What becomes data for the ethnographer is always a collaborative product. For some, such as Aaron Cicourel (1964), the collaborative character of data collected in interviews makes it impossible to base any statements about the informant on that basis. The data is always created out of an interchange of "subject" and interviewer. If data collection drawing on people's experience is always dialogic, what entitles us to claim that we can describe people's doings and how they are coordinated on the basis of experiential accounts?

It should be pointed out here that institutional ethnographers are not using people's experiences as a basis for making statements about them, about populations of individuals, or about events or states of affairs described from the point of view of individuals. For institutional ethnography, the speaking or writing of experience is essential to realizing the project of working from the actualities of people's lives as the people themselves know them. Recognizing and incorporating into the project's ethnographic analysis the actual diversity of perspectives, biographies, positioning, and so on is integral to its ethnographic method. It is people's experience of and in what they do—their "work" (see the following chapter)—and the knowledge based in their work that are the ethnographer's major resource.

Institutional ethnography recognizes, as do those who criticize its value as a research resource, that experience only becomes available dialogically as it is spoken or written. Indeed I would go further to say that what we call *experience* is essentially dialogic. It begins where the body is, in a world known sensually, yet it is always and only an emergent in language and at the point of speech or writing. We generally think of experience as occurring before it has been told. However, if we bring to mind actual occasions of people speaking from their experience, we can see that experience actually emerges only in the course of its telling, and telling is to particular people at particular times and in particular places or, when written, to a future reader or readers. Experiential writing or speaking orients to the occasion, the speaker's and hearer's interests, the social act in which it engages, and the speech genre that is operative for that occasion, even when the writing of experience is to one's self as a reflective procedure.

Rejecting experience as an authoritative resource attends to and problematizes its dialogic production, the latter being viewed as an irreversible contamination. If experience can only arise as it is uttered, then it is determined by a discourse or discourses and cannot be claimed to be an uncontaminated representation of some original state of affairs or event. It is a view that rides with the determinism of the structuralist school, established originally by Saussure (1966). Structuralists and poststructuralists have theorized language as establishing meaning in the binary determinations of its internal relations. Meaning is given prior to the speaker's or writer's intention to mean. She or he speaks or writes within a discourse with its distinctive lexicon, the universe of entities and subjects it recognizes, its exclusions (Foucault 1972), its conventions, and intertextualities. Speaking or writing is never free from such determinants. Discourse, in the poststructuralist view, speaks over our intentions; they are subordinated and displaced. Experiential speaking or writing is no exception. Experience must be spoken or written to come into being; it doesn't exist as an authentic representation of reality before its entry into language; hence, it is already discursively determined by the discourse in which it is spoken. It is reasoning of this kind that undermines for Butler, Scott, and Moya the very possibility that experience can be a kind of truth without claiming universality, for if experience is already shaped in speech, it is so deeply committed by the lexical determinations of discourse that it is already misrepresentation of actuality.

An Alternative Understanding of Experience as Dialogue

In chapter 3, I draw on Bakhtin's concept of discourse (Bakhtin 1981; Holquist 1990)—or, to use Bakhtin's own term (as translated), speech genres (Bakhtin 1986)—as a model for the social process in general. Here we return to his theory as an alternative to the theorizing of discourse as determining what can be said or written. In Bakhtin's view, every utterance is a dialogue between the givens of language or discourse and the speaker's intentions, the hearer, the situation, and so on. The speaker's or writer's part in the dialogue is that of finding in discourse the resources she or he needs; the part of discourse is to make the speaking/writing of intention possible and at the same time to constrain its utterance.

In the women's movement, that dialogue tripped over into struggle. We were aware of how readily what we wanted to find out in speaking or writing could be captured by the discourses in which we were already participants (analogous to the institutional capture in which the reader becomes agent of the institutional discourse described in the previous chapter). Uttering our experiences was a struggle to force the lexical givens of discourse, made in masculinity, to speak what they were not prepared to do. But we could make them speak because the dialogue, as Bakhtin emphasizes, between intentions and the givens of discourse at any moment is indeed fluid. Words can be made to serve what they have not been established to do; new words or ways of combining them can be invented, are invented all the time; language can be changed. Speakers and writers continually create new ways of putting words together to make utterances that haven't been spoken before and are responsive to distinctive situations and particular storytelling motives.

Experience, viewed from a Baktinian perspective, can be recognized as dialogic, but dialogue does not imply that discourse determines the interchange between what is recollected and whatever was happening that is being expressed as the speaker's experience. Too often taking up the concept of discourse following in Foucault's footsteps accords discourse an overpowering role. In adopting Bakhtin's conceptualization, each moment of discourse in action can be seen as both reproducing and remaking discourse. The experiential dialogue has often to struggle with what's given to find ways of speaking experience faithful to the recollections, feelings, details, and thoughts that are evoked, but it is only in dialogue that it becomes experience. In the following quotation from an oral historical interview, we can see "experience" in the making:

> Yes, and Douglas came to the hospital about half past eight in the morning, and he told me afterwards that when he went home, like it was—no, it must have been earlier than that, I don't know whether he was allowed in or something—but he said that he was out early in the morning and somebody came and asked him the time, and he had to tell them that his wife had just had a baby! He was so thrilled he had to tell somebody. I thought it was lovely. I've got an idea that this incident took place when I was just coming out of hospital with my second child & yet it can't have—anyway, we had her home, but do you know?—this is something that *kills* me—it was nothing except . . . I think we had my aunt with us—I don't remember why we had her, but I think she was with us—she must have been, because what I am going to tell you concerns her. Now we had this very nice flat; it had one bedroom and a very nice living room, and directly Douglas came in. . . . I had to have it on the side of the bed with him, with her there, and I was trying to fight him off, but it was no good—I mean he must have had it in his mind while I was away. Just ten days! Just coming out of the hospital! (Rowbotham 1979, 43)

Uttering what becomes experience in the telling is full of hesitations and revisions. It is taking shape as the narrator is telling it to the interviewer. Its dialogic character is visible not only in the moment she directly addresses her interlocutor: "But do you know?" The experience is, in a sense, being made *for* the interviewer; ongoing dialogue generates the story. The point of the story is not just having sex immediately after coming home from hospital, it is also about the presence of her aunt in the flat: "she must have been [there] because what I am going to tell you concerns her." The pains she is taking to get the story right orient to the presence and interest of the interviewer as well as to the past she is giving voice to. The dialogue between interviewer and informant brings the latter's experience into being as an interchange between what she remembers and the interviewer's interest and attention.

Experience, Language, and Social Organization

Experience always has a foot in two worlds: one remembered in the body as well as in the mind and the other in the actuality of speaking or writing it in the company of an interlocutor or the apprehension of a distant audience. In chapter 4 I develop a theoretical account of how language organizes the interindividual territories of experience. What emerges in the experiential dialogue is already deeply organized in language (see chapter 4). The experiential data that Joan Scott views as an uncertain ground for the historian to walk on assumes that experience is a source of knowledge about what was there and happening back then. The institutional ethnographer, however, does not look for accounts of what happened or what was really going on. She or he is oriented to what the informant knows and to producing a knowledge between them of the informant's everyday life in which her or his doings and how they are coordinated with those of others become visible. She or he is oriented toward the *social organization* of people's activities.

The language of experiential accounts is permeated with the social relations and social organization that were already there in what it represents (again, see chapter 4). The notion of experience locates a subject in an everyday world directly known to her or him. In that everyday world, what is perceived, attended to, projected from past to future is already named and organized interindividually in language. David Maurer's account (1981) of pickpockets' "talk" shows us the intimacy of learning a particular kind of work with learning its language or, to use Bakhtin's term (1986), its speech genre:

> When a professional criminal learns his occupation, as, for instance, thievery, with specialization as a pickpocket, he starts with the very specialized techniques of pocket picking in terms of a specific language. More than that, he constantly thinks of his occupation in terms of that language and discusses his work with other pickpockets in terms of their common language. In other words, his entire occupational frame of reference is both technical and linguistic, and the langauge is fundamental not only to the perpetuation of the craft of thievery but to its practice. (Maurer 1981,: 261)

The "language" of thievery constitutes (keep in mind here Luria's notion of words as organizing perception) the relevant objects of her or his activities and organizes his or her working relationships with other thieves and potential victims. Its categories also locate the division of labor among pickpockets on the job: there is the "mark," the focus of the pickpocket attempt; the respectable-appearing "front," who unbuttons the mark's coat so that the "tool" can get into the mark's inside pockets. Hazards are named, including of course police and detectives; similarly, settings and areas are constituted in relation to the relevances of thievery—a locality that is "burned up" is one that has been hit so often that it is "hot" (Maurer 1981, 234–56).

What is highlighted in Maurer's account of this specialized speech genre is just as much the case in the less-specialized speech genres of the everyday. They too embed socially organized activities. People's doings organize attention; they organize the relevance of the everyday objects that provide props, means, guides, conditions, and so on. Many, if not most of these, are already in language before the moment of the dialogue in which experience comes into speech. The terms that characterize them in the experiential dialogue serve not only to identify them referentially but to carry "responses" (for an example, see my account of the social organization of "table" in chapter 4). So the listener doesn't *hear* the experience being told as *words*. She or he hears the experience. The dialogic of recall is not distinguishable from the dialogue between listener (or prospective reader) and the experiencer; the listener's interests and relevances are at work in the lexicon of recall. But it is the dialogic of recall, the experiential dialogue, that makes possible to get spoken, somehow or another, and with whatever incoherences, repeats, corrections, and perversions of ordinary conventions, what has been, in a sense, waiting for the moment of speech to come into being *as someone's experience.* For what is recalled in experience isn't inchoate. It bears social organization from an original setting into the experiential dialogue.

Here is an example. I am interviewing Marco in the context of a study aimed at learning about processes of informal learning on the job among workers in a large steel plant in Ontario. Strictly speaking, this was not an institutional ethnography, although the interview approach I used was similar. Marco has worked in the plant for about twenty years and is a representative on the union local's health and safety committee.

> MARCO: There was a few times where I put myself into positions where I risked my life. [D: Yeah.] The last particular time was, I think, four or five years ago, I got splashed in the face with hot hydraulic fluid and I ended up getting second-degree burns. And back then, like not so much myself but my family, like "Was it worth it? Like look at your face, look in the mirror. Your lips are burned, your nose, you know, you could have lost your eye." "Yeah, you're right, it's not worth it." So I'm at a point now where if I see any danger at all, I just walk away. You know? The machine is the machine but my life is my life.

DOROTHY: So when you look back on that accident, there was something that you did then that you felt [M: I had to do it to keep the machine—] caused the accident but contributed to, yeah, that you shouldn't—

MARCO: Uh huh. I would never do it again, no.

DOROTHY: You were trying to keep the machine going?

MARCO: That's right. Now I would say, "If you want that machine to go," to the supervisor, "Do it yourself!" Like this is back then: I thought, "Well, we got to keep the machine going." Well, it's more important to keep me going. Because I have to go home to my kids at the end of the day, I have to go home to my wife. You know.

DOROTHY: So you were under some pressure from the supervisor at that time?

MARCO: Sure. I was thinking "yeah, that's part of my job, I need to change that hose. And even though it's under pressure, well, it still needs to be done." Well, you know what? I don't think that's safe. And being a Safety and Health rep, I know that the government's always been on my side with the Occupational Safety and Health Act, to say if I refuse to do that job, it's not going to affect my position here. I'm not doing it because I don't feel it's safe and I'm not here to get hurt or get killed. I don't want to do that job because it's unsafe. So I can refuse to do it under the Act, say "That's under pressure there. I'm not touching that." You know? "You cool it down and make it proper for me and then I'll go in there because that's my job. But to go in there and risk getting burned? It happened to me before. It's not going to happen again." And then you look at the liquid steel. If a breakout occurs and I feel that I'm in danger of getting my legs burned and my arms burned, I'm going to run like hell. It's not worth it to me to go home maimed or burned or—to save what, to save a machine that they can rebuild in three days? No.[2]

The facticity of Marco's account is not an issue for the institutional ethnographer. The ethnographer is not interested in using Marco's experience to tell a story about accidents in the steel industry or some such. Nor is the ethnography focused on what can be said about Marco as an individual or as a member of a class of individuals. Nor are we looking for some patterning or situation that we might find again in other interviews. Nor do we have to set aside the feelings that he expresses. What he learned from being burned and from his family members' concern for him was a new way of understanding his relationship to his job. Further, if we were to take up his account ethnographically, it would open up into the social relations and social organization in which Marco's experience is embedded. Throughout we can see the traces of how his activities coordinate with those of others. The language Marco uses is of the everyday of his relationships and work in a steel plant; it is a language that has social organization built into it.

Take, for example, his use of the term *job*. It locates the intersection of his work commitments as he sees them and his work responsibilities as his supervisor sees them and as they have become defined in the contract between the company and the union local. You can see already how much is opened up once we take such an apparently ordinary word and substruct it, that is, go beyond it to envisage the socially organized activities that make its sense. Or notice the characteristic use of *they* in "a machine that they can rebuild in three days." It identifies the peculiar agency of the company for which he works. *They* personalizes as agents the organization of a corporation that nowhere appears as such in Marco's experiential story but that, beyond and behind his supervisor, brings things about—repairs to damaged machinery, new technologies, and the like. In taking authority for his life over against the interests of the company, as represented by his supervisor, he can call on the provincial government's Occupational Health and Safety Act. The authority of government overrides the company's authority as vested in his supervisor. He can refuse to do what his supervisor might consider as being his job if he sees potential danger. Under the law, he has authority to resist his supervisor's pressure.

People who are talking experience use the language of everyday life. Social organization is, as I've suggested here and in chapter 4, implicit or, perhaps better, *present* in that language. The terms people use are used in the organized activities of the original. More than that, they organize those activities. Social organization is not a context for the use of a term; rather, how a term means in a given setting is integral to coordinating the local activity. The problem for the researcher is to avoid taking such terms of everyday talk for granted as the informant speaks his or her experience. When Alison Griffith and I (Griffith and D. E. Smith 2004) were first interviewing women with children in elementary school about the work they were doing in relationship to their children's schooling, one of the topics we introduced was that of the school day. We treated it, as many of them did, as a fixed feature of their children's school and as something that parents were, in a sense, up against. Here was something they knew about; here was something we knew about as women who'd had children in elementary school. It was part of our *work knowledge* (a term developed further in the next chapter) of the school. We learned in the course of our study to explicate the social relations implicit in the term. From the standpoint of teachers, the school day in the school district of largely middle-class families was a highly scheduled sequence of periods allocated to different pieces of the curriculum. Teachers could take for granted that children would be in class on time and that the school day could begin punctually. Not so in the school of a low-income area, where the variability of arrival time of a few children (and it doesn't take many) meant that a tight schedule, such as that of the school in the middle-class area, was not practicable. In a setting of a low-income area, the elementary school day would begin with a period of individual work, which would allow late arrivals to be assimilated without disruption. The working knowledge of teachers recognized a different school day than that which we had known as parents. Our later understanding of the school day, not as a fixed but as a coordinated production of parents and teachers, relied on our drawing on the work knowledge of parents and teachers. It is characteristic of institutions that their standardized features are produced out of people's particular and various doings. Though the school day and the school attendance are regulated in law, we discovered in the course of our research and analysis that the term *school day* was a product of (1) the work that parents did to get their children to school on time, to pick them up at the appointed time, and to bring them back and forth at the lunch hour; and (2) on the school side, the work of the teacher in accommodating the order of class to latecomers or the work of parent volunteers in checking with parents whose children have not arrived, both regulating the daily schedule of the school so that the classes or other activities would conclude on time. The school day appears thus as a social organization of various people's work tied in various ways to the organization of school and the organization of the home, where other activities, such as paid employment, must be coordinated with the school day.

Such terms as the *school day* seem simply referential, denoting an entity of some kind. But to adopt that preconception is to set aside the ordinary observation that they are used in the everyday organizing of people's activities, just as Wieder (1974) found the convict code to be used by convicts themselves. In an earlier study (Jackson 1974; D. E. Smith 1990d), Nancy Jackson and I cooperated in an ethnography of a newsroom in a Vancouver newspaper. We learned during the research process to be critical of our own practices of converting how people talked about what they were doing into abstract nominalized forms. For example, there was a mystery, we were told by a journalist, about what was "news." We came to see that the mystery was created by abstracting the term from the everyday contexts of its use; we learned in time not to do this but rather to explore the term as social organization. What was "news" was particular to the day's work and to that particular day with whatever complex of connections, references, and importance that was generated in the ongoing historical givens of any particular time of work (D. E. Smith 1990d). Jackson describes the progress of our inquiry in this way:

> We began to work on the relation between our sense that we couldn't find things, like news or assignments or stories, and the notion that the descriptive use of language makes an object of the organization of practices in which words arise. What we found was that the understanding of how description works did begin to account for our sense that we couldn't find things. In the case of assignments or stories, if we took the terms to represent an objective phenomenon, as would be conventional, then we were sent off on a search: where do assignments come from; what is a story, etc. We did start with those questions. Only we noticed that there was this kind of gap, this moment in which we saw that "nothing happened, really," or that "they are nowhere to be found." From this we began to see that these so-called objects were . . . organized relations [rather than entities]. (1974, 40)

Stories were assigned to people in the course of the day's work but there was nothing there that could be identified as an assignment independent of what reporters were working on and were responsible for. Nominalizing the ordinary work language of participants in the local setting created abstractions in which the social organization and social relations disappeared. We had recreated at a modest level of investigation the same problem that Marx attributes to political economy. His *Capital* (1976), the first volume in particular, is a critique of political economy because he investigates and displays the social relations and their historical making that underlie and are reflected in political economic concepts such as 'commodity,' 'wage,' 'labour,' 'capital,' 'money,' and so on. Institutional ethnography working at the level of people's everyday lives orients to the discovery of the social relations and social organization that articulate the everyday to the ruling relations; the elevation of concepts to the level of theory bypasses the essential investigatory work of discovering social organization.

The temptation is to jump to a level of generalization beyond that of a particular everyday setting by precipitating nominalizations out of what informants have to tell into ethnographic discourse. It is a move to generalization that is purely in language. It is responsive to the dialogue between discourse and informant where discourse seems to demand the ethnographer to be able to make some general statements. This is one of the hazards of grounded theory. Though Glaser and Strauss (1967) themselves insist that generalizing from a concept such as 'awareness contexts of dying' has to be systematically developed in further research, it is not uncommon to find in grounded theory studies that it has been sufficient merely to locate a concept that is somehow expressive of what the researcher has found in her or his interviews. The concept is a *generalizer* and the researcher may simply rely on that effect to secure theoretical status for her or his study.

The institutional ethnographer, by contrast, must find the generalizing and standardizing processes *in* the ethnographic data, in people's local practices, including language. Hence the direction of inquiry suggests discovering just what everyday activities and their coordinating are going on that make the use of terms such as *job, supervisor, assignment,* and *news* part of the lexicon of everyday work. What social relations are they reflecting? What is their speaking part in those relations? And how do those social relations play a part in generalizing institutional processes beyond the locally observed?

At every point in Marco's story, there, in the vocabulary of his experiential account, are references to forms, relations, and organization that are generalized beyond the particularities of his experience; they could be tracked down and explicated as such. Experiential talk bears necessarily—it is built into the language in which experience is spoken—social relations and social organization in which the individual's personal story is embedded. We cannot speak ordinary language without incorporating and speaking the social organization it carries (see chapter 4).

The Data Dialogues

Speaking or writing experience—the experiential dialogue—happens all the time. Institutional ethnography, however, initiates dialogue with people in interviews or in field situations to create a major part of what becomes its data. Thus the ethnographic dialogue isn't just an opportunity for the researcher to learn; it aims at a particular product. The dialogue between interviewer/observer and informant or between observer and her/his own experience is implicitly a dialogue organized by the ethnographer's participation in institutional ethnographic discourse. The researcher is oriented to a discourse to which she or he will be accountable if the research is written up for publication or as a report to those people or organizations it is intended to serve. The experiential dialogue can thus be viewed as a moment in a social relation, a sequence of coordinated action that organizes the dialogue between informant and researcher as a step or moment in a sequence that hooks back into the institutions of academic, professional, and related specialized discourses. Other moments in the sequence are also dialogic, though here our focus is on the dialogues that generate what we call data, the givens that we work on in creating that dialogue with readers that we call ethnography. Of these, two are most central: the primary dialogue with informants or, in field notes, with an observational setting; and the dialogue with the texts produced in the primary dialogue (reading and indexing transcripts of audiorecordings or field notes).

The primary dialogue has been criticized because it realizes power inequities implicit in the researcher's relation to those she or he interviews. Angela McRobbie (1982) was the first, by my memory, to open up this topic, and though the discussion has accumulated varieties of experience and analysis, the basic dimensions of the issue do not appear to have changed. They are those of the ethnographer's power relation to those with whom she or he is talking and of her or his relationship to them as insider or outsider (Naples 2003, 76). Alison Griffith and I (Griffith and D. E. Smith 2004) encountered problems of this kind in some of our interviews with mothers of school children in a predominantly low-income community. Tracey Reynolds (2002) has explored her experience as a black woman interviewing black mothers. Because Reynolds shares ethnicity with the women she interviewed, she did not anticipate some of the problems she experienced. One of those interviewed was explicit about the differences she saw, pointing out Reynolds's status as a professional and middle-class black woman, comparing it to her own position as a hairdresser (305).

Charles Briggs (2002)—who seems unaware of feminist thinking on this topic—has taken the view that "asymmetries of power" are a general feature of sociological interviewing arising primarily from

> principles that invest interviewers with control over the referential content of what is said (by posing questions), the length and scope of an-

swers (by deciding when to probe or ask a new question), and the way that all participants construct their positionality with respect to the interview and the information it produces. (911)

As can be seen, he identifies the power difference with the interviewer's control over the interview situation and hence his or her ability to impose preconceptions dictated by academic interests on the interview process.

The interview or field observation is work that is itself coordinated in a sequence of institutional action. Issues of "power asymmetries," as Briggs formulates them, diagnose a moment in a social relation in which the researcher is creating resources, data, to be made over into representations within a discourse. The sequence of action from the original observation or interview comprises a series of dialogues. These are organized within a discourse in which the researcher participates and the informant or those observed do not. The first of these, the primary dialogue, is the actual collaborative process of an interview or participant observation. The researcher's part in any talk or in how she or he goes about observation is within the discourse in which she or he is a participant. In a sense, she or he creates or mediates an interchange between a sociological discourse and the informant or those observed. The discourse, as an ongoing historically committed organization of people's work, is brought into an active relation with others, who are not themselves participants. Through the ethnographer, the informant or those whose work is observed are caught up into dialogue largely invisible to them with a scholarly discourse in which they are not otherwise active. They participate, however briefly, in the work organization of a scholarly discourse (he or she will, for example, have signed the ethical review consent form) in that complex net that links university workers (faculty, researchers, and so on); government or private funding agencies and their requirements and controls; publications and publication reviewers representing professional and academic orders of discourse; and so forth with the final readers of whatever work the ethnographer produces. It is the innocence of the informants or those whose work is observed that creates the asymmetry of which Briggs writes. The researcher knows what she or he is hooked into, and the informant does not.

For the ethnographer, a second dialogue supervenes. In reading a transcript from an audiorecording or the researcher's own field notes, the institutional ethnographer rediscovers what was said or observed. In an interview or in participating in the situation being observed, the researcher is as much caught up in the ongoing interchange as is the informant or those whose work is being observed. The researcher hears and responds within the frame of the ongoing social act. But there's much more to the interview or observations than the researcher is aware of or can attend to in the process itself. It's always amazing to me when I engage in dialogue with the interview transcript how much I learn that I had not seen before. When I drew on my interview with Marco for an example of an experiential account, I went back and forth between the passage cited and the themes and language of this book, discovering in that passage what I had not seen before. I could see the dialogues internal to it between Marco and his family and between Marco and his supervisor; I could see the lexicon and references of how he tells his experience. I'm not interested in whether his account is an accurate telling of events; I am interested, rather, in *his* experience and how he tells it and in the traces of social relations and organization present in it. The new dialogue and the new discoveries emerged in the dialogue between what had been produced in the original collaboration between Marco and myself and the context of my exploration of how language carries social organization.

Institutional ethnography recognizes the authority of the experiencer to inform the ethnographer's ignorance. The ethnographer's role is that of an acute, thoughtful, and probing listener who is learning from the informant or observational setting. Hence asymmetries of power in the relationship seem less significant. Yes, it is the ethnographer who initiates the encounter, and it is she or he who imposes the topic and, to some degree, provides its direction. On the other hand, she or he depends on the informant to make available what becomes material for further stages of the researcher's work. Not every informant does this. Those issues raised by Tracey Reynolds (2002) of the status disparities between interviewer and informant have sometimes, in my experience, meant that participation in the interview is given grudgingly with the suspicion that the information is somehow going to be passed on and be to the informant's disadvantage; or simply with a generalized antipathy to people who bring their middle-class clothes, ways of speaking, interrogations, and so on. More problematic, in my experience, have been those interviews in which I have not properly understood where the informant was coming from (Griffith and D. E. Smith 2004). Generally, however, in my experience of interviewing in institutional ethnography in which interest is in the informant's work knowledge, the informant discovers that, for the first and perhaps only time, he or she gets to speak about the ordinary of their lives with someone whose focus is just that and whose job is to listen.

In interviewing steelworkers in Ontario for a study of informal learning in the work setting (D. E. Smith and Dobson 2002), I noticed that they would often start the interview with comments rather like those Reynolds (2002) describes. They would say something like "Why would you want to interview me? I don't know anything," as if knowing was something of which only academics such as Stephan and myself were capable. However, we found that when we asked them to tell us about their work and about how and what they learned outside formal processes—that is, when talk moved to their experiences—they readily and comfortably assumed the experiencer's authoritative status. Once they got going, they had much to tell, and we had a great, great deal to learn. Our job was to get them going on the topics relevant to the study and to follow up with questions where we had not understood what they said or where we wanted to know more. We were studying not a particular job but how the steelworkers learned their job, and in the process preconceptions of the study were being disrupted.

It would seem that if experience is recognized as essentially dialogic so that it isn't there until there is talk or writing, the ethnographer is always trapped. The data is always produced collaboratively. It is always shaped by and to the situation of talk or observation and under particular discursive conventions. Should we treat this as contamination? I think that's nonsense. Let us look at a couple of examples where the ethnographer has made use of his or her own experience as a resource. Gerald de Montigny's (1995a) fine analysis of social work(ing), draws on and analyzes his own experience. It is a dialogue *within an institutional ethnographic discourse.* It is this that makes it possible for him to discover and describe what would not have been described other than in that discursive context. Similarly Kamini Grahame's analysis (1998) of her experience working in a mainstream and largely white organization in the United States concerns issues for immigrant women. What she discovered has the same kind of dialogic character as de Montigny's. Institutional ethnography enabled Grahame to explore just what it was about the organization she was associated with that made it hard for them to find women of color to participate. The mainstream organization took the view that women of color were unorganized and needed training to participate in an organization such as its own. Her own experience, however, told her differently. She knew of and could connect with organizations of women of color that were active in many of the same issues of the mainstream organization. She shows how the organization's "location at the juncture between private foundations, grassroots women, and the state" (1) and its ideology of inclusion precluded awareness of what was already going on among women of color. Organization among women of color was invisible to an institutional discourse schooled by the funding and regulatory practices of government and private foundations. The work knowledges (see next chapter) of de Montigny and Grahame were the major experiential resources on which the researchers drew, and the dialogic within which their stories emerged was with institutional ethnographic discourse. It is a discourse that avoids imposing interpretations and collaborates with informants—or, in these instances, with the ethnographers themselves—in *discovery*.

The power of the dialogue between people's experience and the sociological discourse that the ethnographer gets going is that what he or she learns can, perhaps should, change the preconceptions brought to the meeting. Thus she or he creates or mediates an interchange between the discourse she or he practices and the people she or he talks to or whose work is being observed. The study I was involved in when I interviewed Marco was, as I've said, not an institutional ethnography. I brought with me to the interview a specific frame, namely, that of the informal learning that goes on at the job: this was my interest and my focus in the dialogic of the interview. I was learning from Marco about informal learning. He goes on a little later than the passage cited to describe how he passes on what he's learned from this experience to younger people coming to work in the plant.

> MARCO: That's the first thing I tell any student coming in, [D: You do tell them?] "If ever you feel for your life, a gut feeling even, you turn around and walk back in the lunchroom and then we'll talk about it in the lunchroom, not on the job."

It was not quite what I had been thinking of when I first formulated the topic of the informal learning study. The project was undertaken as part of a larger assemblage of researches all concerned with "informal learning." The overall topic was conceived fairly conventionally in terms of skills learned outside formal educational or training settings. One thing I learned from my interviews with Marco and other steelworkers I interviewed was the inadequacies of the conception of informal learning I had started with. I had somehow taken for granted that what I would be discovering would be the learning of skills relevant to "the job." From Marco and other members of Local 1005 of Steelworkers employed at Stelco in Hamilton, Ontario, that Stephan Dobson and I talked to, I learned that their experiential learning was richer, deeper, and different from the rather conventional view with which I'd started. In a sense, I had created a dialogue among the various informants as I read, noted, and thought. I learned that those who learned from experience were also the teachers of what they had learned and that they thought about what to teach, as illustrated in what Marco told his students. Indeed, one or two of those I spoke to had worked out specific techniques of teaching newcomers to the job. Though I was not doing an institutional ethnography, strictly speaking, I was exposing myself to being taught by those I interviewed beyond my preconceptions.[3]

Discovery in institutional ethnography means, much of the time, not just learning what she or he did not know but disrupting either the concepts with which the research began or the preconceptions not fully formulated. As described earlier, Alison Griffith and I (Griffith and D. E. Smith 2004) discovered in the course of our research what we came to call the "mothering discourse" and to understand how its preconceptions had already been built into our research. At the stage of our study, our data-collection practices were already completed. Preconceptions originating in the mothering discourse had been integral to the conception of our investigation and to the interviewing strategies we adopted. There are unexplored regions apparent in our work that we came to see too late to remedy them. Though we were able to locate at least some of the absences, exploring them remains for others. There is always much more to learn from people's experiences than the researcher can cope with. The asymmetries of power attributed to the researcher–respondent relationship emphasize the researcher's control. They are to be seen in the context of the institutional relations in which the researcher engages informants, however transitorily. Where the interview process is highly controlled, the effects of interchange between informant and discourse mediated by the ethnographer are nullified. For the institutional ethnographer, however, what she or he does not know and what the informant can teach her or him is central to the research project. The controlling interest of the ethnographer does not disappear but is balanced by the institutional ethnographer's deference to the informant's experiential authority and by a commitment to discovery. The ethnographer exposes discourse to being challenged or changed in the course of dialogue either at the first encounter with an informant or in the secondary dialogue in which she or he engages with the transcribed interviews or reviews field notes of observations. The construction of experience in which ethnographer and informant collaborate implicitly engages a dialogue between a sociological discourse and the experienced actualities of the world of which it claims to speak.

Conclusion

Butler and Scott (1992), Scott (1992), and Moya (2000) argue that experience cannot be translated directly into knowledge, because it is fundamentally shaped by the discourse in which it is spoken or is a product of the collaboration of researcher and informant (Cicourel 1964). Institutional ethnography does not reject the notion that experience emerges dialogically. On the contrary, adopting Bakhtin's theorizing of discourse or speech genre (1981, 1986), it views the process in which experience emerges as essentially a dialogue between a speaker who voices her or his experience and the listener or listeners who collaborate in the production of that experience in how they attend to the speaker, how she or he is heard, and the questions they may ask. That experience emerges in this way does not invalidate it as a source of data. If the ethnographer is not so much interested in states of affairs or events but in the institutional modes of coordination to be traced in what people can tell about their everyday lives, then experience is a resource to be probed, expanded, opened up, and taken wherever an informant can take it.

Two stages of dialogue are introduced: the primary dialogue is the conversation in which experience emerges; the secondary dialogue then emerges as the researcher engages with the material produced in the first dialogue, which is now with other sources, her or his data. In this secondary dialogue the social organization implicit in the language used by the informant bears traces of the institutional forms of coordination that are present in and are organizing the everyday that has become a resource for experiential talk. The presence of social organization in the lexicon of both the first and the secondary dialogue creates encounters for the ethnographer in which preconceptions may be changed and new directions opened up.

For the ethnographer, her or his ignorance is a valuable resource; discovering in the first dialogue how little she or he knows is an incentive to listening and treating the informant as the one who has knowledge and can teach. The ethnographer aims to be changed in this relationship, and it is this process of change that exposes her or his preconceptions—the preconceptions of the discourse or discourses in which she or he participates—to being undone. This exposure of conceptualization to the social organization and relations implicit in an experiential account—or, as is more usual, present as indications of connections for which the ethnographer should be looking—is a major test of whether she or he is on the right track in her or his analysis.

The ethnographic work of experiential dialogue between informant and researcher goes beyond the moment of dialogue as a moment in a social relation that catches up the informant's experience and transforms it. It is transformed in the work of transcription which produces the interview as a text. The ongoing conversation in which both ethnographer and informant are active and collaborative is over; the product, whether transcript or field notes, engages the researcher in a new conversation with what is now a text and in her or his job of figuring out what to make of it. Pence (2001) calls such a moment a *processing interchange* (more of this in chapter 8), a work site where a text enters to be worked on to produce a new text to be passed on to the next stage in the sequence. It is at this point the institutional ethnography diverges most markedly from methods such as grounded theory (Glaser and Strauss 1967) that subordinate what informants have said to an interpretation that is not theirs. Yes, we do, as I show in the next chapter, assemble people's accounts to locate a social organization in which their experiences, as told to us, are embedded but not wholly visible. What they have had to tell us, however, is not reinterpreted. The work of the ethnographer is to pass from dialogue with individuals to create a new dialogue, the dialogue between his or her records, whether transcripts, audio- or videotapes, or field notes, and the making of an institutional ethnography. Connections, links, hookups, and the various forms of coordination that tie their doings into those of others can be made visible. No one story overrides; no story is suppressed (though not all stories will be told, and of those that are, not all can be cited); it is finding their articulations and assembling them that is the work of analysis.

Notes

1. Elsewhere I've used the term *primary narrative* for experientially based stories. See D. E. Smith (1990a, 157–63) for an extended discussion contrasting primary and ideological narratives.

2. See Smith and Dobson (2002) for more on the study of informal learning on the job in a steel plant. This passage from my interview with Marco appears in that paper, though in it Marco has a different name. Both names are, of course, pseudonyms.

3. I had undertaken a project in association with others that had a predetermined topic not founded in or oriented by a problematic originating in people's experience.

Work Knowledges

So what should the ethnographer orient to in the data dialogue?[1] The ethnographer is the one who's looking, asking questions, wanting to discover what people are doing and how people are putting things together. As ethnographers, what should we be looking for and asking about? How should we orient questions or observations? How should we frame the informants' attention so that what is learned can become the data on which the researcher relies in analysis? Let me start with a mock ethnography that has not been researched but relies largely on my own work knowledge as a participant. Though my own experience of academic work, both as student and as faculty member, is incorporated, my problematic originates in conversations I had with undergraduate students two or three years ago. The sketch is based on what I've learned of the production of grades in a university setting, my own work knowledge extended by talking to others and learning from what they know.

Work Knowledge of University Grades and Grading: A Mini-ethnography

One of the first things I learned about the job of university teaching when I started my teaching career as a lecturer in sociology at the University of California at Berkeley was about grading. I had produced a midterm examination on which a large percentage of the class got at least a B. I was rather pleased with this outcome because I took it as evidence of the success of the course and of my and my teaching assistants' teaching. The administration, however, did not take this view. The administrators wanted grades that as a whole looked more like a bell curve, so they told me.

I could see in this experience two things about the regime of grading: one was that the instrument, the test or assignment, had to be written so that it would produce differentiation. Tests and assignments don't automatically produce a differentiated set of grades conforming roughly to a bell curve. They must be designed to do so. Yes, my test differentiated between those who had done the reading and listened to the lectures and those who hadn't, but, apart from a few outstanding test results, it didn't produce a graduated set of evaluations. The second was that the overall grading procedure must produce something like a bell curve regardless of students' actual performance. It could be that in a given class, the test results aren't that clearly differentiated and do not conform to a standard distribution. It's up to the instructor somehow to produce at least an approximation.

Grades are identified with the individuals whose work is graded. But that association is itself a product of the institutional process. It's useful to see grades as being *produced* as a particular individual's in the work organization of universities. The organization of courses that dominates in North American universities was established for no particular pedagogical reasons. University administrations wanted to exercise more control over faculty (Barrow 1990). They suspected faculty of putting in less time than they should according to administrative standards. But we can also see that the format of courses, once they have been established, creates a crude commensurability among them. Different unit sizes can be specified. Courses in different fields and of widely varying intensity can be treated as equivalent, enabling grades to be added up and averaged. Students are knowledgeable about how to work this system by balancing difficult courses with those less difficult—that is, courses that must be allocated serious study time and those in which reasonable grades can be achieved without too much work.

The virtual commensurability of course grades makes possible the grade currency that operates in and among universities, at least those in North America. The interuniversity system of representation enables grades from different universities to be formally treated as being of equal value. The university exercises control of its product, some of them as directly as the administration of the University of California that monitored the grades of my midterm exam. The university also maintains records and processes grade information received from instructors, including ensuring that its computerized databases will not be accessible to hackers, and issues transcripts. It also exercises control through its quasi-judicial treatment of plagiarism, cheating in examinations, and the use of essays purchased on the Internet. It must guarantee that the grades accorded and issued under its imprimatur are evaluations of work actually done by the named individual and graded by an appropriately qualified person. All the processes that produce these guarantees are people's institutionally coordinated work.

Courses can be looked at in terms of the work organization of both student and faculty that produce grades. Instructors must design and produce for students ways of testing what they have learned. The subject matter and its tests are not peculiar to that individual, department, or university. The courses are in specific subject matters that are local realizations of academic discourses, organized with their primary bases in universities but having an existence in texts, books, journals, journal articles, conferences at which papers are "read," and, in many instances, forms of professional practice beyond. Hence courses are coordinated within a department to make up programs in a given field, a major, that is accountable to representatives of the discourse. The instructor's work is complemented by the student's work of production, their answering questions on a test, writing a paper, or performing another kind of material product that is made available to the instructor to grade. Grading itself is then the instructor's work and a responsibility for which she or he is accountable both to the individual student (who may complain) and to the university administration (who may also complain).

If we look at this process from the standpoint of students, we can see that it presents a number of problems. A student's grade point average comes to represent her or him in this interuniversity system. If we take up the realities of students' work lives as the actual situations in which they produce tests and assignments for the instructor to grade, we can see that grades may be strongly affected by the number of courses a student is taking and hence the kind of pressure of time and anxiety that hits at the end of term. Students may choose to overload with courses in order to avoid accumulating more debt than they have to. In the present context of the high costs of postsecondary education, students may also be working substantial hours in paid employment. Grades may also be affected by the hours a student is putting in with spouse and children at home. Physical disabilities transform the work of getting to the library, to class, to materials, and so on. All these matters take time; traveling from home to the university takes time. The work of getting to class, to the library, to making what's to be studied into a form in which it is accessible, dealing with the university bureaucracy—all of these also take time, and all of these take longer for a student who's disabled. Time deployed in ways such as these diminish what is available for intensive study and writing or preparation for tests; less time spent in study and preparation means lower grades. The actual conditions of students' working lives are increasingly loaded with contingencies that have nothing to do with their commitment and ability. Yet the process of grading makes the actualities of the conditions under which students' work of taking courses, preparing for tests, doing assignments, and so on specifically invisible within the institutional order that produces the grade records and grade point averages that are acceptable currency among universities. Grade is to be purely based on work that students have handed in to the instructor. Students with a disability may find that some instructors view any accommodation made to the kinds of problems they confront as unfair to other students.

Methods of testing and grading are not standardized on a countrywide basis as they are in the United Kingdom. Publishers may provide for the instructor appropriate tests to be used with a textbook; the multiple-choice examination has become a technically and increasingly refined tool as more and more classes are too large to evaluate using essay-type assignments. However, in general courses, examinations or assignments are the choice of the instructor and oriented to the specifics of the course. Grading is supposed to be objective, but the degree to which evaluation can be objective varies widely with the subject matter and the testing format. In some fields, less objective forms, such as writing essays, are viewed as essential to the students' acquisition of the skills relevant to the field. The use of multiple-choice examinations may indeed impose an objectivity of form on what might otherwise be more appropriately treated as matters of opinion under discussion.[2]

This account is built entirely out of what I've learned in the context of my work in various universities. I've been active in the production of grades, both as a student and as an instructor. I've also talked to other instructors about their work and to students about some of the issues they confront in the contemporary university. A graduate student in one of my courses was in charge of the computerized management of grades at a major university and wrote an ethnographic paper describing the processes. I've also done some, but not extensive, reading, and I've added some inferences about how courses enable widely different subject matters, taught often in widely different styles, to be treated as equivalent. If

I were to start without having had this experience, I'd begin to build up my deficiencies of knowledge by learning from others what they have to tell me about how things work. Our interchanges on what they know from their experience with grades would become the work knowledges on which ethnography would draw. I'd also want to explore further into the institutional order of interuniversity relations to find out about the work that is going on to stabilize the relative value of grades and to deal with the problem of grade inflation that seems endemic at this time. In exploring beyond particular universities, I'd also discover a "grading" discourse sustained by research, journals, conferences, and engagements among university administrators.

In the previous chapter (chapter 6), I describe the dialogue that recovers what becomes data for the institutional ethnographer as one in which the researcher evokes and consults others' experience. If I were to turn the aforementioned sketch into an ethnography proper, I'd get much more detail of how people do the work of their part in the process. I'd want to know from students how they plan and work out the completion of assignments and prepare for taking tests and how they fit their work into the rest of their lives; I'd want to know what instructors are doing when they're grading, how they design courses to correspond to the method of grading, whether they do it at home after the kids are in bed, how large their classes are, whether they have some support from teaching assistants. I'd want to know about the work of the registrar's office, how cheating and plagiarism are handled, and what kinds of discussions go on among university administrators and in relevant journals that address issues of the comparability of grades, and so on. But throughout what I'd be relying on is what I've here called "work knowledge." I would be seeking people who are knowledgeable about the work in the area I was investigating because they are doing it. I would be interested throughout in participants' experiential knowledge of the work involved. They know how they do it, and they can describe it to me—if our dialogue does what I want it to do. In drawing on people's work knowledge, the researcher is learning from their expert and exclusive knowledge of what they do and of the contexts and conditions that complement their work. Transcripts of interviews reproduce that learning process; the data is the account of the informants' work knowledge that has been collaboratively produced but is no more or less problematic than any other account of what someone knows by virtue of their experience of doing.

Work Knowledge as the Institutional Ethnographer's Data

The work knowledge that the institutional ethnographer produces from the interview process is not essentially different from the knowledge produced in participant observation. In the former, the dialogue is spoken: informant and ethnographer collaborate to create the work knowledge. In the latter, the work knowledge is produced in the experiential dialogue of the ethnographic observer with her or his field notes and journal. My knowledge of university grading is acquired as a participant. Participant observers are also doing the work in addition to talking to others about theirs. They experience it as they do it. A special dimension, the insider's, is added to the story. But extensive experiential data is produced in the ethnographic interview (Spradley 1979), and, at a fundamental level, the participant observer is not differently grounded other than that the written record is in the observer's own words. It too is based in the experiential, but this time it is based on the experiences of an observer who is looking, watching, and asking questions as well as doing the work. Sure, the observer keeps field notes and checks out guesses about what's going on by consulting others or observing further. Nonetheless the data is no less experientially based than what people can tell the ethnographer in an interview. Participation, however, engages the ethnographer in the institutional complex, and if the ethnographer is also an activist (G. W. Smith 1990; Turner 2003), dimensions of the institutional process come into view to which the ethnographer is alerted by his or her activism. George W. Smith (1990, 1995) wrote of his experience of activism as ethnography, describing what he experienced as an activist as a practice of ethnographic discovery.

> The constant political confrontation between AIDS ACTION NOW! and its respective, politico-administrative regime, often designed on the basis of the analysis as it had so far developed, continued to orient my collection and examination of data. The ongoing analysis of the data was intended to extend my working knowledge of a regime. In every instance, this involved the acquisition of the knowledge people working in the setting had, with the kind of reflexivity that entailed. My ethnographic work, in this respect, was intent on describing, from inside, the social organization of a world that was constantly emerging, and one of which I, too, was a member. (1995, 31)

Smith was learning in the work of activism. He was learning in his own practices and learning from others' work knowledge of what he calls a "politico-administrative regime." The process of learning as ethnographer was not essentially different from learning as an activist, other than that he had to write and report.[3] Turner (2003) used a very similar approach in an investigation that started with her own activism with other residents opposing the development plans for a ravine close to their homes. She first learned what was involved in raising issues with the city council. From there she went on to learn from those working in relation to the municipality's development-planning regime, building a map of the institutional processes that delivered the development outcomes against which the residents protested.

Work Knowledge

There are at least two aspects of what I'm calling work knowledge. One is a person's experience of and in their own work, what they do, how they do it, including what they think and feel; a second is the implicit or explicit coordination of his or her work with the work of others. George W. Smith's (1990, 1995) own work knowledge as an activist was complemented by what he learned from others of theirs. In the passage in the previous chapter from an interview I did with a steelworker, Marco, there were other unexplicated presences. His supervisor was one; his family members were others; and then there was the nebulous other, the "they" representing the company. We might think of this aspect of people's experiential accounts of their work as doors through which the ethnographer may go to open up further resources of knowledge from those at work on the other side of a particular story. Of special importance (reserved for the following chapter) are the texts that enter into the organization of people's work and how the text coordinates different work processes. Here are often to be found the key linkages between one person's work and that of others. My notion of work knowledge comprises both of these. In what follows, however, I examine the two separately because they raise some rather different practical issues in the data dialogue.

Work in a "Generous" Sense

There are problems with using the concept of work, in large part because it's treated as being equivalent to paid employment. By institutional ethnographers, "work" is used in a generous sense to extend to anything done by people that takes time and effort, that they mean to do, that is done under definite conditions and with whatever means and tools, and that they may have to think about. It means much more than what is done on the job. In developing the concept to ground institutional ethnography's dialogue with informants, I've drawn on the thinking of a feminist group called Wages for Housework (D. E. Smith 1987), a group that put forward the notion that housewives do work that actually sustains the paid work in the society and sustains capitalism. Hence, it was argued, housewives should be paid for housework. I found most useful their expansion of the concept of work to include a whole range of activities that are unpaid, not by any means done exclusively by women, such as driving your car to work, taking your clothes to the cleaners in order to look decent for the office, and so on. The group argued that the capitalist economy was sustained by this underground of unpaid and invisible work that people don't recognize as work nor as a contribution to the economy. The other day I was lined up in the bank for about forty-five minutes (during lunchtime in a big bank in downtown Toronto). I was reminded of Tim Diamond's description (1992) of senior citizens in a retirement home who were waiting for breakfast to arrive:

> There each sat before breakfast, bib in place, eyes glued to the elevator. They waited quietly, with a wild patience, practicing patienthood, actively practicing the skills of silence. (129)

I and others in that long line at the bank were at work, practicing the skills of silence, shifting from foot to foot, easing our backs, trying not to get mad.[4] This, for the institutional ethnographer, is no less work than digging a ditch, filling in a form, or putting out a fire. Much of my story of grading in universities expands the notion of work in this way. We don't usually think of getting to class or the library as part of students' work (and, hence, part of the work producing the university as an everyday actuality), but with this concept of work, that's exactly what we would do.[5]

An elegant literary example of invisible work is Virginia Woolf's account in her novel *To the Lighthouse* of Mrs. Ramsay's artful organization and facilitating of a dinner party. Woolf shows the detail of Mrs. Ramsay's supervision of the preparation of the dinner, her management of the interaction among diners, and—important point—that she is conscious and intentional in what she does (Devault 1991, 6–8). That it is work is not recognized by those about her. Marjorie Devault uses the story of Mrs. Ramsay's work to introduce her own study of the invisible work that is her focus. She uncovers the work of feeding the family, putting in place not only what we'd usually think of under that term, such as preparing food, but also aspects of what is done that we wouldn't think of as work, such as planning a meal; shopping; how the person doing the work anticipates the routines, likes, and dislikes of family members; and so on.[6] She writes,

> My topic is activity without a name, activity traditionally assigned to women, often carried out in family groups; activity that I know from experience but cannot easily label. When I began to think about this research, I wondered how I might study the ways that women care for those they live with. Unable to see how such a goal could be framed as a "proper" sociological topic, I resolved to approach the topic through a study of "housework." For reasons that were only partly conscious, I began to concentrate on the work of providing food. The term is awkward and sounds rather odd, but I could find no term that said precisely what I meant. I meant more than just cooking, more than "meal preparation" (the efficiency expert's term). And "providing," of course has been used for what the traditional husband does—it is linked to the wage that a woman transforms into family meals. While planning the research, I struggled with a variety of definitions, but found no simple and adequate label for the activity I had in mind. (4–5)

Devault sees what she calls an "insufficiency of language" as an instance of "the pervasive lack of fit between women's experiences and the forms of thought available for understanding experience." This insufficiency is a common problem for institutional ethnographers. It comes in various forms. When Stephan Dobson and I were interviewing steelworkers, we'd sometimes run into that problem of language insufficiency, particularly in describing aspects of technological processes to two people who were largely ignorant of steel processing. We did not share the everyday lexicon of the shopfloor. We had no store of visual references that filled out their descriptions. Some informants would resort to gesture. In reading one of my interviews (conducted without Stephan), I found that in one lengthy passage describing a particular process in the plant, I am responding "Yes," "Oh, I see," and so on. And yet reading his account several times left the process unintelligible. How could I have been understanding what my informant was saying at the time, but not now? I didn't think I had been faking it. When I thought back to the interview, I realized that his gestures had been vivid and expressive of the motion of the machine, the shifts in the stages of processing, and so on.

These, of course, had been edited out by the technology of audiorecording. Being aware of such problems means aiming at greater and explicit detail in words. Devault is very successful in getting her informants to describe the work they do in feeding the family; the account she builds on their descriptions expands our understanding of family life as work in ways that go behond what was anticipated by the Wages for Housework group (its roots in an ideological Marxism inhibited such expansions) and way beyond the attenuations of much writing about family and family relationships.

Work is intentional: it is done in some actual place under definite conditions and with definite resources, and it takes time. The merit of this kind of a conception of work is that it keeps you in touch with what people need to do their work as well as with what they are doing. Nona Glazer (1993) has drawn attention to a general transfer of work in contemporary society from paid to unpaid work, which is also a shift of time and costs.[7] One example she gives is the work done by customers in a contemporary grocery store. She contrasts it with a period when customers did not walk up and down the aisle picking out what they wanted to buy, putting them in a basket or cart, and moving them to the checkout. Everything was done by the sales clerk. You could even go into the corner store in the morning, leave your list of groceries, and it would be delivered to your house while you went to work. In 1912 the self-service grocery store was invented and began to transform the grocery store business. In any grocery store we go into now, the work of finding the stuff on the shelves and toting it down to the checkout is the customers' work. It's no longer the work of the sales people and other staff to go and find things for you.[8] You tote it out to the car; nobody delivers it to your door. You transport it home, and that's work, too (and the costs of transportation are yours). These activities take time. In the days when you thought out a list in advance, you took it down to the grocery store and someone would deliver your box of groceries to your door; it was the store's time—paid time, not unpaid time (Glazer, 1993, pp. 48-67).

Talking work in the generous sense of Wages for Housework means speaking experientially and concretely. But there's something else about the concept of work in this general sense: it incorporates the individual's subjectivity and his or her experience. These indeed are what the interviewer (as contrasted with the participant observer) relies on. She or he is interested in collaborating in drawing on the informant's experiential knowledge of her or his work; it is precisely here that informants can speak as experts. Not only does the experiential give a distinctive view of someone's work, but when people are speaking of what they do as work, they can also include how they think about it, how they plan, and how they feel. Andree Stock's ethnography (2002) explores with elementary school teachers the work they do in the making of school reports. She describes the work of writing reports, the practice of a distinctive discourse, how the classroom is managed to yield reportable information on individual children, and, along with these, the emotional aspects—the stress and anxiety that some of the teachers experience in doing the work.

Here again is an important difference between experiential and institutional accounts. The latter is likely to be describing a work process as if it were performed by a position or category rather than by the person the researcher's talking to, and if there's any reference to subjectivity or meaning, it will be attached to a category: "If the child care worker thinks that there may be a problem of child abuse, she . . ." is a typical formulation of subjectivity in institutional discourse. Properties of subjectivity are assigned—the child care worker "thinks" when, for example, what she or he is actually doing is working through the checklist (making telephone calls, checking the records, visiting the family, consulting a supervisor) that is a step in a standardized risk assessment procedure (Parada 2002). The problem for the child care worker may be more one of deciding whether what she or he has learned from the investigation is accountable as an instance of the institutional category that makes the case not only actionable but one that must be acted on. The concept of work and work knowledge as they are conceived in institutional ethnography orients the researcher to learn from people's experiences regarding what they actually do, how their work is organized, and how they feel about it.

The Problem of Institutional Capture

Work knowledges are a major resource for the institutional ethnography, but they are not always accessible to the researcher. I'm not talking about the ordinary barriers that may be presented to the fieldworker (people may refuse to be interviewed; institutional authorities may present barriers; and so on). This is a barrier created by the ways in which institutional discourse may enter into and, from the point of view of the ethnographer, pervert the dialogue that produces work knowledge. The researcher is up against the capacity of institutional discourse, described in chapter 5, to subsume or displace descriptions based in experience. The interview situation is subject to "institutional capture" (DeVault and McCoy 2002; D. E. Smith 2003b), particularly where both informant and researcher are familiar with institutional discourse and know how to speak it. The process of subsuming the actual under the institutional sometimes becomes a feature of an actual rather than a textual conversation. The researcher may not, indeed, notice having been captured by the institutional discourse until she or he reads the transcript of an interview only to find that the informant's account is in institutional terms and is descriptively empty. Anderson and associates (Anderson, Hughes, et al. 1989) locate the same effect, which they describe as a problem of getting past the "organizational rationale" of a particular informant:

> The task we face is how to describe in actual cases precisely what her work tasks consist in and how the co-ordination and sequentiality of her work is achieved. Saying that she is an accounts processor really tells us very little at all. Neither does describing her place in the organizational setting. The problem is one of researchability. What materials are there which we could use to capture and preserve the displayed organizational unity of her work? Taping her own account of what she does simply gives us back the problem. She does not tell us how to do it for ourselves, how to compile the documents, find the missing invoices, transfer the necessary numbers, and so on. She gives us, instead, a description of the organizational rationale to what she does. In asking her to take us through her work, what we get is a description of how everything she does is fitted together. What is done first, second, and so on, and how once the base figures have been "picked up" the rest can be derived. What she gives us is the organization's organizational account, premised in the fact of its inherent co-ordination and sequential unity.[9] (127)

The particulars of the informant's local work are displaced by "the organization's organizational account."

Institutional ethnographers share Anderson and his associates' problem of how to go behind or get beyond the institutional discourse spoken in an informant's accounts of her or his work.[10] The sense of work used here is precisely to create work knowledge that is as close as possible to what an individual does in time, in a particular actual work setting, and in relation to particular others. Institutional discourse swallows perspective, the local, the particular, and the subjective experience of workers. As we saw in chapter 5, institutional discourse selects those aspects of what people do that are accountable within it. What is not discursively recognized will not appear. Long ago I read an account of filmmakers who went to a Navajo reservation in the Southwestern United States to film silversmiths at work.[11] They also gave cameras to some of the Navajo people themselves, who made their own films of silversmiths at work. The films made by the white filmmakers showed beautiful scenes of the craftsmen at work and of their products. The films made by the Navajo were rather different. They did not focus exclusively on work that is specific to the craft of making silver jewelry. They included things such as the craftsman walking to work in the morning or going to get fuel for the fire. There was a whole range of doings that appeared as the work of a silversmith to the Navajo filmmakers but that didn't appear as such to the white filmmakers. I remember also when one of my sons, then in elementary school, had done a science experiment in school and wanted me to tell him how to write it up. I said, "Well, you just write down what you did." "Don't be stupid, mother,"[12] he said. "They don't want you to write down everything. They don't want to know that I filled the thing with water and took it over to the bench." Institutional ethnography's concept of "work" is meant to direct attention to what someone is/was doing; it wants to include the actual doings that go on to making institutions happen, whether they are recognized in institutional discourse or not. For the institutional ethnographer the craftsman's morning walk to his smithy and the child's getting water for his experiment are as much part of the work as those that are recognized and become accountable within institutional discourse. The problem for institutional ethnography is to get behind such ordinary barriers of language and to learn from people about what they are actually doing. The concept of work as defined here helps to direct the ethnographer. It is a reminder to constantly return to the particularities of what people are or have been doing, to their thinking and feelings as well as to the circumstances, means, time, and other resources of that activity.

Assembling and Mapping Work Knowledges

In mapping the institutional process that has been selected for focus, research begins with the everyday experience of those who are related to the process in similar ways. This constitutes the problematic of the study (see chapter 2). Those consulted might be patients with AIDS visiting physicians (McCoy 2002, forthcoming; Mykhalovskiy 2002; Mykhalovskiy and McCoy 2002); they might be mothers with children in elementary school (Griffith and D. E. Smith 2004); they might be residents protesting a city's development plans for a treasured wild ravine (Turner 2003). This starting place does not constitute a sample of a population. It is a starting place that orients the direction of research. In the experiences of members of this group, the researcher can identify the relations that are to be explored and the first level of categories of persons who should be interviewed.

The concept of social relation is useful here. It is not to be confused with relationships such as those between mothers and daughters. Indeed the term does not identify an entity. Rather it is a guide to inquiry that reminds the researcher not to treat description of a given work knowledge as an end in itself, but to look for the *sequences* of action in which it is embedded and which implicate other people, other experience, and other work in the institutional process on which research is focused (G. W. Smith 1995). The importance of the concept is in the direction of research that it proposes. Starting in the everyday experience of people caught up or otherwise participating in an institutional process, it directs the researcher to explore how their work (in the sense in which the term is used here) is articulated to and coordinated with others active in institutionalized processes.

The ontology of institutional ethnography proposes that the differences in perspective and experience of participants be recognized and taken advantage of in mapping given processes or organization. Indeed it is indispensable. The experience of one informant may include references to other positions or people involved in the same institutional process. As suggested earlier, it is useful to imagine these as doors that can be opened by interviewing someone on the other side whose perspective and experience complements (and may correct) the work and experience of the first informant. Talking with mothers of children in elementary school about the work they do in relation to their children's schooling tells us about the ways in which what they do in the home complements the work of teachers; moving through the door of the school to talk to teachers and beyond them, to the school board administrators, gives a different perspective and shows different interests as well as a different scope of work knowledge (Griffith and D. E. Smith 2005). The teachers whom Alison and I talked to in the school in the middle-class area could count on mothers being available to support their children in home or remedial work. Not so with the teachers in the low-income community school, who rather took for granted that they would not get that support, even though it may well have been available if they had sought it (Manicom 1988). At the school-board level, administrators take into account the different bases of "support" for a school contributed by middle-class communities as contrasted with low-income communities. They, the administrators, may use the institutional language of "community"; but, explored ethnographically, their perspectives on how schools vary with income levels and kinds of families subsume both the varying work organization of mothering under different conditions and the varying practices of teachers. By exploring the work knowledges of those situated differently in the institutional division of labor, the researcher can begin to assemble the sequences of action built from complementary work.

In the previous chapter, I draw attention to how the telling of experience carries into the ethnographer's presence the tracks of the social organization of the everyday actualities in which the experience originated. That social organization does not begin and end with what's within a particular individual's experience. Methods of selecting from the always-more-than-can-be-used material that ethnographic research generates are, of course, guided by the original problematic; but, more important, they are guided by the interlocking character of work knowledges of people differently located in a process. In a sense, different pieces of the puzzle select other pieces and select those aspects of other work knowledges that fit. It is as if it were a jigsaw puzzle that grows piece by piece into its own direction. For example, Ellen Pence (2001) tracks the sequence of institutional action that constitutes a case of domestic abuse. Pence introduces into her ethnography the standpoint of women whose abusive spouses are processed through the judicial system. People differently placed and at work in different parts of the sequence have different work knowledges. The police making an arrest and writing it up as a report have a work knowledge quite different from that of the probation officer, whose job it is to assemble the history of the case and make a recommendation to the court at which the person found guilty will be sentenced.[13] In between these two is the work of the city attorney, the defense lawyer, the judge, and others involved in producing the work of the court, including that of the defendant, witnesses, and so on. The different work knowledges that are produced in the researcher's dialogue with police or probation officers are not reinterpreted in the analysis. Rather, they are fitted together so that the organization of the sequence, circuit, or other organizational form can emerge.[14] Drawing on others' work knowledge of those standing in reciprocal positions is a major resource for the ethnographer as she or he learns about how people are coordinating their work in a given institutional setting.

Informants' work knowledge and the work knowledge of participant observers, including activists, are based in experience and hence authoritative (see chapter 6) for the ethnographer. She or he does not reinterpret them or assign them a value that they do not claim. Analysis remembers that each informant contributes only a piece of a social organization that is the coordinated achievement of people's doings. In writing the ethnography, the researcher assembles the different work knowledges of people situated in and contributing differently to the process on which research focuses. Assembly procedures vary and depend, as we shall see in later chapters, on the particular conformation that the problematic brings into focus. But in every case what is being explicated is how people's work is coordinated in a given institutional process or course of action. This is where institutional ethnography diverges from ethnographic strategies such as grounded theory (Glaser and Strauss 1967). The latter method of transposing the researcher's impressions or intuitions into concepts that have the formal property of universality combines to displace diverging perspectives and to subdue the social organization that generates difference to a monologic interpretive scheme. Of course, various informants are heard from, but they are subdued to examples or instances of the ethnographer's theory. By contrast, here social organization is not a concept imposed externally on and used to interpret data; rather, the concept is to explicate what is discovered in the process of assembling work knowledges and finding out how they articulate to and coordinate with one another. In a sense the ethnographer's analysis assembles the work knowledges produced by her or his collaborative work with informants to create a map or model of that aspect of institutional organization relevant to the research problematic. Different ways in which complementary work knowledges are assembled depends largely on the institutional processes or relations identified as key to the problematic.

The notion of mapping institutions central to Turner's study (and see D. E. Smith 1999d) draws attention to the difference between mainstream sociological studies and institutional ethnography. Though institutional ethnography's mapping does aim to be accurate, it does not aim to be an objective account that stands independently of the actuality of which it speaks. It refers back to an actuality that those who are active in it also know. Garfinkel's early critique (1967) of mainstream sociology undermines its methodological claims to an objectivity independent of the setting it describes. Making sense of sociological writing relies implicitly on the reader's background knowledge of what the writing refers to. Similarly, institutional ethnography always refers back to, is interpreted in relation to, and may be corrected or added to on the basis of others' work knowledge of what it describes.

Making maps is a useful metaphor for institutional ethnography because maps do not claim to be read independently of the terrain they map. My ethnographic "sketch" of grading in universities was composed dialogically; writing this evoked my experiences and what I remembered of having learned from others. Strictly speaking, it was not participant observation, but it was based in participation. I wrote it for this chapter as an example of what an exploration of work knowledges in an institutional setting might look like and for readers who most probably are themselves familiar with these processes. You could tell me things about the process I don't know; you could point out where I am mistaken; you could add what I've told you that you didn't know into your own work knowledge of the process of grading.

The indexicality of a map is dialogic. The reader of the map is referring it to the actual terrain on which they're traveling or plan to travel. In a sense, it explicates those aspects of the terrain that will enable the traveler to find where she or he is and where she or he is going. It does not stand independently of the terrain it maps. Analogously, the work knowledge that's the source of the ethnographer's data builds, with other resources, an account of an aspect of an institutional regime that a reader can refer to with her or his own work knowledge of the same regime or can incorporate into one's work knowledge. The ethnography is to be interpreted as an explication and expansion of the work knowledges people have of the social terrain it claims to describe.

Conclusion

In sum, the collaborative work of the researcher and informants produces out of the informants' everyday doings the informants' work knowledges. The concept of work becomes an important guide in entering into the data dialogue. It orients the ethnographer to what people are doing and to the forms of coordinating people's doings that make up that complex of work organization relevant within the general framework of the research problematic. It is important to hang on to an understanding of the notion of work that makes possible a focus on what goes into the relations and organization that coordinate people's everyday doings with those of others and to avoid being misled by institutional conceptions of work, such as that which equates it with paid employment. Selecting items off the shelves in a supermarket and bringing them to a cash register is work; waiting in line to speak to a teller in a bank is work; walking to the mailbox is work; so is filling in your income tax form; and so on and so on. Getting down to the everyday organization of people's doings is not as easy as you might think. Ordinary uses of the concept of work easily deflect us. But this puts into place not only what people do but the time it takes to do it, the conditions under which it gets done, and what people mean to do. It suggests that there may be skills involved; that people plan, think, and feel; and that what others are doing and what is going on is refracted by the perspective of the doer's activity.

Experience is a bridge between what is not yet spoken and what becomes, through dialogue (chapter 6), the substantial ground of ethnography. Assembling the different work knowledges gives institutional ethnography a practical means of exploring the social as the coordinating of different people's doings. Though scarcely as precise as conversational analysts' dovetailing of sequences of talk, it follows an analogous logic, first formulated in George Herbert Mead's account of symbolic communication (Mead 1962). Each stage or step orients to the work with which it coordinates sequentially; each next stage or step articulates to the foregoing and defines it as well as orients to what follows. Assembling the stages helps to locate a sequence of action or a set of sequences, a social relation, as in our study of mothering and schooling (Griffith and D. E. Smith 2004); alternatively, it maps a complex—as in McCoy's work (1999; see following chapter) and in Turner's study (2003)—that cannot be located in any one site of people's work. Nor is it produced abstractly, as are those representations of organization characteristic of mainstream organizational studies or the management studies examined by Giltrow (1998). The product is ethnographically grounded, drawing relevant passages of dialogue with informants into the text to stand not as illustrations or examples but as accounts of the work people are doing that coordinate with the work of others in an organized process. Ethnography discovers the institutional order rather than imposing it.

In the following chapter, "text" and "texts" are introduced as an important component in the organizing of institutional courses or circuits of action. Their general significance in the translocality of institutions has already been emphasized. Introducing texts as ethnographically observable presences in coordinating people's work opens up the forms in which power appears. It enables the ethnographer to reach further into the social relations and organization of institutions as they are connected with the larger relations of ruling and the economy.

Notes

1. Majorie Devault and Liza McCoy, in a chapter that appears in this book's companion volume, *Institutional Ethnography as Practice* (forthcoming), describe how institutional ethnographers have learned about people's activities and how such activities are coordinated with those of others.

2. Personal communication, Liza McCoy.

3. George Smith's observations as an activist were never written up as an ethnography. He died too soon. They were, however, used and made available to others in his work as an activist.

4. We were and are also doing unpaid work that at one time was done by paid staff and has been transferred so extensively to automatic teller machines, or ATMs (Glazer 1993).

5. Deborah Brown (2004) has made innovative use of the concept of work as it is explained here. In her research into child protection institutions in British Columbia, she met with women who were under the supervision of a child protection agency in a focus group setting (she calls them her "research consultants"). Collectively they drew on their experience in describing their relations with the agency as work. They identified work activities as well as the skills they developed over time. Brown then went on to explore, with the help of a child protection counselor, the textual sequences regulating the work of the child protection agency.

6. Devault rejects notions such as "caring work" that classify ideologically without giving access to the local practicalities that are involved in producing family meals.

7. This fine study of work, contextualized by changes in the organization of capitalist institutions, isn't strictly speaking an institutional ethnography. It is, however, congenial in providing excellent descriptions of changes in women's work imposed by changes in the work organization of capitalist enterprises. It is also rare in avoiding subordinating accounts of work and work organization to the frames and concepts of political economy that generally operate as institutional discourses do to subsume, rather than explicate, actual social relations and organization.

8. I note also the technologies of packaging that facilitate the consumers' work. Packages packed in plastic are draped on stands and often contain, for example, nails and combs—more than the one or two items that the customer wants.

In the past, nails or screws might be weighed or counted out by a clerk. Now it's hard to find a package of screws with fewer than ten—unless they're large. The plethora of discarded packaging contributes significantly to garbage disposal problems in municipalities. Most of that discarded is required by the packaging of standardized units and/or the exigencies of display and access.

9. Anderson and his associates are, of course, using the term *capture* in a context that implies almost the opposite of how it is used in the phrase *institutional capture*.

10. See also Devault and McCoy in the accompanying volume, *Institutional Ethnography as Practice* (forthcoming).

11. I've lost the reference but remember the story.

12. He used the term *mother* when he wanted to speak to me in a fashion incompatible with the less formal *mom*.

13. See my chapter describing an interview with a probation officer around a presentencing investigation in *Institutional Ethnography as Practice* (forthcoming).

14. McCoy's (1999) study, discussed at some length in the following chapter, describes a circuit.

CHAPTER 8

Texts and Institutions

The move to expand ethnography beyond the local of people's everyday experience requires drawing texts into ethnographic practice. In chapter 1, I introduce the notion of the ruling relations. It is meant to locate for us a phenomenon so deeply embedded in our time and our lives that we are hardly aware of it. The contrast that brought these relations into view was the recalcitrance of the gendered body as experienced within the women's movement. It wouldn't ascend with the Cartesian uplift that separated mind from body. Stuck with embodiment, the sociological inquirer starting from women's standpoint becomes aware of the extraordinary complex of relations that, in our contemporary world, has the power to locate consciousness and set us up as subjects as if we were indeed disembodied. And, oddly, it has the power to do so even when it speaks of the body.

The foundation of these relations is textual. It does not matter for the purposes of this general observation whether the text is print, film, television, audio, computer, or whatever. Of course, these media differ. They have in common, however, this one effect, that they are forms of writing, speaking, or imaging that are replicable and hence can be read, heard, and watched by more than one individual, in different places, and at different times. The words written here are read by me, the writer, as I write them and as I read them over as you the reader are reading. Yet we are separated in time and space. We have set up this odd connection that the publication of this book has made possible. The book appears independent of me; it appears in multiple copies in libraries; it may be being read by others as well as you.

My use of the term *text* needs some firming up. It is a term used in linguistics to refer to stretches of talk as well as to what is inscribed in some
more or less permanent form (of course, stretches of talk by the time they
come under the technical gaze of the linguist are so inscribed). But here,
in this context, it is important to hang on to the association of words or
images with some definite material form that is capable of replication. It
is the *replicability of texts* that substructs the ruling relations; replicability
is a condition of their existence. The capacity to coordinate people's doings translocally depends on the ability of the text, as a material thing, to
turn up in identical form wherever the reader, hearer, or watcher may be
in her or his bodily being. And when we are addressing institutions, as we
are for the most part in institutional ethnography, we must be particularly
aware of the role of texts in the generalization of social organization that
we take for granted when we use the term. How is it that hospitals or
schools or universities or corporations can be recognized as the same kind
of social form in the multiple different sites of their local practice? Replicable and replicated texts are essential to the standardizing of work activities of all kinds across time and translocally. It is the constancy of the text
that provides for standardization. The multiple replication of exactly the
same text that technologies of print made possible enabled historically an
organization of social relations independent of local time, place, and person. Texts suture modes of social action organized extralocally to the local
actualities of our necessarily embodied lives. Text–reader conversations
are embedded in and organize local settings of work.

The complementary organization of work that the researcher can assemble from the work knowledges that people provide remains no more
than a particular work organization in a particular site unless and until
we can find the institutional dimension of its organization. And that
means finding the texts that coordinate the work done by different people
not only in that setting but in other settings so that the work done in one
place is coordinated with that done elsewhere and at other times.

Two things need emphasis before we go deep into the topic: one is
that—and this may be a generational effect—I am a reader. I know more
about written texts than about images or sound or texts involving numbers. So I tend to neglect the aspect of textual coordinating that, for example, Liza McCoy (1995) addresses in her work on the photographic
image or that is represented by television or film, musical scores, mathematics, architectural drawings, and so on.[1] Texts, particularly texts in
writing, are ubiquitous in institutional organization and are certainly of

major importance in producing the generalization and standardization of people's doings that are integral to the institutional. The second point of emphasis is that what I can say here is limited by the state of the developing art of locating texts in the sequences of action and how they are implicated in coordinating them. Hence the aim of this chapter is to make texts ethnographically visible, to show some of the ways in which institutional ethnographers have incorporated them into ethnography, and finally to encourage others to recognize the textual as active.

My account of the ontology of the social has stressed that the social is in motion, but it is difficult to conceive of texts in that way. Drawing texts into an ethnography based on this ontology is up against their ordinary inertia as I stressed in chapter 5. In the process of writing or creating an image, the text has not yet come into being. It is on the way. Once it arrives in textual time (D. E. Smith 1990a), the text–reader conversation catches the reader up into the text's temporal order. Her or his focus is contained within it. It is detached from the local setting of the reader's/watcher's local bodily presence. When we read, the text contains our consciousnesses; it lifts us out of locally oriented awarenesses—they don't go away of course, but we don't attend to them. Texts have their own internal temporal structure, but it is not the temporality of the everyday living in which the work of reading is being done. This containment of consciousness, the break of everyday temporal experience, the focus on the work of reading that captures attentional focus—these make it hard for us to see texts as entering into an ongoing conversational relation with the reader, such as that I describe in chapter 5, let alone to recognize the "active" part they play in coordinating people's work.

Figure 8.1 is designed as an aid to conceptualize texts as "occurring" in time and in the course of, indeed as part of, courses of action. We can

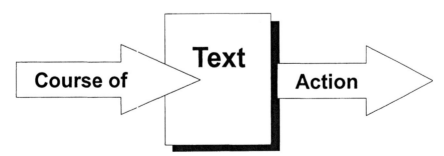

Figure 8.1. Conceptualizing Texts in Action

imagine one individual reading in the library as part of preparation for writing a paper or for checking what's available on the Internet relevant to her or his work. She or he is engaged on a course of action, and reading the text is integral to that action; the text being read enters into the text she or he is writing. Imagine notes being taken (another text) that then become built into the text of the paper being written as a course assignment or as an article to be sent to a journal to be reviewed for publication. The course of action is in time and in definite local places. The text as a material entity, maybe a book or a journal publication, is with her or him in that particular place in which the work is getting done, and it takes time (she or he is checking a watch to make sure she or he is going to be able to finish it before she or he has to leave).

The key to incorporating texts into the ethnographic mode is to be able to recognize that their reading is situated in an actual time and place; that it is an integral part of a course of action; and that there's a text–reader conversation going on that involves an actual person (maybe more than one). For example, when I first began to think about how to make texts recognizable as part of the action, I was in a hotel in Evanston, Illinois, waiting for a friend to arrive from the airport. At a coffee table in the lounge close to where I was sitting, four or five people were seated. I couldn't hear what they were talking about, but I could see them talking and could see a text on the coffee table open in front of one of them, who seemed to be dominating the group interaction. He talked more than the others and looked around into each face as if collecting their attentions. Every now and again, he'd pause; his eyes would go down to the text in front of him. The others would wait—it was as if the text had its turn (to use a notion from conversational analysis) that displaced others. Then he'd look up and speak again, as if he was reporting or responding to what the text had said to him.[2]

A first step is recognizing the text as a material presence in local situations in which it is activated by a reader. When I was teaching a graduate course in textual analysis in the Department of Sociology of the University of Victoria, British Columbia, I asked students to bring a text to class with enough copies for every member. It was enlightening in more ways than I anticipated. Members of the class went about reading texts in different ways depending upon the genre. When they read a handsome brochure for an eastern Canadian university, they did not start at the beginning and work through. Rather they flipped back and forth, picking out sections to scan, glancing at the pictures, and moving on or back to others. A form for referees supporting a student's application for admission to graduate school was read differently; it was scanned but not generally read through from top to bottom. Either of these procedures differ from the reading of a novel. Or from the reading of a telephone directory—if indeed it can be described as reading. The text–reader conversations were observably different and appeared to be specific to the genre of text with which the reader was engaged.

Such observations do not take us far enough in exploring texts ethnographically since it is what their side of the text–reader conversation commits the reader to that is central to the text's coordinative work. Introducing these observations here is meant to anchor the notion that texts happen, that text–reader conversations take place in real time and in the actual local setting of their reading: "Texts represent—are in themselves—certain kinds of human acts" (McGann 1993, 4). Noticing how people go about activating texts helps to escape our experience of them as passive and enables us to see them as in action. Recognizing texts as people activate them in their work, as they occur, makes possible the expansion of ethnography beyond the local to explore and explicate institutional order. It makes visible the presence of institutional relations in the everyday of people's lives. If we can fix our attention on the ongoing actualities of people's doings, we can see them/ourselves as we pick up a newspaper or a book, write an e-mail message, follow a recipe, switch on the television, bring up a file on the computer monitor, fill in a form, and so on and so on. We are actively engaged with texts as we read them or as we continue to carry on a silent conversation with what we have read (D. E. Smith 1990a). Textual materials that are on the shelves, in files (whether in computer directories or in file cabinets), or are otherwise out of action exist *in potentia*, but their potentiating is in time and action, whether in ongoing text–reader conversations or in how the "having read" enters into the organization of what is to come. Even Julia Kristeva's argument (1986) that the text is the reader's production presupposes a text that can be treated as recognizably the same in the varieties of readings that can be created. Reproducing the same managerial and accounting procedures across many local settings hooks their local work organization into "centralized" regulatory and decision-making processes that are themselves located in particular settings. These relations could not exist without the possibility of a standardized reproduction of texts, enabling them to be recognized as "the same" in the multiple local contexts in which they occur (McGann 1993).

The previous chapter describes how ethnographers might go about drawing on the work knowledges of participants in an institutional process. Introducing texts into the analysis of coordinated sequences or circuits of people's work inserts the institutional into what is otherwise just an account of a local work organization. The coordinating provided by texts is both in the local work process *and* in relation to the work being done in other sites and at other times. Locating the texts involved in such a process and including in the ethnographic process an account of how they enter into courses of action identify for the ethnographer dimensions of organization that reach beyond the local and open up doors for further exploration, particularly, of how local work is governed extralocally.

How Texts Coordinate

The textual dimension of institutional ethnography is, in institutional settings, inseparable from the accounts of people's work based on the informant's work knowledge that interviewer and informant create together. Texts, however, do not become a focus in and of themselves. While we have valuable things to learn from discourse analysis as well as from the field of rhetoric, institutional ethnography recognizes texts not as a discrete topic but as they enter into and coordinate people's doings. Indeed, as activated in the text–reader conversation, they *are* people's doings.

In coordinating a work process, texts in institutional settings also produce the institutional observability of the work of those involved; that is, there's a two-way coordination, one that is involved in coordinating a sequence involving more than one individual in an institutional course of action and the other with those responsible for overseeing the process and for ensuring that what is done meets regulatory requirements. This double coordination can be found in various forms in all of the instances that I will use to illustrate some of the different ways in which the role of texts can be recognized ethnographically.

Cases as Linear Sequences

Pence's investigation (1996, 2001) of the judicial processes involved in domestic abuse cases locates the "case" as a major organization of the sequence starting with a violent interchange between husband and wife that results in a 911 call. It is from this point that every institutional step is mediated and made accountable in texts. The call taker records the details of the call in the fields set on the computer monitor. The fields are activated as soon as she or he initiates the process. The police officers follow a protocol during their intervention that enables them to produce a report acceptable to their supervisor. It includes whatever may be relevant to a decision about whether to take further action, including the possibility of making a charge. The textual procedures of the judicial process conform to a more general genre of textual organization: the "case," or, in the judicial context, the "file." Cases are organized textually as records of individuals; such records are then passed through a sequence of institutional stages.

Pence (2001) introduces the notion of a "processing interchange" to identify a characteristic work organization. At each processing interchange, a text enters and is processed. It may then be passed on as modified or checked, or a new text built from the resources of the original is produced and passed on. The individual whose case is organized in this process has been constituted textually. The institutional schedule organizes the lives of both husband and wife. Who they are, how they are recognized, and how they may be required to perform are established in the texts that make up the records of the case.

A detective who was an informant for Pence created the following account as one typical of a sequence in which the text of a police report travels through various processing interchanges, being modified or supplemented as it travels.

Jan. 1, 1993, a Friday: A domestic between a co-habiting couple occurs in the city. The victim gets a black eye and bloody nose and calls the police. A sqd. responds and finds the offender gone and is not able to locate him within the 4 hours. They go back to their business.

Jan. 2: The sqd. dictates a report.

Jan. 4: The report is transcribed and returned to the Patrol division.

Jan. 7: The report is signed by the supervisor and taken to the traffic division where it is logged as a warrant request.

Jan. 8: It is placed in the city attorney basket. It is Friday.

Jan. 11: It is logged into the city attorney's office and sent to an attorney. Some time within the next couple of weeks, an attorney will review it, decide to issue, direct a clerical to fill out the necessary forms.

Jan. 25: The file is returned to the DPD [Duluth Police Department] Detective Bureau clerical person with a summons attached.

Jan. 27: The clerical types out the summons information and mails the package out, including all of the reports, the victim and witness information and statements.

Jan. 28: The victim and offender, having continued to live together, share the first day since the assault that they have not thought or argued about it.

Jan. 29: The offender opens his mail and notes that his court date is set for Feb. 22.

Feb. 22: He doesn't appear for court. At the end of the day, the court file is carried back into the Clerk of Courts offices.

Feb. 23: It is placed into a basket where it sits for the standard two week minimum grace period.

March 10: It is removed from that basket and placed into the "return to city atty for warrant basket." It may sit there until a stack "worth" picking up or mailing back accumulates but to be charitable, let's say it goes within a couple of days.

March 12: It is received in the city atty's office and sent to the issuing attorney.

March 17: It is dictated as a warrant and returned to the DPD.

March 18: Sgt. Nichols carries it to the court, swears to it and has it signed by a Judge. He then carries it into the Clerk of Court's office. There it is placed into a basket of complaints to be filed when they have time. This may take a week.

March 24: It is placed into the warrants basket to be picked up by the Sheriff's warrants office.

March 26: It is received into the warrants office, logged in, entered into the computer and placed into the basket for service.

March 27 and 28: The couple spends first weekend since his failure to appear not worrying and arguing about what will or should happen.

March 30: He calls and agrees to come in the next day.

March 31: He appears and pleads not guilty. A jury pretrial is set for the first week of May (jpt's are always the first week of the month and he is now too late for April). (Pence 1996, 67–68)

The scheduling of the sequence is legally prescribed: every step is marked by a "move" of the text of the report, and each such move is marked (this isn't described, but we must suppose that there is a date stamp or something similar that registers the arrival of the file at each major location). This account shows us a sequence of text-initiated steps in a course of institutional action that concludes in arrangements for the court appearance of the accused. First, the report is produced; then it travels from one site to another, becoming a "file" as the summons and other material are added to it. When the offender fails to appear at his arraignment, a new text is introduced, the warrant, and the file moves on to the next processing interchange for further action. The text and its transformations coordinate people's action; each move initiates a new action on its arrival at someone's work site; the product is then passed on, transformed or not, to the next site, where it again initiates an action.

The police officer's description locates the producing, authorizing, accumulating, reading, and forwarding texts as integral to people's work and as coordinated in modes that are legally regulated. Thus, not only do texts mediate the process of coordinating each stage of work with the next, but they also coordinate the whole work process and each of its stages with the law of, in this case, the state of Minnesota. The distinctive coordinative practices are key to transposing people's local work into the institutional (more on this in the following chapter). As an ethnographic practice, assembling the various work knowledges of participants to expose how they are coordinated textually discovers, or begins to discover, the institutional regime that they are part of and produce. Wife and husband are no less implicated in this process as participants, each of whom is active, even though they are not institutionally identified as agents in the process.

The sequence of processing interchanges creates a course of institutional action, one that is indifferent to the actualities of the lives of those on whom it imposes its order. And, of course, as pointed out, the whole of this sequence has implicit reference to legislation and, specifically, to the legislation that has established domestic abuse within criminal law as well as to other like texts that regulate local practices. The institutional character of local events is accomplished in the coordinating of local doings with a text-based order applicable translocally.

Accountability Circuits

The "case" as a genre of textually organized work is a sequence. It is organized around individuals. But this is not the only form in which the ethnographer finds the text as "active" in coordinating people's work. Liza McCoy (1999) explores a work organization of accountability.[3] It does not follow the sequential order of the judicial process in domestic abuse cases that Pence describes. It explores the textually mediated relations of the hierarchy of administrative process in a community college. Her ethnography catches community colleges in Ontario at a time of change. Constrained by governmental initiatives, colleges were, at the time of her study, shifting from funding based exclusively on enrollment to a system that funded skills training more responsive to local corporate needs and that used cost–revenue systems of accounting. Basic funding was provincial, but the federal government was promoting the development of a competitive market with private providers of training. That meant that colleges had to bid for jobs and administer short-term training contracts. To function effectively in competitive markets, colleges needed more precise knowledge of the unit costs of training activities, and they needed to redesign administration to respond to and service clients' needs.

Reorganization involved creating, redesigning, or adapting the texts through which people's work became accountable within the new framework. McCoy analyzes the text of the program costing for one division in a particular community college to show the relations it organizes: specific features and types of calculations enabled people's performance in various positions to be evaluated by their superiors; calculations evaluating the status of programs in terms of costs and revenue made it possible to decide on the retention or removal of programs on the basis of cost–revenue comparisons among them.[4] Relations among administrators, financial officers, department chairs, instructors and union representatives were reorganized. The cost accountant of Fulton College describes such change:

> INFORMANT: Um, in the old system the president had control over everything. We try to make the deans responsible for the operations.
>
> LMcCOY: Of their divisions?
>
> I: Yes. Right, so the only way we could make them responsible is to tell them, okay, this is what you're bringing in, this is what it's costing you, right? So the only way we could do that is to go through the costing exercise across the board and so, okay—"short programs are not making money, post-secondary programs are making money, the division as a whole is looking good, but you have certain programs that are being carried by other programs." This is the reason for doing this kind of exercise at this stage. (McCoy 1999, 196)

McCoy comments:

> Here we see the powerful organizing potential of the document. The accountant describes the way the program costing document is being used by him and the administrator in charge to "make the deans responsible for the operations." (196)

A conversation with another administrator shows, from his perspective, the major changes in relations of accountability to which the academics in the college would now be subject. Given the programs for which government funding had been allocated, the academics had considerable independence in how they went about their teaching work and how they allocated their time to different aspects of it. The new cost–revenue system transformed the relationships between academics and administrators, creating what the administrator cited in the following describes as wreaking "mental havoc" among the staff.

> LMcCoy: What would be involved in putting that [program costing] in place?
>
> INFORMANT: The—first of all you have to get the academic side to buy into the importance of it. Um academics are peculiar beasts. They live in a world of, let me get on with doing my job, and don't bother me with dollars and money. Unfortunately the current system is putting us in a position of being a business. Okay? We're a business. And we have to very carefully balance the humanistic side of our aspect against the bottom line. We can't afford to lose money. Ford can lose 9 million dollars, they can borrow from the bank and get it back next year and next century. We can't, we're not allowed to run a deficit budget. We have to remain within our budgetary factors, which means we all of a sudden now have to look at what we're doing as a business. And I'll tell you right now that's creating a lot of mental havoc with our staff. (McCoy 1999, 198)

In bringing the academics within the new structuring of accountability, administrators took advantage of a form that had been established in union–management negotiations following a teachers' strike in the mid-1980s over the maximum teacher hours that could be required of a teacher. Limits had been set in the collective agreement, but administrators often ignored them—they were "trying to increase enrollment while holding staff salaries down." One outcome of the strike settlement was the development of a standard formula for calculating teacher "workload" (McCoy

1999, 211), which was embodied in a form: the Standard Workload Form (SWF). Until the restructuring of accountability, the form had little direct significance for instructors other than allowing them to bring a grievance if they believed that the collective agreement had been contravened; under the new cost–revenue regime, it could be used to assess the effectiveness of the dean and the department chairs in deploying their teaching resources within the new focus of being a business.

> Teacher "workload" as a routine calculation is not determined by teachers figuring out how much they work, but is rather determined independently of their experience of doing the work. It is the work of the department chair to fill out (or cause to be filled out) and approve SWFs for all the teachers in the department. This is not a representation after the fact. SWFs are filled out in the process of determining what courses a teacher will teach in the upcoming semester and what other work will be expected of her or him, such as developing curricula or going to speak in high schools. The process of SWF thus applies the terms of the collective agreement to the work any one teacher is being asked to do, and by calculating workload by means of the formula, it can be seen whether this proposed set of tasks fits or contravenes the terms of the agreement. (McCoy 1999, 212)

Again McCoy introduces the text of the SWF into *her* text and spells out for the reader how it translates the instructor's work into time and hence cost. She goes on to examine how the form is activated (read) by people positioned differently in the college organization. For one teacher, the form is for her to complete at the first stage, almost as a proposal to be discussed with the department chair. The chair then signs off on the teacher-completed form if it is acceptable to her or him. McCoy's conversation with this teacher shows up the disjuncture between the formalities of the representation of the teacher's workload and the actualities of what the teacher is doing. The department chair, with whom McCoy also talked, recognizes the quasi-fictional character of the representation produced by the workload form. McCoy was also provided with an opportunity to work through with the instructors in the department just what they were committing themselves to for the coming semester. What became apparent, however, as the new organization of accountability was introduced was that the SWFs began to play a new role; they ceased to have the fictional character they had before. Overall time and the time allocated to different categories of teaching and related activities began to be taken seriously as a means of managing how instructors did their work in terms of its contribution to the overall cost–revenue status of programs:

> SWF process was being pulled into the program costing, as the documentary resource for breaking teachers' salaries down into bits of cost that could be allocated to different programs and courses. (McCoy 1999, 227)

These are what Pence would describe as processing interchanges in the circuits of accountability coordinated by texts. Rather than focus on the processing of a text from one position in a sequence to another, McCoy works out from the text (two texts in particular) to explicate how, as they are activated by people at work in different positions, they coordinate the work of administrators and instructors, conforming the work of both to the new cost–revenue regime.

Other Ethnographic Uses of Texts

The examples given here do not exhaust the types of maps that have been drawn by institutional ethnographers, using texts to anchor the sequencing of work processes. In this section, I want to contrast two very different ways in which texts are recognized in institutional ethnographies.[5] The first of these explores and maps an institutional process in which the work that texts coordinate is primarily in texts; the second is an ethnographic account of the work that is profoundly physical and in which texts appear in distinctive work sequences that make the embodied work accountable within an administrative process.

Susan Turner's study (2001, 2003) of the processes of municipal government decision making in land development maps a complex sequence of texts and work based on and producing or modifying texts. She describes her project as addressing

> the practices of reading and speaking that go on in the concrete settings of the peculiar public text-mediated discourse of land use planning, as institutional. In the dialogic organization of people's activities, a public governing institution is produced; a public knowledge is produced and so are concrete outcomes on the land. (2001, 300)

The sequence she maps begins with the early stages of interchange between developer and the city planning office, and it proceeds through the stage at which the site of the proposed development became public and local residents were notified, through council meetings, the various steps of checking with agencies and government departments to the point where the bulldozers started uprooting trees, and beyond that to the final approval of the development plan. Her account is powerful not only because of the complexity of the work–text–work sequences she explicates vividly and with clarity but also because she is particularly successful in showing the connections between work primarily in textual modes and how texts mediate work done at one stage at one site and the multiple connections set up by a text with work done in multiple governmental sites.

The problematic of her study is given in her experience as a resident neighboring on an undeveloped ravine that people in the area had treasured as a place to walk and picnic. Residents in neighborhoods where land is to be developed are notified; the date and time of the council meeting at which it will come up for discussion are provided so that they can attend. Her map of the sequence shows that the residents' intervention comes at a point relatively late in the decision-making sequence where the effects of their protest is minimal—the municipality is already committed to development, and all that the residents achieve are relatively minor changes in situating the development in the ravine and in the character of the housing to be built there.

Turner's ethnography examines carefully how texts enter into and organize work. She details the interchanges that pass from text to talk and from talk to text, making visible the work that is carried on primarily in a textual mode—in the sense that the work is oriented to texts, is based on texts, and is producing texts. Though in the long run the bulldozers began to change the ravine, in between the original plan of the developer and that irrevocable moment that enters the "real world" there has been, as she shows, another real world, one that exists in time, in people's doings, and in the texts that are produced by and organize their work.

Tim Diamond's study (1992) is based on his work experience as a nursing assistant in nursing homes for seniors in Chicago.[6] While Turner's study maps the text–work–text sequences implicated in and organizing the sequence of work that leads to, or perhaps better, *is*, a decision to go ahead with a housing development project planned for a ravine previously left in its natural state, Diamond focuses on the day-to-day work practices of nursing and the day-to-day work practices of being a resident. The study is through and through located in the everyday sensualities of such work, and it is full of people talking. Texts, however, are there; they are present as part of the work, and at the same time they are present to coordinate the local work of nursing assistants and residents with the institutional regime of the nursing home management, with the welfare system and municipal departments responsible for standards of care in seniors' residences, and so on. They appear in, as well as organize, the everyday working lives. Here is an example of how the textual requirements of accountability within the senior nursing home setting appears as a dimension of nursing assistant work:

> After most residents have gone to bed, and before the night shift arrived, we hustled to finish our charting of the bedmaking, bath schedule, bowel and bladder regimens, restraint and position sheets, weights and vital signs. Then nursing assistants were considered by the authorities to have performed their tasks. But these documentary requirements had little to do with how the night closed or with much of what had gone on during the day, in terms of human contact. The coming of night meant coaxing brittle bones into night clothes, while negotiating with those who wore them to get into bed, calm down and try to sleep. Then it meant slipping out the door and turning off the light as quietly as possible. (Diamond 1992, 156)

The charting Diamond describes has less to do with the residents than with the administrative surveillance exercised, first, in the supervisory organization of the residence and, second, by the municipal department responsible for the oversight of the residence, which, though privately owned and managed, was funded through welfare. The nursing assistants' documenting and filling in charts at the end of a shift are themselves work. Documenting and charting make the assistants' work accountable to the authorities. Each task also makes invisible the work of caring and the human encounters involved. From another aspect, we find again how institutional discourse subsumes and displaces the actualities of the work that people do.

In these two examples, I emphasize less the shape of text-mediated organization than the differences in the kinds of work that the two studies describe and analyze. Turner's study of work in texts and work mediated by texts makes visible the possibilities of institutional ethnographies that, working from a problematic in experience, engage with the ruling relations as such; Diamond, by contrast, describes a work situation in a definitely embodied world that is subordinated textually to an institutional regime. Ethnographic strategies in the two are clearly different. In the first, the ethnographer must learn how to read the texts from those whose work it is to read and write them; she must learn the institutional speech genres and discourse; and she must be able to recognize as work what people do with texts and talk to complete the sequence concluding, in this case, with the decision to go ahead with the development of the ravine. By contrast, the ethnographer of situations comparable to that of Diamond's nursing home must be able—whether through participant observation or highly skilled, long, and detailed interviews with informants—to describe the detail of the daily work and doings, the routines, and the texts and to be able somehow to see that those who might not be accessible to interviews are also at work. In Turner's account, being an activist was central, but so also was talking to people about their work and about the part played by texts in what the people were doing. Diamond's study, by contrast, depends on his own direct experience as a nursing attendant to describe the work thereof, and it is hard to image an institutional ethnography of work of this order in which observation does not play a significant role.

Conclusion

In formulating texts so that they can be incorporated into ethnography, I have emphasized two: first, recognizing texts as "occurring" or "activated" (McCoy 1995) in actual local settings and at particular times; second, exploring empirically how they coordinate institutional courses of action. Pence's ethnography (2001) of the judicial process in domestic abuse cases makes visible the key role of texts in coordinating the work of those involved in the institutional course of action that constitutes a case. She introduces the notion of a processing interchange to identify those work sites that are key in coordinating courses of action—texts come in, are worked on, and are passed on in a new form to the next person in the line of responsibility. The organization of a "case" can be contrasted with McCoy's investigation (1999) of what I call an "accountability circuit." Her ethnography addresses the texts of the new regime of accountability being introduced in community colleges in Ontario at the time of her study. Her textual point of entry to the work of administrators, teachers, and so on makes visible a reorganization of relations from those that had been the local practice under the previous regime.

In the work of both Turner (2003) and Diamond (1992), texts can be seen as inserting the institutional into people's activities; otherwise, the two studies are quite different. Turner's mapping of the land development planning and decision process makes it possible to track the work of the various people involved, including the residents who came together to make their protest. The work of residents, municipal officials, municipal councilors, the developer, and so on is work in texts—producing texts, reading texts, and oriented to texts. The texts are key components of the process: they are produced by those involved; they pass to multiple others; those others take up their work from that text on. In the course of this sequence of text-based activity, the ravine beloved of its neighbors is irrevocably transformed. Though they contrived to save some of its features, in terms of what it had been, it is gone. Diamond's focus is, by contrast, deeply embedded in the immediacies of the world of working (Schutz 1962b). He shows us the life that is organized by the institutional and the presence of that institutional in that life. Yet, contrasting as they are, they are complementary. In Turner's story, there is a ravine; there are neighbors who take pleasure in it; when it is threatened, they try to protect it, and they fail. That everyday world isn't central to her inquiry, though it does provide the problematic of her study. In Diamond's story, the presence of the institutional is examined in people's everyday work but is open to being connected further into the intersections of private and public in the provision of residential care for seniors. The coherence established by institutional ethnography's ontology preserves the interconnections discovered in any study for further discovery and exploration or for the making of connections with other studies. No study stands alone; each opens into the interconnections of the ruling relations regardless of the ethnographic level of its major focus.

Once we begin to see how to locate and analyze texts ethnographically as integral to institutional organization, it becomes possible to trace connections that might otherwise be inaccessible. In such examples we can begin to envisage the potentialities of an ethnographic investigation that deploys many of the traditional skills of sociological ethnographers but supplements them with an incorporation of texts grasped as "in action" in the local settings of people's work and with a recognition of just how texts and textual systems coordinate at a distance and across time. It is this combination, not the one or the other, that enables institutional ethnography's claim to reach beyond the local everyday worlds of people's doings into the organization of powers generated in the ruling relations—the topic of the following chapter.

Notes

1. Leanne Warren (2001) has made an institutional ethnography focused on a musical score.

2. Conversational analysts have analyzed conversations in which texts, to my eye, are clearly "active" in the sense used here, but they are not incorporated into the analysis.

3. Many thanks to Liza McCoy for her help in getting my account of the community college circuit accountability reasonably faithful to her fine description and analysis.

4. An abridged version of the text analyzed is reproduced in McCoy's dissertation. It is preferable to make focal texts, if only in abridged form, available in the ethnography *as part of the main story,* where this is practicable. The complete version of important texts can be assigned to appendixes, but where possible, some version of the text subject to analysis should be directly accessible to the reader and introduced to make clear that it's an integral part of the ethnography.

5. Both Turner and Diamond contribute to this book's companion volume, *Institutional Ethnography as Practice* (forthcoming), giving accounts of how they went about doing their distinctive and different institutional ethnographies.

6. Many thanks to Tim Diamond for checking up on my account of his account of nursing assistants' and residents' work.

CHAPTER 9

Power, Language, and Institutions

There is a certain innocence to what has been developed so far as institutional ethnography's method of inquiry. Working from people's experience of their own doings, knitting different perspectives and positions together, and exploring the text-based forms of organization provide means of constructing representations of how things work. But however useful this might prove to those who want to change those workings and however successful it may be in expanding people's everyday knowledge of them, there is yet a missing piece, and that is the dimension of power.

The ruling relations are a complex and massive coordinating of people's work. Intentions, desires, opportunities, impediments, blockages, and powerlessness arise within them. The texts that constitute and regulate (D. E. Smith 2001a) establish agency, that is, textually specified capacities to control and mobilize the work of others. Textually sanctioned agency produces a power that is generated by the concerting and mobilization of people's work. It is specific. It has limits, and it would be a mistake to conceive such forms of power as mobilized simply within a single formal organization, such as a business corporation. Corporations exist within the ruling relations and their interconnectedness—financial markets, banks, legal systems, mass media, government departments and agencies at all levels, and so on. Turner's study (2003) of the decision processes of municipal land development planning is an explication of a course of institutional action in which the interconnectedness of the relations of ruling is made visible. Though she does not engage directly with the interconnections between development as business and the municipal governmental process, it is clear that what she is describing is an organization designed

183

to facilitate the interests of the developer rather than those of the residents of the area and perhaps of the community more generally. The further explication of these relations and how they organize the political processes in which the land-use planning decisions go forward would yield no less to the same ethnographic practice that Turner employs.

Texts and language in general are central to this phase of inquiry. They are not to be taken as the exclusive focus for any actual investigation. The sequences that go into the making of a judicial case (Pence 2001) or circuits of accountability (McCoy 1999) are sequences in which work is tied into text and text into work. While keeping in mind that a text always *occurs* in and as part of someone's work, it is handy to think of text–work–text or work–text–work sequences in orienting ethnographic practice. These formulae are helpful in reminding us not to focus exclusively on texts, particularly since in this chapter that is just what we are going to do.

The emphasis on texts and the language of texts might suggest that institutional ethnography moves in a direction that has been recognized among Marxists as idealism, a theory holding that ideas and beliefs—consciousness—determine the social. I'm not as much dismayed by such an interpretation as I am concerned that it may be all to easy to slip into the illusion that we, as members of an intelligentsia (D. E. Smith 2004), may all hold, of the power of consciousness and intention and to see these somehow as ruling the ordering of society and the course of history. The ruling relations in general are specified in chapter 1 as an objectification of consciousness and agency. It is a conceptualization that is both *in* and *at odds* with Marx and Marxist tradition. I would argue that Marx's own method requires such a concept through which contemporary actualities can be recognized as existing materially in people's activities coordinated textually. Marx did not live to experience the historical developments that have objectified consciousness and organization in the varieties of discourse, large-scale organization, institutions, and so on, which the term *ruling relations* generalizes. The ethnographic of institutional ethnography addresses the ruling relations as coming into being only in people's work as coordinated by the materiality of texts activated in text–reader conversations.

In relating texts, language, and power, institutional ethnography might be seen to address a problem that Pierre Bourdieu (1992) has explored in his work on language and symbolic power. However, it diverges radically from Bourdieu's theory that pursues an economic metaphor to display dimensions of power in language. The image he offers is confrontational, distinctly masculine in style. Speaker and hearer engage with each other in a relation of exchange:

> A relation of communication between a sender and a receiver, based on enciphering and deciphering, and therefore on the implementation of a code or a generative competence, is also an economic exchange which is established within a particular symbolic relation of power between a producer, endowed with a certain linguistic capital, and a consumer (or a market), and which is capable of procuring a certain material or symbolic profit. (66)

This is clearly a model of language and power very distant from that being put forward in this book. For Bourdieu, symbolic power is associated with authority and domination among people. It focuses not only on individuals passing messages back and forth but also on "the capacity of various agents involved in the exchange to impose the criteria of appreciation most favourable to their own products" (67). It is a different conception of language and communication than that put forward in chapter 4, which develops a conception of language as coordinating people's subjectivities. To conceive of language as coordinating is to open up for exploration dimensions of organization that are presupposed in the kinds of communicative encounters Bourdieu envisages.

Texts and language in general are central to phases of inquiry reaching into those regions of the ruling relations where capacities to design and impose the texts, language of texts, and even, more generally, institutional discourse are lodged. For the most part, the intertextuality of institutional texts is organized hierarchically, and changes in conceptual design and the terminology of texts are imposed. Gerald de Montigny's account (1995b) of the hierarchical organization of the texts involved in child protection services in a Canadian province traces this distinctively hierarchical form of intertextuality:

> It is through texts that mundane activities appear or stand as proper social work, hence as matters of record. A home visit becomes an entry in a Running Record, an apprehension becomes a Report to the Court, a decision to request custody of a child becomes a Notice of Hearing, and so on. . . . Through various organizational procedures, including file storage, file audits, mandatory reports from local offices to central offices and budgeting, the routine record-keeping activities of social workers become the statistics for the office, and ultimately for the department.[1] (209–10)

The hierarchal organization of intertextuality is a two-way street: de Montigny describes how work at the front-line level becomes accountable within the hierarchal organization of the "department"; at the same time the concepts and categories providing the terms in which what is done at that level become accountable are governed by the law and, presumably, also by the administrative rules of the department.

This chapter focuses on these two distinct but interrelated coordinating functions, those textually coordinated work processes that produce the institutional realities that make the actual actionable and the distinctively hierarchical forms of intertextuality in which texts at one level establish frames, concepts, and so on, operating on and in the production of institutional realities.

The first of these functions is the fashioning of institutional representations. People's actualities become a resource on which work is done to extract formalized and highly restricted representations.[2] Extraction procedures may involve the completion of a form by a nonemployee; it may be a line of questioning by an institutional representative designed to fill the fields on her or his computer monitor or to produce a report for which she or he is accountable. In all cases, the representation is designed by the conceptual organization of an institutional discourse to which the actuality it represents must be fitted.

Whatever the method, these are key processes. They are general. And they are of central importance for three reasons: one is that they transform the local and particular into the generalized forms in which they become recognizable and accountable across the local settings of institutional work; two, the objectification of institutional realities overrides individual perspectives (see quote from Code in chapter 2); three, the translation of the actual into the institutional is an essential step in making the actual actionable institutionally.

Though we are not here focused on the social organization of scientific knowledge, Lynch's analysis (1983) of perception in the context of scientific discourse is useful in demonstrating the mediation of the text in standardizing the observable. He describes how the local actualities of observation are geometricized in a series of graphic abstractions made on paper. Each step of the series takes the process a stage further in rendering the object measurable. He argues that this graphic work constructs from the actualities in their raw or savage form those measurable abstractions that are the currency of scientific discourse. Though the technical and discursive aspects of the process that Lynch describes are specific to the science he is observing, the general features and steps that transform local actualities into an object that is recognizable within the discourse are essential features of the construction of the textual realities of the ruling relations.

In institutional settings, such procedures subordinate people's experience to the institutional; in that transformation, local actualities become institutionally actionable. Hence the frames, concepts, and categories (and the technologies) that structure the selection and assembly of the actual as institutionally actionable are central in subordinating individual subjectivities to institutionally generated realities. So the first topic of this chapter is the making of institutional realities.

The second topic is that of the hierarchical organization of intertextual relations. Note that *hierarchy* is understood here as strictly a textual and conceptual relation; it is not necessarily or simply related to hierarchies of position. The regulatory frames of institutional discourses structure the relevances and select the categories, concepts, and methods that organize institutional representations. They also provide instructions for how texts are to be read in the text–reader conversations built into sequences of institutional action. Here the primary focus is on regulatory frames, those higher order texts that regulate the "scripts" (Campbell 2002) more directly involved in producing institutional realities from the actualities of people's lives.

Making Institutional Realities

Disjunctures between the artificial realities of institutions and the actualities that people live are not avoidable; they are *of* the transformation, the process of going from the actual to words or images that represent it. Nor are they necessarily malign. When the call taker in an emergency center works successfully with a caller in trying to describe an emergency situation to allocate it to the appropriate response service (D. E. Smith and Whalen 1996; Zimmerman 1992), the caller's engagement with the institutional process works, or should work, to benefit the caller or those on whose behalf he or she calls. Yet in that process there is a transfer of agency from caller to institution that is integral to how the institution assumes the capacity to act. The necessary disjunctures at the point of transition from actual to institutional reality dump or distort the experience of those who are caught up in and subject to institutional forms of action.

In the volume accompanying this, *Institutional Ethnography as Practice* (D. E. Smith forthcoming), in which various institutional ethnographers write about different aspects of their work and experience doing institutional ethnography, Alex Wilson and Ellen Pence (forthcoming) describe a project of investigating the U.S. judicial system in domestic abuse cases by Mending the Sacred Hoop, a group of Native women in which the Native epistemology that structures the project raises issues about systems of institutional categorization:

> We observed how the work of institutional practitioners in the U.S. legal system is regulated through devices such as rules, regulations, guidelines, officially authorized definitions, matrices, forms, protocols, and directives that are standardized across particular jurisdictions and work settings. These devices ensure that workers operating in different locations, agencies and time frames are coordinated in their actions. It is a distinctly westernized way of pulling highly individualized situations or events into clearly delineated categories to organize how their practitioners perceive, discuss, and handle institutional business. The categories operate in selective fashions that don't necessarily represent what had occurred, but what of institutional concern had occurred. The information selected by the practitioner at the intersection of an institution and people's everyday lives was put into a category as an expression of a given rule or procedure. Hence, the institutional order in the U.S. legal system puts together a picture of an event that is very different from the way it was actually lived. No one calls 911 to report, "I'm the *victim* of an *in progress misdemeanor, physical no weapon, violation of a protection order.*" Most of the time, neither the categories nor the action that follows make sense in terms of how people are living. Practitioners working at the front-line are not required to make a fit between institutional categories and actualities.

Wilson and Pence express a disjuncture that goes beyond the ordinary and necessary problem that no representation ever reproduces or can reproduce the actuality that is its original. They propose that the categories imposed institutionally are at least indifferent to the actualities of "how people are living" and may be more seriously disjunctive. At the same time, the formalized and authorized categories to which people's actualities are fitted by those working at the front line are the only means by which those actualities can be made actionable.

The work of transposing people's experienced actualities into institutional realities generally involves some form of interrogation. The social worker visiting a home where child neglect has been reported comes with questions for which she or he must find the answers; the questions are not for the most part spoken but focus how the social worker surveys the apartment, the child, the parents, and so on. The answers to the implicit questions make up the report that is filed (de Montigny 1995a). Surveys and forms as textual genres of interrogation set out as fields the equivalent of questions to which "subjects" or "clients" or "patients" must respond, transposing aspects of their everyday worlds into shapes that fit the topic-assigned spaces provided; or, as in the case of the Needs Assessment Schedule examined by McLean and Hoskin (1998), the questions built into the form are *about* the patient, who plays no part in responding to them:

> During case discussions in which community workers gathered together to discuss the progress and allocation of patients, the form, and in particular the ratings within the summary sheet, were viewed to provide a useful basis upon which to move a patient to a different level of care. Community workers are divided into three groups and in general the decision to allocate patients is made in terms of level of client need, with . . . workers dealing with clients with high needs, case managers with medium needs, and clients deemed to have simple needs being allocated to Community Psychiatric Nurses (CPNs). (534–35)

"Needs" are thus "objectively" determined; patients do not participate; their desires and concerns are not to be confused with formalized and standardized interrogation built into the "summary sheet." Patients' needs are determined by the community workers in their work of responding to the interrogatory structure of the Needs Assessment Schedule.[3]

McLean and Hoskin do not orient to the potential disjunctures between patients' experiences and the needs assessment that represents them. Campbell (2001), however, shows us this process in her account of a case manager interviewing an applicant for home support services. She shows an assessment form being used as the case manager's script in interviewing an applicant to determine his eligibility for home support services. In principle, the commitment of the service is client centered; recognizing the client's need and choice is to be paramount, and this is expressed by the case manager in introducing the process to the client. The case manager is filling in the form in the course of her conversation; its interrogatory structure is superimposed on the conversation of quite a different kind that the client, Tom, is attempting:

> As the interrogation unfolds, the . . . case manager's interest in collecting certain kinds of data means that she doesn't "hear" Tom's experiences, including his current state of emotional turmoil about his medical condition and his trouble with pain. The following excerpt offers a glimpse of how this happens:
>
> CASE MANAGER: Can I see that bottle? I'd just like to get the correct spelling and the correct dosage off the bottles. . . . When do you take these . . . at night?
>
> TOM: One a night, yup. I just started that one yesterday, I take one a week. . . . And I take Ibuprofen at night time.
>
> CM: Now does this hold the pain for you, Tom?
>
> TOM: Not really, um, I think that—. I just stopped taking that.
>
> CM: You've stopped, OK I won't put that down. You're not taking it anymore.
>
> TOM: I don't know, I thought Advil did more for me than these things, but I don't know. See I was taking it for knee pain in the middle of the night, I'm getting pain in the elbows, and knees and hips. I'm getting pain everywhere where there's a joint there so . . . (voice trails off)
>
> CM: Do you smoke, Tom ? (Campbell 2001, 239)

The case manager's primary concern is to complete the formal assessment on the basis of which Tom's case will become actionable, slotting him into a course of institutional action specified as a "service plan." Her responsibility for the scripted interrogation interferes with her ability to *listen* to what Tom has to tell her about the reasoning that led him to stop using the prescribed medication, undermining the clinic's client-centered commitment.

De Montigny (1995b) writes of the power of being professional. The story he tells to illustrate this is one that reflects on his visit as a social worker to a family home where there is suspicion of child neglect or abuse and how the report he will write will catch that family up into the judicial regime of child protection in the province in which he was working. But even as he is telling his story and speaking of the power he has over that family as a professional, he is displaying layers and levels of power that stretch beyond his formal capacity, his training, his knowledge of what to look for and how to write a report. He is accountable to government; he is subject to the legislation; there is something else going on that doesn't become entirely visible in his story. The frontline work of converting people's experienced worlds into the textual realities of institutions is articulated to regulatory texts—laws, administrative rules, systems of accountability, policies, and so on—that frame and authorize the institutional capacity to act. In back of each of these front-line examples is a textually defined framework that is concretized in the interrogatory devices that in various ways perform the transformations.

Regulatory Frames

The term *frame* is used here as a general term for the wide varieties of conceptualizations, theories, policies, laws, plans, and so on that operate at a general level to structure the institutional action and reality coordinating people's work at local levels.[4] In this chapter, the focus is primarily on the organization of institutional realities in relation to institutional action. In the process of constructing a factual account on institutional terms, some aspects of lived actuality get picked out and worked up as an event, a state-of-affairs representation of a person, or the like. The shaping of facts, news, information, cases, and other forms of knowledge is circular in this sense: frames govern the selection of what will be recorded, observed, described, and so on. In some institutional settings, they are specified as categories used at the front line in the work of interrogation; they are built into the technologically refined sets of questions or ratings, such as those used by community workers in the McLean and Hoskin's account (1988). What is assembled in this way is then interpretable by the frames that structured the selection procedures. It can be fitted back into them in the fashion characteristic of institutional discourse (see chapter 5).[5] Frames, established from positions of power in the institutional regime, control facticity; they control and are specified as the categories and concepts that come into play at the front line of building institutional realities.

In a transcribed recording of a telephone conversation, Marilee Reimer (1988) shows how a reporter's questions to a representative of the union local on strike at a senior citizens' residence follows a protocol that fits the information collected to the paper's preestablished frame. The reporter describes the protocol as follows: After getting information about who is on strike and whether a strike vote had been taken, the next issue is the effects of the strike on the public and industry; after that, the extent of the strike, the status of negotiations, and, finally, the wage demands and offers. This is the order of importance: the items closer to the end of the sequence are those most readily dropped from the story in response to exigencies of space. The one side of the reporter's phone conversation with a union representative that Reimer recorded shows him following this protocal, though there is no final reference to either the status of negotiations or wage demands and offers. Here is her transcription:

REPORTER: Hello.

R: This involves the operating engineers?

R: Any movement by the hospital toward your demand?

R: The hospital has nothing to lose by going to arbitration.

R: Was the hospital full when you started?

R: 24 hour round the clock study sessions?

R: How many patients now? But they're still trying to keep things going with the supervisory staff?

R: What kind of public reaction has there been?

R: Is this the first time there's been a withdrawal of services?

R: No contact with the government?

R: Has the hospital applied for a labour arbitrator?

R: The hospital is sort of a hotbed, no?

R: You don't think the hospital can continue to operate much longer?

R: How are the trustees taking this whole thing?

R: Who is preparing the meals? (Reimer 1988, 43)

As can be seen, the direction of the reporter's questions, in addition to the progress of the strike and negotiations, emphasizes the problems the strike creates for the residents. The issues and problems for workers that led to the strike do not appear as a topic at all; they were not included in the protocol described by the reporter; they have disappeared. In the story that resulted from this phone interview, the lead sentence read, "Another 20 patients will be sent home today as Kelowna General Hospital cuts down its services because of a hospital workers' walkout" (Reimer 1988,

44). Clearly the frame that's guiding the encoding in the quoted sequence of questions is "the effects of the strike on the public." The paper's politics are built into the institutional devices—in this case, the reporter's work knowledge of the *protocol* for producing a story of this kind. *Bias* would have been avoided by consulting both sides of the dispute (Bagdikian 1983).

Exploring the regulatory dimensions that have been designed into the textual genres that structure the transformation of actuality into "information," "data," "news," and so on, takes ethnography further into contemporary forms of the organization we call "power." In McCoy's account (1999) of the accountability circuit in the community college described in the previous chapter, the form that instructors must complete and that represents her or his work in the process of the financial management of the college has little to do with the actualities of the work being done or the variations from instructor to instructor that depend on differences of field, variations in how a given course is taught, individual approaches to teaching, differences in the kind of preparation required or the kind of out-of-class supervision required for different groups of students, and so on and so on. Whereas, formerly, instructors and their departments would have had a good deal of autonomy in filling in the form that made the allocation of instructors' time accountable, the articulation of the old form to the new system of financial accountability subordinated instructors, departments, and department heads to the financial administration of the college and its new orientation to cost and revenue. Thus in exploring the regulatory dimension present but relatively invisible in the frontline textual devices and the frontline work of those who implement them, we begin to explicate institutions as forms of power to be located in the language or discourse that coordinates people's work at different levels of institutional organization.

George W. Smith (1988) initiated an inquiry that opened up the regulatory process and its relation to the production of the report that transmogrified[6] the sexual pleasures of gay men in a bathhouse in Toronto into criminal behavior for which all those present, as well as the owner of the bathhouse, could be charged. The police officers who did the investigation produced a report intending these items of the criminal code. Here is their report:

> Constables Coulis and Proctor attended at the premises, entering separately, where they approached the cash area. It was at this location that

the officers first saw the accused, who was later identified as [John Doe]. [Doe] was the only employee that the officers saw that night. [Doe] was the one who permitted the officers access to the premises once they had paid the fee for either a room or a locker. When the officers first entered the premises they walked around and noted the lay-out of the premises as well as any indecent activity that was taking place at that time. It was at this time that both officers saw a number of men laying nude in their private booths with the door wide open. Some of these men were masturbating themselves while others just lay on the mattress watching as other men were walking about the hallways. The officers took periodic walks about the premises and they saw that the same type of indecent activity was taking place each and every time.

During the course of the first visit the officers made certain purchases from [Doe], who was working in the office area. The office area was equipped with numerous sundry items available to the patrons for a fee: pop, coffee, cigarettes, Vaseline and various inhalants. The officers watched [Doe] on two separate occasions when he left the office area to clean rooms that had just been vacated. On each of these occasions, [Doe] walked past a number of rooms that were occupied by men who were masturbating themselves. At no time did [Doe] make an effort to stop these men, or even suggest that they close the door to their booth so that these activities would no longer be visible to other club patrons. (168–69)

We might imagine their procedure to have been much like that described to Pence by a police officer she interviewed. In describing how he went about writing a report in domestic abuse cases, he told her, "I'm looking for the elements of a crime. . . . Was there infliction of bodily harm or the fear of bodily harm? . . . Was there intent? . . . Did the person knowingly commit the offense?" (2001, 212). The observations reported are designed to fit to the categories of the criteria for domestic abuse in Minnesota just as the observations incorporated into the bathhouse report orient to Ontario's "bawdy house" laws. Smith, who takes the standpoint of the gay men in the establishment, points out that they were there for their own sexual enjoyment. That this is absent from the report is obvious; at the same time, the disjuncture between the experienced actualities of those caught up in such a process and what is recognized in the form of words that represents them institutionally is an important dimension of institutional power. The regulatory frame and procedures preclude admission of the experience, interests, and concerns of those charged with a crime. The specifics of the report are precisely articulated to sections of the criminal law. It reads as follows:

179. (1) In this Part . . . "common bawdy-house" means a place that is
    (a) kept or occupied, or
    (b) resorted to by one or more persons for the purpose of pros-
        titution or the practice of acts of indecency;
193. (1) Everyone who keeps a common bawdy-house is guilty of an in-
        dictable offense and is liable to imprisonment for two years.
    (2) Every one who
        (a) is an inmate of a common bawdy-house,
        (b) is found, without lawful excuse, in a common bawdy-house,
            or
        (c) as owner, landlord, lessor, tenant, occupier, agent or other-
            wise having charge or control of any place, knowingly per-
            mits the place or any part thereof to be let or used for the
            purpose of a common bawdy-house, is guilty of an offence
            punishable on summary conviction. (quoted by G. W. Smith
            1988, 174)

The specifics of the report are designed to make just that transformation of the actual into the institutional that can be fitted to the categories
that will enable charges to be brought against those identified in section
193. Chapter 5 describes institutional discourse's characteristic procedure
of subsuming actualities as integral to the production of the institution.
Here we see the inverse process: rather than find how the institutional
subsumes a preexisting experiential account, we have an account *designed*
to be subsumable by the institutional discourse. To be *subsumable* under
the category of "bawdy house," the report has to establish that the bathhouse could be recognized as an instance of a place "resorted to by one or
more persons for the purpose of . . . the practice of acts of indecency." Gay
sex is not, as such, an indecent act in Canada; masturbation is not, as such,
an indecent act. To render what was going on accountable as an act of indecency, it must be observable and observed by others; it must be public.
So the police report must show not only that men were masturbating but
that they were doing so where others could see them, both those specifically watching and others walking by. Figure 9.1 shows the match between passages in the police report and the categories of the criminal code.

Similar procedures are operating to ensure that not only the person
who owns the bathhouse but also those actually engaged in indecent acts

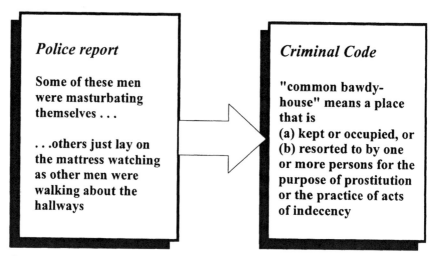

Figure 9.1. Fitting the Observation to the Regulatory Text

can be subsumed under the relevant categories. Anyone "found in" a common bawdy house without lawful excuse is also chargeable. So those neither masturbating nor otherwise involved in directly sexual activity are included in the report, as illustrated in figure 9.2.

There is a work process here. The investigating officers could not just write their report on the basis of having visited the bathhouse. They had

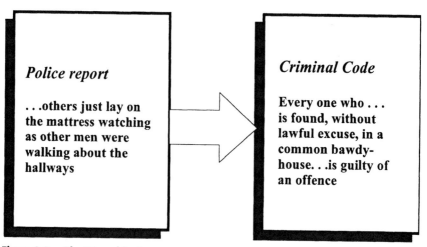

Figure 9.2. The "Found-ins"

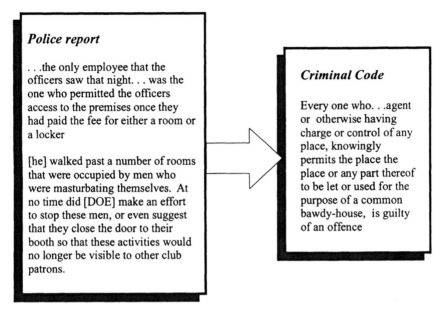

Police report

. . .the only employee that the officers saw that night. . . was the one who permitted the officers access to the premises once they had paid the fee for either a room or a locker

[he] walked past a number of rooms that were occupied by men who were masturbating themselves. At no time did [DOE] make an effort to stop these men, or even suggest that they close the door to their booth so that these activities would no longer be visible to other club patrons.

Criminal Code

Every one who. . .agent or otherwise having charge or control of any place, knowingly permits the place the place or any part thereof to be let or used for the purpose of a common bawdy-house, is guilty of an offence

Figure 9.3.   Who's Responsible

to be able to describe what they themselves had witnessed, when and if the case came to trial. They had to have personally seen men masturbating in plain view. There would be no problem about charging the owner, but to charge his employee, the officers had to hang around to observe the manager of the bathhouse engaged in activities that would necessarily imply that he could see just what they themselves could see, the "acts of indecency" (see figure 9.3).

The police investigation, the work of the police when they scrutinized the premises and the activities of the men enjoying themselves in it, aims at a report of observations that fit the criminal code categories and thus enable the case to be subsumed under the section of the criminal code defining "bawdy houses."

So Smith's investigation finds for us the regulatory text at work in the first stage of transforming the actual into the institutional. The criminal code regulates the local work of producing a representation in a form that enables institutional action. The text of the law is a shell analogous to Schmid's conceptual shells (2000; see chapter 5), the substance of which is to be found elsewhere. Giving the shell substance draws the actual into an institutional capacity to act. The investigating officers' work is to produce descriptions to fill the shells—bawdy house, acts of indecency, "found-ins," and so on—established by the criminal code. Each instance cited earlier—the caller–call taker interchange, Campbell's case manager's conversation with Tom, McLean and Hoskin's community workers filling Needs Assessment Schedules for patients—could be hooked in this way into regulatory texts analogous to those that Smith exhibits as organizer of the police report. In de Montigny's study (1995a), he describes his experience of visiting a home where there was suspicion of child neglect or abuse. He describes how his focus on the state of the home, the parent present, and the child is oriented to making observations that fit the legal framework within which he acts and in terms of which his report must be framed. For example, he finds the child lying on a bed and raises his head to check whether there's a flattening of the skull that would indicate that the child had been confined in a supine position for a long period. We hear from his account of his observations how they are structured to be subsumable under the categories of the law that govern child abuse or neglect in the province in which he was working at the time. Though he does not explore the specifics of the regulatory texts, he provides an illuminating account of the orientation of the frontline worker to the implicit interrogatory character of writing the report.

These accounts are of the moment of transformation into the institutional. If we begin with the experience of those who are caught up into the institutional process through such transformations, Smith's study (1988) invites us to take the next step that engages with the regulatory frames vested in texts and hence with the organization of institutional process at a level beyond the local and particular. Though he does not pursue the origin of the "bawdy house" legislation, it has a history of survival beyond the date implied by the term *bawdy*, which is an anachronism in contemporary North America. Smith's investigation explores how the moment of inscription (Latour and Woolgar 1986) is hooked up into a regulatory organization that has been *designed* to realize objectives that are not those of the people whose lives get caught up in the institutional transformations that subjugate them. The experience of disjuncture expressed by the Native women of Mending the Sacred Hoop (Wilson and Pence forthcoming) locates a political issue at ground level that is organized at levels within the relations of ruling that can only be made visible in a process of inquiry that reaches into them to discover the textual connections invisible but present in the everyday of people's participation in the institutions. Ethnography can reach beyond the moment of disjuncture to the regulatory process organizing it.

Conclusion

Exploring power as it arises in the textual coordinating of institutional work is not meant to deny, by implication, the existence of powers that arise in other forms of the social. It is meant rather to make social relations and organization based in or mediated by texts ethnographically observable. This chapter has given special focus to the processes through which people's everyday experience becomes subjected to institutional action by being fitted to institutional categories. Such categories, however, don't stand alone. They are specifications of and are responsible to regulatory texts that authorize and subsume the local particularities resulting from the work of translation.

Disjunctures between the actualities of people's experience and the actionable institutional realities are imposed by the regulatory frames—law, code, policy, discourses, or other regulatory corpora—governing the structure or organization of textual devices and the categories and questions embedded in them—the forms, scripts, or computerized fields that are used by frontline workers, such as the case manager determining home care eligibility (Campbell 2002), the social worker visiting a family suspected of neglecting a child (de Montigny 1995a, 1995b), the Needs Assessment Schedule operated by community workers (McLean and Hoskin 1988), and others. The forms and other textual genres are designed to select from the actual that which fits the institutional frame. The reporter's questions are not responsive to what the union representative might have to tell and want to make public about the conditions at the senior residence. The case manager in the clinic is clearly not responsive to what Tom is trying to tell her about his situation and feelings. The police officer describing how he focuses on the specifics of the categories defining domestic abuse in Minnesota bypasses altogether the issue of the extent of danger to which a woman may be exposed. The work of fitting the actualities of people's lives to the institutional categories that make them actionable is done at the front line. The categories, questions, or other specified particulars are governed by and responsive to frames established at a more general level.

The previous chapter introduces the possibility of an ethnographic practice reaching beyond the observable into larger social relations. This chapter has taken that a step further. George Smith's research and analysis shows us an apparently simple sequence, starting with making a text, and then the product, the text itself, and eventually the reading of the text, implied by charges having been brought against the bathhouse owner, the man in charge, and the "found-ins." He shows just how items of that report are designed to articulate to the criminal code under which the owner, the manager, and those present in the bathhouse on that particular occasion could be charged. In so doing, he shows us something else, namely, the text as it is oriented to a higher order regulatory frame. The "bawdy house" law "controls" the police report through the work the police do to observe and record so that what they write, the text they make will fit, or is subsumable by, the frames and shells of the law. The discovering work of institutional ethnography engages with social relations applying standardized forms of regulation to multiple local sites of people's work. As an institutional ethnography works from the specific local settings from which it takes its direction, it discloses beyond them not just specific institutional forms but also the ruling relations in which institutions are embedded. This ethnographic move from the moment of transition from people's experienced actualities into a formalized and text-based representation that frames and authorizes it offers a model for exploring other regions of power via the texts that organize them.

I do not mean to reduce institutional processes to texts. Nor do I intend to suggest that the various instances described in this chapter exhaust the ways in which texts mediate institutional regimes. The aim rather is to make visible the ethnographic significance of texts as coordinators of people's work and, hence, in the ethnographic exploration of relations and organization beyond the local settings of people's work. This general capability of texts is foundational to the very existence of the ruling relations, including institutions, large-scale organization of all kinds, discourse, and so on. Once texts are recognized as key coordinators of the ruling relations, possibilities are opened up of ethnographically exploring economic relations, higher levels of the organization of the ruling relations, and the interconnections between them. As institutional ethnography develops, its practitioners discover how to recognize and integrate textual materials into their ethnography. Thus the interplay of work and other forms of action and texts brings the organization of power in contemporary society within ethnographic reach, at least in principle (of course, the ethnographer may well be denied access to key regions of power). Recognizing texts as they enter into action and as coordinators of institutionally organized processes creates the possibility of investigating the macrosocial ethnographically.

Notes

1. De Montigny's ethnography predates the computerization of these forms of accountability.

2. Richard Darville (1995) calls this process "textualization."

3. Buckholdt and Gubrium (1983) describe similar procedures, though they focus less on the role of texts and do not explicate the social relations into which the systems of categories are hooked and by which they are regulated.

4. I have used the term *schema* as an alternative, but the plural *schemata* is awkward, and since I intend the term *frame* to direct attention to a general and not specifically defined set of phenomena, I have preferred its metaphorical character, much as Schmid (2000) has chosen the term *shell* to describe terms that need a filling to complete their sense. Frames have shape but are empty; what fills them must conform to their shape. That's my metaphorical sideways step.

Note that this usage should not be confused with Erving Goffman's use (1974) of the term in his frame analysis approach. He writes, "I assume that definitions of a situation are built up in accordance with principles of organization which govern events—at least social ones—and our subjective involvement in them; frame is the word I use to refer to such of these basic elements as I am able to identify. That is my definition of frame. My phrase 'frame analysis' is a slogan to refer to the examination in these terms of the organization of experience" (10–11).

I go with Goffman, however, in his notion of specifying the concept in the course of inquiry into, in his case, the organization of experience and, in mine, institutional forms of the social.

5. See also, my account of ideological circles (D. E. Smith 1990a).

6. It's rare to have a chance to use this word. It means to change something into a grotesque form.

PART 4

Conclusion

CHAPTER 10

Where We've Got To and Where We Can Go

In this concluding chapter I want to do three things: the first is just to summarize where we have got to in providing a basis for institutional ethnography to work from; the second is to project possibilities into the future that build on this basis—I have given many examples as we went along. I'm not disavowing these. Each institutional ethnographic study contributes to our knowledge of the ruling relations. I want here, however, to give an idea of possibilities of ethnographic research reaching beyond what has been done so far. Finally, I want to address briefly the uses of institutional ethnography.

Where We've Got To

In taking up those intellectual discoveries of the women's movement identified with the concept of women's standpoint, I describe my own experience of two forms of subjectivity: one in the local particularities of my everyday world as mother and housewife, the other in the academic world based in texts and transcending the locally embedded body. Resolving to do away with this disjuncture, I begin to seek a sociology that would start from just these local actualities of my and others' lives and would explore from there to explicate the social relations organizing everyday worlds across multiple local sites.

What I call the ruling relations (chapter 1) come into view from a standpoint in the everyday world as a distinctive organization of translocal relations that are based on or mediated by texts. The replicable text makes it possible for the same words and images to be present to people in different places and at different times and hence to introduce into people's doings the same organizing—though not determining—component. What I am calling institutions are those complexes of relations and hierarchical organization that organize distinct functions—hospitals or, more generally, health care; universities; welfare; corporations; and so on and so on. They are distinctive in that they appear in many local settings as specialized forms of action while at the same time they participate in relations that standardize their operations and generalize them across particular local instances. They are, however, embedded in and rely on the ruling relations. No institutions, no large-scale organizations stand outside laws, government, financial organizations, professional and academic discourses, the discourses of the natural sciences, managerial discourses, and on and on.

Institutional ethnography itself must necessarily participate in the ruling relations; insofar as ethnographers are at work in universities or other research bases and are teaching and publishing the results of research, or otherwise making it available to people, institutional ethnographers cannot avoid being part, directly or indirectly, of what we are investigating. It proposes, however, to reconstruct the social organization of knowledge of the social from a form that objectifies, creating representations of the social as if we could see it from outside. The concept of standpoint becomes in this context a methodological device. It opens up research from a position in people's everyday lives, from within people's actual experience, aiming to explore what lies beyond the scope of an ordinary knowledge of the everyday into the social relations that extend beyond us and catch us up in organization and determinations that we cannot see from where we are. The aim is to create something like maps of how things work beyond the scope of our everyday knowledge.

The Problematic

In chapter 2, I introduce the notion of a problematic as a way of realizing the concept of a standpoint in the everyday world as a project of inquiry. Institutional ethnography doesn't begin, as much mainstream sociology does, by formulating a problem theoretically. This is often done quite formally. From the theory, hypotheses may be derived that research will test or at least subject to empirical scrutiny. Sometimes this procedure is highly formalized, and sometimes it is more a matter of ensuring the theoretical relevance of a given study. In any case, institutional ethnography doesn't go that route. It doesn't begin in theory but in the actualities of people's lives with a focus of investigation that comes from how they participate in or are hooked up into institutional relations. This is what is called the problematic of a given study.[1] It translates the more general notion of the everyday world as problematic (Smith 1987) into an orientation specific to a given study.

The problematic of a study isn't developed theoretically. It may be developed from what the researcher already knows about the everyday experiences of an institutional process. Sometimes preliminary interviews are done, or the researcher relies on her or his experience, as did Alison and I (Griffith and D. E. Smith 2004) in our study of mothering and schooling, or as Gerald de Montigny did in his study (1995a) of social "work(ing)" in which the ethnography is entirely based on his own experience as a participant who was also an ethnographer, or as George W. Smith (1995) did in his ethnographic uses of his experience as an AIDS activist. Ellen Pence (2001) had years of experience in advocacy work with battered women whose spouses were going through the judicial process under the domestic abuse laws of Minnesota. She knows well their experience that this process and its outcomes have little to do with giving them safety from their abusers. Her investigation takes their standpoint, exploring the police and judicial process in terms of the issue of the safety of women who are abused. Sometimes the ethnographer proceeds, as Alison and I did (2004), by talking to a number of people who are participating in pretty much the same relation to the institutional process that is problematized. This is not a sample of a population. The ethnographer isn't studying the people she or he talks to.[2] She or he is establishing a standpoint as the starting point of investigation of the institutional process. She or he may not interview very many at all. It depends on the range of different experiences needed to avoid an overly narrow focus. Interviews are conducted with those whose everyday experiences establish the standpoint and orientation that structure the direction of investigation.

Though a study's problematic may originate in the researcher's political concerns, those concerns must be translated into an investigatory focus that is not simply critical. It must be taken up only as the actualities of people's everyday lives as they are experienced. In a sense, the political concerns must be transcended or set aside in formulating the research problematic. Institutional ethnography is essentially a work of inquiry and discovery; it must move beyond what the ethnographer already knows or thinks she or he knows, and the ethnographer must be prepared

for and open to finding out that matters are not as she or he may have envisaged them. Institutional ethnographic findings will be relevant to critique, making institutional ethnography more specific, locating sites of
potential change that are within reach of those participating in the institutional process, suggesting major reformulations, or simply informing
the activist of the workings of institutional processes beyond the reach of
his or her experience and power to change. Its uses in such contexts depend on the reliability, accuracy, and analytic power of the ethnography.

The Ontology of the Social

The ontology of the social written in chapters 3 and 4 provides a theory
defining the object of institutional ethnographic study. The actualities in
which it starts and to which it is oriented at every stage of research are not
already shaped up into precursors of ethnographic representation. I remember well, having gone from the safety of the halls and offices of the
University of California sociology department, where I did my graduate
work, to the wards of Stockton State Hospital in California's Central Val-
ley to do fieldwork; how bewildering I found it. I'd been given no more
instructions than simply to observe. Once started on the work of simply
observing, I was bewildered. The instructions to observe were disorient-
ing. What should I be observing? Actuality was not, after all, shaped up
for observation. Though I did notice on one occasion—that of attending a
court where a judge made decisions about whether patients held on a
temporary basis should be committed—that there were some occasions
that were shaped precisely to be observed. Not so, however, for the day
room where patients spent much of the time doing, in the words of Diamond (1992), the work of waiting. Institutional ethnography would have
told me to not only attend to what people were doing, in the nursing station as well as in the day room, but also to look for how their activities
were coordinated and, I am now thinking of it as an institutional ethnography, for forms of coordinating that hook into the institutional order in
which, so to speak, we were all sitting and waiting. I would have found
them. Looking back I can even see them—for example, a little episode
when everyone had gone to lunch except staff and ethnographer and one
other woman who was merely sitting. A staff member approached her po-
litely to remind her that it was time to go to lunch; she did not move nor
appear to respond; the staff member then tried to take her elbow to guide
her toward the door leading to the cafeteria; she did not move; finally a

second staff member came from the nursing station, and, taking the other elbow, they lifted and pushed and got her going. I wondered at the time why she might not be allowed simply to sit in peace, but I learned subsequently that it was indeed the hospital's custodial responsibility to ensure that patients were fed. The staff members exerting physical pressure—not such as could be called violence—were doing their job, the hospital's job.

The actualities of the everyday world don't tell you what to observe and record. In addition to its problematic, it needs theoretical specification to guide the direction of the ethnographer's gaze. I've called that theoretical specification an *ontology* because I want to emphasize that what we are aiming to discover really happens or is happening. It is this that justifies a project of inquiry and the possibility of discovery. The ontology explicated in chapters 3 and 4 starts from Marx and Engels's ontology of a social science that sets asides concepts, speculation, and imagination in favor of engaging with actual people's actual activities. To that I have added another and, in my view, essential dimension, namely, the ongoing coordinating of those activities. That is how the ontology specifies the peculiar investigatory domain of sociology.

The social as the focus of sociological investigation is, in this view, people's activities as and however they are coordinated. The social in this sense does not form a discrete phenomenon or theoretical entity that can be treated as external to people and even causally implicated in their doings. It is not to be equated with social system, social structure, society, or any other of sociology's many reifications of the social. Coordinating people's activities actually happens; how it is in a particular setting can be explored and explicated, but it cannot be separated from those activities and treated as if it were a discrete phenomenon. I have emphasized also that when we look at people's doings and how they are coordinated, at whatever level of organization, we find how coordinating always presupposes that people's experiences and perspectives are different. In any given work process, people are doing different things; they are positioned differently; those differences are based on and generate differences of experience, perspective, interest, and so on.

It is here that the fourth dimension of the ontology comes in. Thought, concepts, beliefs, ideology, et cetera, et cetera, are not allowed to escape into a metaphysical space set up for them in people's heads and outside their doings. They are also people's doings, their activities. For the institutional ethnographer, these become phenomena for observation as they are observable and, hence, in talking or writing. For this reason, language becomes an essential final piece of the ontology built in chapters 3 and 4. Language, following Vološinov (1973), Mead (1962), Bahktin (1981), and Luria (1961, 1976; Luria and Yudovich 1971), is treated as both essentially social and as the coordinator of subjectivities. In exploring the word–object relation in the formation of what Vološinov (1973) calls *interindividual territories*, we could also begin to see how words for objects carry social organization. Further, as Mead insists, words organize a community of responses among speaker and hearer that both picks up on what has been going on and projects control into what comes next in a social act. Vološinov's concept (1973) of interindividual territories also became useful in differentiating experiential from text-based forms, the former grounded in people's experience and the latter in textual resources (chapter 4).

Data and Analysis

Opening up the region of institutions to ethnographic research picks up first on the centrality of language by introducing institutional discourse and by identifying some of what are held to be distinctive ways in which institutional texts are read and come into play. Reading is explicated as an active process using the idea of a text–reader conversation, foreshadowing the later specifications of chapters 8 and 9 that investigate further the incorporation of texts into ethnography. The major data resource for institutional ethnographers is people's experience of their work; such experience may be accessed through participant observation, in interviews with informants, or, of course, both. The institutional ethnographer relies on people's own ordinary good knowledge of their doings to produce in collaboration with them what I call "work knowledge"—that is, descriptions and explications of what people know by virtue of what they do that ordinarily remains unspoken.

I should emphasize here that when institutional ethnographers use the concept of "work," we aren't just talking about what people do on the job. Like the discovery of housework or mothering as work, institutional ethnographers use a generous conception of work that applies to anything people do that takes time, depends on definite conditions, is done in particular actual places, and is intentional. We do the work in supermarkets and banks that was once done by paid employees (Glazer 1993). When I'm going from Vancouver to the University of Victoria to teach institutional ethnography, I don't think of my online check with the bus company for the time when the number 9 bus will stop at Larch as work, but I would if I were doing institutional ethnography. Though it may seem trivial, it was an important moment in the study Alison and I (Griffith and D. E. Smith 2004) did of mothering and schooling when we recognized getting the children off to school in the morning as work.

The ethnographer proceeds by learning from people about their work in various positions in the institutional process on which the formulation of the problematic has focused. What she or he learns isn't treated as a collection of individual accounts; it is assembled into sequences or other socially organized forms. Apart from taking measures to ensure that the ethnography is based on more than one individual account and that it represents some kind of a range of potential differences (this doesn't mean a large sample), observing the work or using informants in different positions and assembling them as sequences gives the ethnographer means of checking out what she or he has learned from others as she or he discovers how the person positioned next in a sequence picks up and builds on what has been done at the previous stage. It is in these connections, the modes of coordinating sequences or circuits of institutional action, that we return to texts as major coordinators. Ellen Pence has described the textually mediated sequence from the moment of contact at the 911 call between a woman who has been abused and the judicial institutions. She tracks the work organization and, most strikingly, the significance of texts, such as the police officers' report of their original visit, in how the different stages or steps of the processing of a case are coordinated. A different kind of sequence is shown by Liza McCoy (1999), who examines the reorganization of relations among financial administrators, deans, department heads, and instructors with the introduction of new cost-recovery procedures of accounting into community colleges in Ontario. A circuit has been put into place such that department heads and instructors are responsible (and accountable) for producing the information that allows the financial administrators to exercise control over them. These two instances are just that; they are intended not to be exclusive but to illustrate the relatively straightforward analysis of how institutional processes are coordinated as people's work mediated by texts.

Texts

The focus is always on the social, understood as the coordinating of people's actual activities, their work in the generous sense. In institutional settings, texts are integral and ubiquitous in how people's work is concerted. There is a problem, however, in integrating them into ethnography. It comes from what I'm calling the inertia of the text. We don't experience texts as being in motion; their materiality as texts gives them a kind of stasis that is difficult to overcome. While we see people's talk as part of the organizing of a sequence of action, it's harder for us to see texts that way. Hence a first move is enabling us to see texts as being in motion, first as they occur in text–reader conversations (chapter 5) and then as they play a part in organizing courses of action (chapter 8). Incorporating texts into an ethnography makes it possible to expand exploration of institutional relations into higher levels of organization.

Intertextuality in this context has a hierarchical structure where hierarchy is not conceived as an ordering of positions but of texts at one level that establish the frames and concepts that control texts at lower levels and, inversely, of texts at lower levels that are fitted to the frames and concepts of higher order texts. The order of "authority" is conceptual. The texts that transpose actualities into the forms of representation that make them institutionally actionable select and elaborate from the actual to fit the frames and concepts of the higher level authorized text. There are regulatory texts that set up the frames that are particularly important in the organization of the frontline work that transposes actualities into the institutional texts that become the realities enabling institutional action. For example, George W. Smith's study (1988) shows how police observations and the resulting report of gay men engaged in sex in a bathhouse was framed to fit the categories of the law. The police report that became central in coordinating the further work involved in the judicial process was organized both by the observational procedures that produced it and by the items selected for and worked up as description to fit into the "bawdy house" law.

Expansion

Because institutional ethnographers are exploring the ruling relations—though from different angles and with different focal concerns—our studies begin to add up in a way that was originally surprising to me. Recognizing texts and the frames and concepts they carry as coordinators, indeed as key to the coordination of what we are calling institutions, makes it possible to recognize, even in research that is focused on a different institutional region, aspects of social organization and social relations that are also to be found in the sites of our own explorations or are relevant to us in terms of where we might look. Incorporating texts into sequences of action establishes a double reach: the first as coordinator of work done by people positioned differently in a social relation (conceived as a sequence of action); the second as the textual coordinating of a particular person's or group of people's work in a particular local setting with the regulatory intertextuality of the institutional hierarchy that standardizes across multiple settings and through time.

In this section I would like to look further into the possibilities of projecting exploration of text-mediated relations beyond those hitherto described. The interrelations and interconnections among different foci on the ruling relations are not accidental. We are exploring a complex of interrelations that cannot readily be bound within one corporate entity, agency, or even one institutional complex. Once we begin to see how to locate and analyze texts ethnographically as integral to institutional organization, it becomes possible to trace connections that might otherwise be inaccessible. This section suggests two expansions of institutional ethnography into the extended social relations of economy and ruling relations and their intersections. The two examples draw on research that is not institutional ethnography and that is, indeed, only partially ethnographic. I aim to show how developing problematics from particular everyday world settings can be opened up to show the social relations in which the problematics are embedded; it is an aim that reaches into the macrosocial level of organization. The first of these examples is ethnographic; it is a study by Steven Vallas and John Beck (1996) of the changing work relationships and organization of four U.S. pulp mills owned by one company. The second example begins with an account of a welfare applicant who dropped out of a California program realizing the new welfare principles of the U.S. Personal Responsibility and Work Opportunity Reconciliation Act of 1996 (Lioncelli 2002).

Since in the second case I've had other research to draw on, I have been able to follow it further than in the case of the pulp mills. But the procedure proposed is the same. It goes from a problematic in the everyday of people's lives to proposing lines of investigation that would explicate the social relations that organize its actuality.

The Pulp Mills

Vallas and Beck (1996) interviewed workers and managers at pulp mills into which management had recently introduced new technologies combining automated continuous processing with computerized regulation.

Before the introduction of new technologies, workers were directly involved in production and in overseeing mechanically automated processes. Slight variations at one stage could have significant consequences down the line. Workers learned on the job over time, gaining carefully guarded skills. In introducing new automated controls and "total quality management" strategies, the corporation sought to achieve "greater stability in the operations and appreciable reductions in crew sizes" (Vallas and Beck 1996, 346). Operators now oversee and regulate processes at a distance through computerized controls. Process engineers are increasingly in command at the shopfloor level, and the experience-based knowledge of older operators is further displaced by devising new computer "loops" minimizing dependence on the operators' experiential knowledge.

An institutional ethnography of such a setting would introduce two distinctive phases of the organization of investigation. The first would be the adoption of a standpoint in the everyday lives of some people active in the organization. The Vallas and Beck study is clearly focused on the experience of workers in the plants. There is, however, a major limitation that adopting workers' standpoint would displace. Deciding to study four pulp mills owned by a single company means adopting the institutional order of the company as the framework of study. Beginning with the workers' standpoint means beginning in a particular local site of their work. The pulp mills are in different parts of the United States and in regions differing economically. For example, a pulp mill in the Pacific Northwest is in a region in which working-class communities have already been depleted by declining lumber and fishing industries. The everyday of pulp mill workers in that region will have seen significant reductions of the workforce in their plant contributing further to undermining employment opportunities. A pulp mill in, say, Louisiana would be located in a region where preexisting poverty and unemployment would enable a corporation to take advantage of lower wage levels. Working from within the boundaries of the corporation as Vallas and Beck do is analogous to institutional capture. The perspectives and experience of workers in different localities disappears; more than that, for the institutional ethnographer, they are displaced as perspectives and experience of the changes introduced by the corporation on which ethnography could build.

While much of Vallas and Beck's ethnography would be relevant, a major aspect of the second phase of an institutional ethnography would take up a textual trail. The introduction of the new continuous process technology and the consequent reduction in "crew size" and displacement of workers' skills and experience are hooked into other technologies, those of the managerial and financial accounting that represent shopfloor processes at the level of international financial markets. McCoy (1999) locates the changes in accounting practices and in the organization of relations among financial managers, administrators, and instructors to the federal government's changed policies attempting to create competition between community colleges and private sources in responding to the training needs of corporations. In the case of the pulp mills, an analogous though more complex chain of accounting texts and practices tie the workings of the corporation into the stock market. The public representations of the financial workings of a corporation are regulated by various bodies, notably in the United States, the Securities and Exchange Commission. Regulatory texts operate very much as we saw the "bawdy house" law operating to specify how actualities are to be translated into the commensurable forms of accounting texts. Investigation would not take for granted the representational procedures governed by the authorities that preside over accounting practices in the United States. United States accounting practices give labor costs greater weight in measuring profitability than that given in some other jurisdictions, hence encouraging managers of United States business corporations to give primacy to the reduction of labor costs in improving the visible profitability of their company and hence its standing in capital markets. What goes on at the shopfloor level, what goes on in the everyday lives of workers considered, as Marco comes to consider his own life as existing outside as well as on the shopfloor, is organized by and penetrated by the dynamic of markets, markets both for products and for money, over which workers have no control and to which they are connected through the textual hierarchy that translates their work at the shopfloor level and their wages into representations of the financial status of the company. An institutional ethnography, adopting a standpoint in the everyday lives of workers, could expand exploration into the text-based organization of financial accounting, including the bodies that regulate it both nationally and internationally.

The Welfare Trail

My second example introduces some rather different connections. Rather than track direct textual connections (at least in principle; in practice, of course, the researcher may not be able to gain access to the ethnographic detail she or he needs to trace the circuit as McCoy did), the linkages here are to a hierarchy of discourses supplying the organizing frames and categories specified and embodied in institutional texts that interpret and render accountable people's activities.

The restructuring of welfare institutions in the United States, beginning in the 1980s and progressing rapidly in the 1990s with a Republican majority in Congress, imposed radical changes. Personal rather than public responsibility for economic well-being was concretized as programs that set up schedules to be followed by welfare applicants that put preparation and the search for employment first, without reference to the realities of local economies or such personal constraints as the care for small children. Stephanie Lioncelli (2002) wrote an ethnography of a program funded by the U.S. Personal Responsibility and Work Opportunity Reconciliation Act of 1996. The program blended a feminist ideology of work as central to women's independence with the stringent principles and scheduling imposed by the act. It worked for some, but for women with small children, the stress on finding and keeping employment was not always practicable in the realities of their local economy. Here is one who dropped out:

> I had a job where I commuted four hours on the bus (she holds up four fingers for emphasis). . . . I took my kids on the bus to my mom's and then went to work. I was giving my paycheck to my mom for watching my kids so I quit. (86)

From a standpoint such as this, the local practices of the agency could be hooked up to the categories and frames of an institutional discourse that is tied into the disbursement of federal funding. The extent to which welfare workers can respond in a way that is responsive to the individual realities of people's actual circumstances, particularly those living in economically disadvantaged areas, is sharply limited by the textual technologies rendering their work accountable to supervision within the general framework of federal legislation (Ridzi 2003).[3]

The design of the principles of the new welfare regime can be traced back to the U.S. congressional hearings of 1987–1988. Nancy Naples (1997) examines the textual residues of the hearings to show how the *master frames* (her term) of the new welfare discourse regulated the process of the hearings and their product. No doubt, research of the kind that Turner applied to the process of municipal land development planning could explore the text–work–text sequences that produced the master frame and categories established in the hearings (little doubt that they were prepared well in advance of the hearing themselves).

There is, however, a further step to be taken. The institutional discourse of the new welfare regime is a specification for that institutional complex of a more general ideological discourse. The term *ideology*, as John B. Thompson (1990) shows, has been variously theorized. The coherence Thompson achieves overlays a conceptual jungle that I want to avoid. I am using the term *ideology* here to identify a metadiscourse that regulates others that are specialized for specific contexts such as institutions.[4] The ideological discourse that has come to govern public discussion on the economy since the early 1980s in North America is the discourse known as neoliberalism. Neoliberalism, as an ideological discourse, is based on economic theories that stress the paramount significance of a free market for general prosperity; government is viewed as costly and inefficient; concepts of citizenship stress individual responsibility for economic well-being and so on (Brodie 1996; Martinez and Garcia 1997; Naples 1997). More specialized and subordinate discourses have been developed that mediate ideological discourse at the general level and the specifics of institutional discourses. Canadian institutional ethnographers have noted the *new public managerialism* as a discourse mediating neoliberalism and institutional discourses in a variety of institutional settings, such as health care (Rankin 2003), education (McCoy 1999), and child protection (Parada 2002).[5]

Other connections can be made: traditional Marxist accounts locate ideology as an expression of the interests of a ruling capitalist class. How such interests are linked to the concrete processes of transforming the dominant ideological discourses in society are not specified. It is, however, possible to research these relations rather than assigning them to theory. Ellen Messer-Davidow (1993, 2002) describes an institutional complex created by a powerful section of the capitalist class, together with leaders of the right wing, designed to achieve right-wing control over public discourse in the United States. These organizations include think tanks—that is, institutes for training journalists to replace what were seen as the predominantly liberal professional journalists of the day, supporting financially right-wing initiatives in universities, and preparing young people for developing and administering right-wing policies in the public service.

> They pitched plans to donors, spun issues in the media, mobilized supporters, delivered proposals to public officials, and clinched the sales by mustering squads of paid lobbyists backed by citizen letter-writing campaigns. Although some organizations had multi-issue agendas and others had carved out niches, such as family policy or business deregulation, they were able to mount cross-sector operations because they drew their associates from overlapping conservative networks in government, business, the professions, education, and the media. (2002, 221)

Messer-Davidow's research uncovered the massive funding of US$80 million to eighteen conservative think tanks between 1992 and 1994 (2002, 223). Lewis Lapham (2004) picks up the story for 2001, describing the route of funding from the conservative foundations, nine leading members of which have US$2 billion in assets (32), to twelve national think tanks disposing of over $100 million (35). Add to these the $300 million spent on what Lapham calls the "conservative message machine," which includes the various conversation television channels, such as Fox News Channel (37). Research could, of course, go further in tracing the intermediary stages by which major investments in foundations translate into transformations of public discourse in the media,[6] into generalized discourses of new management, and into the specified discourses and textual practices described by ethnographers such as McCoy (1999) or Rankin (2003), including the new textual technologies of accountability that characterize contemporary welfare organization sketched earlier.

These two examples illustrate some of the possibilities of institutional ethnographies beyond what has already been described. They are possibilities opened up by institutional ethnographies such as those I have drawn on in writing this book. As discoveries are made, it is possible to see how institutional ethnography can be expanded into regions that it has not yet addressed and into levels of social relations beyond those as yet encompassed. Translated into ethnographic practices, research practices would not be essentially different from those that have been already described in various ways. They would lead to further discoveries.

In both these sketches, the significance of the textual can be seen as clearly central to investigations of social relations that connect the local into the extended social relations of ruling. Research that adopted the pulp mill model would engage with the circuits of accountability that

McCoy's work introduces us to. It would go beyond hers to engage with the textually mediated organization of international financial markets, but it would not be essentially different in its ontological grounding. Tracking the frames, concepts, and categories organizing the experience of the welfare applicant quoted here suggests more than one alternative. Such an investigation would yield to the type of research modeled by George Smith's study of a hierarchy of intertextuality wherein the regulatory frame of the law structures the representation of actualities through which they become institutionally actionable. And these, of course, are not the only models, as you have seen.

The Collective Work of Institutional Ethnography

Institutional ethnography does not, however, depend on large-scale projects such as those conceived here. The ordinary economies of funding generally restrict individual projects to a modest scope. Yet as institutional ethnography describes and analyzes the workings of one aspect, it extends its capacity to see and go further. As it evolves, studies that appear to be dispersed and fragmented can be seen as focused on a common object. No institutional ethnography is a case study; each is an investigation of the ruling relations explored from a given angle, under a given aspect, and as it is brought into being in people's everyday work lives. Generalization from a particular study is not a matter of populations or even just the forms of standardization and generalization that institutions themselves produce and reproduce; it is, more important, an effect of the phenomenon of the ruling relations themselves—that they are interconnected in multiple ways as well as deeply informed by the dynamic of capital accumulation (Smith 1999b).

That forms of coordinating characterizing the ruling relations rely on texts creates, I suggest, a distinctive vulnerability. At an earlier period the ruling relations generated bases in the public service (radically expanded in the United States during the period of the New Deal), universities (Veblen 1957), education, and the mass media for an intelligentsia independent, at least to some degree, of capital; recent developments of almost every arena are integrating these bases into capitalist organization and social relations. Designing and disseminating ideological discourse, creating special subordinate discourses, and, finally, specializing and sometimes technically developing institutional discourses are appearing as highly effective and largely invisible regulatory transformations, as the example of redesigning welfare institutions to fit the neoliberal frame has shown. Herbert Schiller (1996) makes a severe statement of the problem that this assemblage of various ethnographic pieces has suggested:

> Today, a remarkable edifice of invisible control has been constructed, permitting the most far-reaching measures of social domination to escape significant public attention. (1)

Schiller's focus is primarily on the mass media, but what he is describing applies also to developments within other regions of the ruling relations, as some institutional ethnographies are showing (McCoy 1999; Mykhalovskiy 2001; Parada 2002; Rankin 2003).[7]

Postmodernism has brought about a deep distrust of the Enlightenment faith that knowledge instantly disposes of illusion, falsehood, and ignorance. I have learned from that critique of the massive arrogance of knowledge claims to master the totality of knowing, but I am confident that methods of patient inquiry into the social can make discoveries, can create knowledge, and can make the invisible visible. Institutional ethnography, as a sociology for people, aims to make visible the forms of ruling that are largely not observable from where we are.

Institutional ethnography relies essentially on accumulating the work knowledges of individuals and assembling them to display how they are coordinated, particularly in the medium of texts. Institutional ethnographers have found that other institutional ethnographies, including those focused on other institutions, are relevant and useful to us. Sometimes this is a matter of their technical research innovations, but more important, it seems that they contribute different perspectives into that more general complex of the ruling relations with which individual inquiry engages. We begin to learn how to see and how to make visible the translocal relations of ruling. This job becomes all the more important in the historical context that Schiller locates. Institutional ethnography discovers other dimensions of the "far-reaching measures of social domination" that are remaking the institutional forms in which we participate. A knowledge of just how these forms of domination are being put together can make resistance and progressive change more within our reach.

The problem remains of how to make what institutional ethnographers learn through research more accessible. Academic publishing has its limitations, though we should not underestimate it: not only does it reach other sociologists, but it percolates into the teaching of students, including those in professional schools. Institutional ethnography has been used to locate sites of institutional change within the reach of local practitioners. Ellen Pence has been a leader in this respect. Her careful ethnography (2001) of the judicial work organization that produces cases of domestic abuse out of people's everyday lives has been used to locate a number of places where it has been possible to make changes that contribute to increasing the safety of women who are subject to violence from their spouses. There are facets of how the judicial processes are coordinated that could be and have been changed. For example, the police report on a domestic abuse case, as Pence shows, plays a central role in producing the institutional reality on which the case goes forward (see chapters 8 and 9). The Duluth, Minnesota, police were persuaded to redesign the protocol for writing reports so that the reporting of what might indicate the degree of violence to which a woman was exposed would be included. Their practice has become a model for other police forces concerned to do better in safeguarding women in such situations. Institutional ethnographic forms of inquiry and analysis can also become a skill outside the research setting. Pence has developed methods of organizing the participation of those—police, attorneys, probation officers, child protection workers, and so on—involved in domestic abuse and child protection cases in coming together to examine how their local practices are put together so that they produce outcomes, or "side effects," other than those desired. Criticism is shifted away from focus on the competence or incompetence of individuals to the work process and its intertextuality. Likewise Turner used her work–text–work cartographies to involve people in analyzing their own workplaces. She is specifically interested in extending institutional ethnography as a skill that activists can use not as a research tool but as a way of making visible the invisible that permeates their everyday work lives.

These are modest possibilities and proposals. The emphasis always is on inquiry and discovery and on working from what people are experiencing to bring the beyond-their-experience into the scope of ordinary knowledge. What for the institutional ethnographer may be a technical and sometimes difficult enterprise can, once completed, be translated into the language of the everyday world so that institutional participants can integrate it into their everyday work knowledge. Keep in mind that the participants include people who are not paid as well as those who are paid—the women being investigated and disciplined by child protection agencies, the client in the clinic trying to get a word in edgewise, the woman who gives up her job because costs of child care absorb her wages. Institutional ethnography's explorations of social relations beyond the

local contribute now, and will in the future contribute more, to figuring
out for us how things actually work.

Notes

1. See Campbell and Gregor (2002).

2. See McCoy's chapter in the accompanying volume, *Institutional Ethnography as Practice* (forthcoming).

3. Henry Parada (2002) has a comparable account of how the procedures
used by child protection workers in assessing the risk in cases of suspected child
abuse are also the means through which their practices are made accountable to
supervisors and administrators.

4. This is analogous to how Lillie Chouliaraki and Norman Fairclough (1999)
write ideology as drawing on, appropriating, and "colonizing" other discourses
(27), except that I am inverting the relationship. Rather than appropriate and colonize subordinate discourses, I suggest that the institutional discourses subordinate to and regulated by ideological discourses are specifications that apply the
general frames of ideological discourse to more specialized areas.

5. Stefano Harney (2002)—not an institutional ethnographer—has a fascinating account of the change from public administration to public management in his
study of "state work."

6. David Brock (2002) his written a fascinating autobiographical account of
his experiences mediating neoconservative thinking and public discourse.

7. George Smith and I, in the 1980s doing research on the training issues in
the plastics industry, noted a shift from concepts of education and training that
emphasize human capital to concepts of human resources. The former joins public and individual interests of the individual in education or training that will produce a line of income. The latter, however, orients to how training and education
serve the labor force needs of capital. When acting as consultant on a project proposing to research the work implications for teachers of new curriculum and assessment procedures that gave the Ontario Ministry of Education greater control
over how teachers teach and what they must teach, I learned that these changes
were coupled with others that minimized the role of teachers in determining educational policy at all levels. Changes that standardized the curriculum and curriculum outcomes were coupled with a reduction of school board functions,
increases in size of school boards (attenuating the role teachers can play in board
policy), a change of school administrator positions (principal and vice principal)
out of teachers' associations into managerial positions, and the introduction of a
college of teachers imposing standards on teachers independently of teachers' associations. In general, the change is from the exercise of teachers' professional
judgment whether collectively or as individuals to the management of teachers
ensuring their responsiveness to government objectives.

When a definition uses a term defined elsewhere in the glossary, the term's first appearance is in CAPITAL LETTERS.

actual, actuality/ies   I don't give the terms *actual* or *actuality* content because I want them to be always directing us to the outside-the-text in which we are living and in which the TEXT, this book, is being read. *Actual* and *actuality* point outside the text to the world to be explored by the ethnographer, which is the same world in which she or he is doing the work of exploration. Actualities are always more than can be described, named, or categorized.

agent, agency   *Agency* is a term used in sociology to reassure people that, in explaining their behavior, the sociologist does not view them as puppets of a social system. Since INSTITUTIONAL ETHNOGRAPHY does not explain people's behavior but works from where people are and learns from them to discover the translocal relations in which they participate (knowingly or not), it does not have to tell them that they have agency. Hence, in institutional ethnography, the term *agent* is used analogously with how the term *subject* has come to be used in poststructuralist thinking, where it is treated as a property of DISCOURSE. Discourse creates positions for subjects; it also creates positions and performances for agents, those who are identified as the protagonists of institutionally specified acts. Hence, *agent* and *agency* identify discursive functions.

coordinate, coordination   Rather than treat the SOCIAL as existing over and above individuals and determining their behavior, INSTITUTIONAL ETHNOGAPHY takes the social as a focus on how ACTUAL people are coordinating their activities. The focus on coordinating is extended to language so that it is understood as coordinating individual subjectivities, providing us with a way to avoid using concepts that hide the active of thought, concepts, ideas, and so on in people's heads.

data dialogues   The dialogue between interviewer and informant that evokes the informant's EXPERIENCE, or that between observer and his or her own experience, always has a third party in back of the ethnographer, those for whom the ethnography is being written. The experiential dialogue becomes the researcher's data in relation to the DISCOURSE in which researcher and her or his future readers participate in a further dialogue.

difference   Difference is incorporated into INSTITUTIONAL ETHNOGRAPHY'S concept of the SOCIAL. In addition to differences in physiology, EXPERIENCE, and biography, differences among individuals in perspective and concerns are generated in the social process of COORDINATING activities.

discourse   The term has been used in many senses: it is used by linguists to denote streams of talk or TEXT, and it is used by Michel Foucault (1981) to identify conventionally regulated practices of using language that formulate and recognize objects of knowledge in distinctive ways. The conception of discourse used in this book builds from Foucault's use. Discourse refers to translocal relations COORDINATING the practices of definite individuals talking, writing, reading, watching, and so forth, in particular local places at particular times. People *participate* in discourse, and their participation reproduces it. Discourse constrains what they can say or write, and what they say or write reproduces and modifies discourse. Though discourse is regulated in various ways, each moment of discourse in action both reproduces and remakes it.

experience   The term *experience* is used to refer to what people come to know that originates in people's bodily being and action. Only the experiencer can speak of her or his experience. It emerges for the ethnographer in dialogue, spoken or written, among particular people at particular times and in particular places, including self-reflection. Institutional ethnographers sometimes refer to *lived experience* to locate those interchanges of awareness, recognition, feeling, noticing, and learning going on between body and world that are prior to and provide sources for experience as it is evoked in dialogue.

ideological discourse   Ideological DISCOURSES are generalized and generalizing discourses, operating at a metalevel to control other discourses, including INSTITUTIONAL DISCOURSES.

indexicality   Any account of ACTUALITIES of whatever kind depends on referring back to those actualities to make its sense. That is the account's indexical character. INSTITUTIONAL ETHNOGRAPHY does not claim to transcend indexicality. Its ethnographies depend on and refer back to the actualities from which their findings are extracted.

institutional capture   INSTITUTIONAL DISCOURSE has the capacity to subsume or displace description based in EXPERIENCE. Institutional capture can occur when both informant and researcher are familiar with
institutional discourse, know how to speak it, and hence can easily
lose touch with the informant's experientially based knowledge.

institutional discourse   Institutional discourses select those aspects of
what people do that are accountable within it, subsuming ACTUALITIES
as integral to the production of the institution. Their TEXT–READER
CONVERSATIONS involve procedures for treating actualities as instances
or expressions of institutional discourse's frames, concepts, and categories. Typically, perspectiveless representations are created in which
people disappear as subjects and AGENTS.

institutional ethnography   Institutional ethnography explores the SO-
CIAL RELATIONS organizing INSTITUTIONS as people participate in them
and from their perspectives. People are the expert practitioners of
their own lives, and the ethnographer's work is to learn from them,
to assemble what is learned from different perspectives, and to investigate how their activities are COORDINATED. It aims to go beyond
what people know to find out how what they are doing is connected
with others' doings in ways they cannot see. The idea is to MAP the
institutional aspects of the RULING RELATIONS so that people can expand their own knowledge of their everyday worlds by being able
to see how what they are doing is coordinated with others' doings
elsewhere and elsewhen.

institutions   I am using the terms *institutional* and *institutions* to identify
complexes embedded in the RULING RELATIONS that are organized
around a distinctive function, such as education, health care, and so
on. The terms identify the intersection and COORDINATION of more
than one relational mode of ruling. State agencies are tied with professional forms of organization, and both are interpenetrated by relations of DISCOURSE, including the INSTITUTIONAL DISCOURSES that are
systematically developed to provide categories and concepts expressing the relationship of local courses of action to the institutional function. It is a specific capacity of institutions that they generalize and are
generalized. Hence, in institutional settings people are active in producing the general out of the particular. The institutional is to be discovered in motion, and its distinctive modes of generalizing
coordination are themselves being brought into being in people's local doings in particular sites and at particular times.

interindividual territories   Valentin Vološinov's concept of language (1973), in which words are a "two-sided act, the product of the reciprocal relationship between speaker and hearer." The relation between subjects that the two-sided act of the word or utterance constitutes is *between* them; it is interindividual. EXPERIENCE-based and TEXT-based interindividual territories are to be distinguished. While the experiential is never displaced, the basis or ground on which interindividual territories are built differs radically in the move from experiential to text-based territories.

interrogatory devices   The work of transposing people's experienced ACTUALITIES into institutional realities involves generally some form of interrogation. Surveys and forms, as textual genres of interrogation, set out as fields the equivalent of questions to which "subjects," or "clients," or "patients" must respond, transposing aspects of their everyday worlds into shapes that fit the topic-assigned spaces provided.

intertextuality   Intertextuality is a term used largely in literary theory. It expresses the view that TEXTS do not stand alone; their sense is not independent of other texts; they are essentially intertextual. In INSTITUTIONAL ETHNOGRAPHY the notion of intertextuality is borrowed to recognize the interdependence of institutional texts. In particular it is used in this book to refer to the interdependence of texts in a hierarchy: higher level texts establish the frames and concepts that control and shape lower level texts.

mapping   Maps are always INDEXICALLY related to actual territories. Analogously, INSTITUTIONAL ETHNOGRAPHY's project of mapping INSTITUTIONS always refers back to an ACTUALITY that those who are active in it know (the way that the phrase YOU ARE HERE works on a map). A map assembles different WORK KNOWLEDGES, positioned differently, and should include, where relevant, an account of the TEXTS coordinating work processes in institutional settings.

ontology   Ontology is a theory of being. In this book, the term is used to denote a theory of how the SOCIAL exists. INSTITUTIONAL ETHNOGRAPHY's ontology provides a conceptual framework for selective attention to ACTUALITIES. It moves toward inquiry that goes on in the same world as that which the ethnographer is exploring; it moves away from an ontology that affords AGENCY to concepts.

power   In INSTITUTIONAL ETHNOGRAPHY, INSTITUTIONS are seen as generating power through the COORDINATING functions of language and TEXTS.

Even the uses of physical force to control others, such as that by the police or military, are INTERTEXTUALLY coordinated. The texts that constitute and regulate institutions establish AGENCY, that is, textually specified capacities to control and mobilize the WORK of others. Textually sanctioned agency produces capacities for action accountable within the institutional hierarchy creating powers that are generated by the textual concerting and mobilization of people's work.

problematic INSTITUTIONAL ETHNOGRAPHY begins in the ACTUALITIES of people's lives with a focus of investigation that comes from how they participate in or are hooked up into institutional relations. A problematic sets out a project of research and discovery that organizes the direction of investigation from the standpoint of those whose EXPERIENCE is its starting point.

processing interchange A term used to identify a WORK process particularly characteristic of INSTITUTIONS in which a TEXT enters the work setting of a given individual and is processed or incorporated into a new text to become the focus of another or others' work.

regulatory frames (see also, INSTITUTIONAL DISCOURSE) Frames are discursive procedures that organize how something is to be interpreted. They orient the production of a TEXT to the frame that will interpret it and, in TEXT–READER CONVERSATIONS, provide instructions for interpreting the text. In the INTERTEXTUAL hierarchies of INSTITUTIONS, the frames of higher order texts regulate those produced at lower levels. Such regulatory frames are of special significance in regulating how ACTUALITIES are selectively incorporated into textual realities.

ruling relations The concept of the ruling relations directs attention to the distinctive translocal forms of SOCIAL ORGANIZATION and SOCIAL RELATIONS mediated by TEXTS of all kinds (print, film, television, computer, and so on) that have emerged and become dominant in the last two hundred years. They are objectified forms of consciousness and organization, constituted externally to particular people and places, creating and relying on textually based realities.

social, the People's ongoing activities viewed under the aspect of their COORDINATION with the activities of others.

social organization When distinct forms of COORDINATING people's doings emerge that are reproduced again and again, we use the term *social organization.*

social relations The term does not refer to relationships such as those between instructor and student, boyfriend and girlfriend, or parent and child. Rather, it orients the researcher to viewing people's doings in particular local settings as articulated to sequences of action that hook them up to what others are or have been doing elsewhere and elsewhen. It is useful analytically to think of social relations as temporal sequences in which the foregoing intends the subsequent and in which the subsequent "realizes" or accomplishes the social character of the preceding. It reminds the ethnographer to attend to how the object of focus is embedded in sequences of COORDINATED action.

text   Unlike some theorizing of "text," the term is used here strictly to identify texts as material in a form that enables replication (paper/print, film, electronic, and so on) of what is written, drawn, or otherwise reproduced. Materiality is emphasized because we can then see how a text can be present in our everyday world and at the same time connect us into translocal SOCIAL RELATIONS. Texts—printed, electronic, or otherwise replicable—produce the stability and replicability of organization or INSTITUTION. The capacity to COORDINATE people's doings translocally depends on the text as a material thing, being able to turn up in identical form wherever the reader, hearer, watcher may be in her or his bodily being. INSTITUTIONAL ETHNOGRAPHY recognizes texts not as a discrete topic but as they enter into and coordinate people's doings, and, as activated in the TEXT–READER CONVERSATION, they *are* people's doings.

text–reader conversation   The concept of a text–reader conversation recognizes reading a TEXT as an ACTUAL interchange between a reader's activating of the text and her or his responses to it. Text–reader conversations take place in real time, in the actual local setting of their reading, and as moments in sequences of action. Noticing how people go about activating texts helps us to escape our EXPERIENCE of them as inert, enabling us to see them as embedded in SOCIAL RELATIONS and, hence, as being in action.

women's standpoint   A methodological starting point in the local particularities of bodily existence. Designed to establish a subject position from which to begin research—a site that is open to anyone—it furnishes an alternative starting point to the objectified subject of knowledge of social scientific discourse. From women's standpoint, we can make visible the extraordinary complex of the RULING RELATIONS, with its power to locate consciousness and set us up as subjects as if we were indeed disembodied.

work   The term is generally used to refer to what people are paid to do. The Wages for Housework group expanded the concept to refer not only to housework but to anything that people do that takes time, effort, and intent. INSTITUTIONAL ETHNOGRAPHY has adopted this conception of work in exploring the ACTUALITIES of INSTITUTIONS. It orients the researcher to what people are actually doing as they participate, in whatever way, in institutional processes.

work knowledges   The term refers simply to what people know of and in their WORK and how it is COORDINATED with the work of others. Work knowledge is a major resource for the institutional ethnographer. It is dialogically evoked in the interviewer–informant interchange when it is based in the informant's own EXPERIENCE or in the observer's experience/observations of people's activities in a given setting. The different work knowledges that are produced in the researcher's dialogues are fitted together so that the organization of the sequence, circuit, or other organizational form can emerge.

Abercrombie, N., and B. S. Turner. 1982. The dominant ideology thesis. In *Classes, power, and conflict: Classical and contemporary debates*, ed. A. Giddens and D. Held. Berkeley: University of California Press.

Adler, Paul S. 1993. "The learning bureaucracy": New United Motor Manufacturing, Inc. *Organizational Behavior* 15:111–94.

Aglietta, M. 1979. *A theory of capitalist regulation: The U.S. experience*. New York: Verso.

Alexander, J. C. 1989. Sociology and discourse: On the centrality of the classics. In *Structure and meaning: Relinking classical sociology*, ed. J. C. Alexander, 8–67. New York: Columbia University Press.

———. 1995. *Fin de siècle social theory*. London: Verso.

Althusser, Louis. 1969. *For Marx*. London: Penguin Books.

———. 1970. *Reading "Capital."* New York: Pantheon Books.

———. 1971. Ideology and ideological state apparatuses. In *Lenin and philosophy and other essays*. New York: Monthly Review Press.

Andersen, E. 2003. Women do lion's share at home. *Globe and Mail*, February 12, A7.

Anderson, R. J., J. A. Hughes, et al. 1989. *Working for profit: The social organisation of calculation in an entrepreneurial firm*. Aldershot, Eng.: Avebury.

Anyon, Jean. 1997. *Ghetto schooling: A political economy of urban educational reform*. New York: Teachers College Press, Columbia University.

Arnup, K. 1994. *Education for motherhood: Advice for mothers in twentieth-century Canada*. Toronto, Ont.: University of Toronto Press.

Austin, J. L. 1962. *How to do things with words*. Cambridge, Mass.: Harvard University Press.

Bacon, Francis. [1620] 1939. Novum organum. In *The English philosophers from Bacon to Mill*, ed. Edwin A. Burtt. New York: Random House.

Bagdikian, Ben H. 1983. *The media monopoly*. Boston: Beacon.

Bakhtin, M. M. 1981. *The dialogic imagination: Four essays*, ed. M. Holquist. Austin: University of Texas Press.

———. 1986. *Speech genres and other late essays*. Ed. C. Emerson et al. Austin: University of Texas Press.

Bal, M. 1997. *Narratology: Introduction to the theory of narratives*. Toronto, Ont.: University of Toronto Press.

Bannerji, H. 1995. Beyond the ruling category to what actually happens: Notes on James Mill's historiography in *The history of British India*. In *Knowledge, experience, and ruling relations: Explorations in the social organization of knowledge*, ed. M. Campbell and A. Manicom, 49–64. Toronto, Ont.: University of Toronto Press.

Barrow, C. W. 1990. *Universities and the capitalist state: Corporate liberalism and the reconstruction of American higher education, 1894–1928*. Madison: University of Wisconsin Press.

231

Bazerman, Charles. 1988. *Shaping written knowledge: The genre and activity of the experimental article in science.* Madison: University of Wisconsin Press.

Beniger, J. R. 1986. *The control revolution: Technological and economic origins of the information society.* Cambridge, Mass.: Harvard University Press.

Berger, P., and T. Luckman. 1966. *The social construction of reality.* New York: Doubleday.

Bernstein, Basil. 1966. Elaborated and restricted codes: Their social origins and some consequences. In *Communication and culture: Reading in the codes of human interaction,* ed. A. G. Smith, 427–41. New York: Holt, Rinehart and Winston.

Blalock, H. M. 1969. *Theory construction: From verbal to mathematical formulations.* Englewood Cliffs, N.J.: Prentice Hall.

Blumenthal, Sidney. 1986. *The rise of the counterestablishment: From conservative ideology to political power.* New York: Times Books.

Blumer, H. 1969. *Symbolic interactionism: Perspective and method.* Englewood Cliffs, N.J.: Prentice Hall.

———. 1997. Foreword to *Violent criminal acts and actors revisited,* by L. Athens. Urbana: University of Illinois Press.

Boden, D. 1994. *The business of talk: Organizations in action.* Cambridge: Polity Press.

Bourdieu, P. 1973. The three forms of theoretical knowledge. *Social Science Information* 12 (1): 53–80.

———. 1990. *The logic of practice.* Stanford, Calif.: Stanford University Press.

———. 1992. *Language and symbolic power.* Cambridge: Polity Press.

Bradford, Richard. 1997. *Stylistics.* London: Routledge.

Briggs, Charles L. 2002. Interviewing, power/knowledge, and social inequality. In *Handbook of interview research: Context and method,* ed. J. F. Gubrium and J. A. Holstein, 911–22. Thousand Oaks, Calif.: Sage.

Brock, David. 2002. *Blinded by the right: The conscience of an ex-conservative,* New York: Three Rivers Press.

Brodie, Janine. 1996. *Women and Canadian public policy.* Toronto, Ont.: Harcourt Brace.

Brown, Deborah. 2004. Working the system: Re-thinking the role of parents and the reduction of "risk" in child protection work. MA thesis, Department of Sociology, University of Victoria.

Buckholdt, D. S., and J. F. Gubrium. 1983. Practicing accountability in human service institutions. *Urban Life* 12 (5): 249–68.

Burawoy, M., J. A. Blum, et al. 2000. *Global ethnography: Forces, connections, and imaginations in a postmodern world.* Berkeley: University of California Press.

Burawoy, M., A. Burton, et al. 1991. *Ethnography unbound: Power and resistance in the modern metropolis.* Berkeley: University of California Press.

Burrows, G. 2004. Clean water, not education, is most effective tool in fight against poverty. *Guardian Weekly* (London), 23.

Butler, J., and J. W. Scott. 1992. Introduction to *Feminist theorize the political,* ed. J. Butler and J. W. Scott. New York: Routledge.

Button, G., ed. 1991. *Ethnomethodology and the human sciences.* Cambridge: Cambridge University Press.

Campbell, M. L. 1984. Information systems and management of hospital nursing, a study in social organization of knowledge. PhD diss., University of Toronto, Ontario.

———. 2001. Textual accounts, ruling action: The intersection of knowledge and power in the routine conduct of community nursing work. *Studies in Cultures, Organizations, and Societies* 7 (2): 231–50.

Campbell, M., and F. Gregor. 2002. *Mapping social relations: A primer in doing institutional ethnography.* Toronto, Ont.: Garamond.

Chandler, Alfred Dupont. 1962. *Strategy and structure: Chapters in the history of the industrial enterprise.* Cambridge, Mass.: MIT Press.

———. 1977. *The visible hand: The managerial revolution in American business.* Cambridge, Mass.: Harvard University Press.

———. 1979. *Managerial innovation at General Motors.* New York: Arno Press.

Charmaz, K., and R. G. Mitchell. 2001. Grounded theory in ethnography. In *Handbook of ethnography,* ed. A. Atkinson, S. Coffey, J. Delamont, and L. Lofland, 160–74. London: Sage.

Chomsky, N. 1968. *Language and mind.* New York: Harcourt Brace.

Chouliaraki, L., and N. Fairclough. 1999. *Discourse in late modernity: Rethinking critical discourse analysis.* Edinburgh: Edinburgh University Press.

Cicourel, A. V. 1964. *Method and measurement in sociology.* New York: Free Press.

Clark, H. H. 1996. *Using language.* Stanford, Calif.: Stanford University Press.

Code, L. 1995. How do we know? Questions of method in feminist practice. In *Changing methods: Feminist transforming practice,* ed. S. Burt and L. Code, 13–44. Peterborough, Ont.: Broadview Press.

Collins, R. 1979. *The credential society: An historical sociology of education and stratification.* New York: Academic Press.

Darville, Richard. 1995. Literacy, experience, power. In *Knowledge, experience, and ruling relations: Studies in the social organization of knowledge,* ed. M. L. Campbell and A. Manicom. Toronto: University of Toronto Press.

Davidoff, L., and C. Hall. 1987. *Family fortunes: Men and women of the English middle class, 1780–1850.* Chicago: University of Chicago Press.

Dehli, K. 1988. Women and class: The social organization of mothers' relations to schools in Toronto, 1915–1940. PhD diss., University of Toronto.

de Montigny, G. A. J. 1995a. *Social work(ing).* Toronto, Ont.: University of Toronto Press.

———. 1995b. The power of being professional. In *Knowledge, experience, and ruling relations: Explorations in the social organization of knowledge,* ed. M. Campbell and A. Manicom, 209–20. Toronto, Ont.: University of Toronto Press.

DeVault, M. L. 1991. *Feeding the family: The social organization of caring as gendered work.* Chicago: University of Chicago Press.

DeVault, M. L., and L. McCoy. 2002. Institutional ethnography: Using interviews to investigate ruling relations. In *Handbook of interviewing research: Context and method,* ed. J. F. Gubrium and J. A. Holstein, 751–75. Thousand Oaks, Calif.: Sage.

———. Forthcoming. Institutional ethnography: Using interviews to investigate ruling relations. In *Institutional ethnography as practice,* ed. D. E. Smith. Walnut Creek, Calif.: AltaMira Press.

Diamond, T. 1992. *Making gray gold: Narratives of nursing home care.* Chicago: University of Chicago Press.

Diamond, Tim. Forthcoming. "Where did you get that fur coat, Fern?" Participant observation in institutional ethnography. In *Institutional ethnography as practice,* ed. D. E. Smith. Walnut Creek, Calif.: AltaMira Press.

Dobson, Stephan. 2001. Introduction: Institutional ethnography as method. *Studies in Cultures, Organizations, and Societies* 7 (2): 147–58.

Douglas, M. 1966. *Purity and danger*. New York: Penguin Books.

Dowling, William C. 1999. *The senses of the text: Intensional semantics and literary theory*. Omaha: University of Nebraska Press.

Duranti, A., and C. Goodwin. 1992. Rethinking context: An introduction. In *Rethinking context: Language as an interactive phenomenon*, ed. A. Duranti and C. Goodwin, 1–41. Cambridge: Cambridge University Press.

Durkheim, E. [1895] 1966. *The rules of sociological method*. New York: Free Press.

Emerson, R. M., R. I. Fretz, et al. 1995. *Writing ethnographic fieldnotes*. Chicago: University of Chicago Press.

Engeström, Y. 1987. *Learning by expanding: An activity-theoretical approach to developmental research*. Helsinki, Finland: Orienta-Konsultit.

Engeström, Y., R. Miettinen, et al. 1999. *Perspectives on activity theory*. Cambridge: Cambridge University Press.

Fauconnier, Gilles, and Mark Turner. 2002. *The way we think: Conceptual blending and the mind's hidden complexities*. New York: Basic Books.

Fine, M. 1993. [Ap]parent involvement: Reflections on parents, power, and urban public schools. *Teachers College Record* 94 (4): 682–710.

Foucault, M. 1970. *The order of things: An archaeology of the human sciences*. London: Tavistock.

———. 1972. *The discourse on language*, 213–37. New York: Pantheon Books.

———. 1981. The order of discourse. In *Untying the text: A poststructuralist reader*, ed. R. Young, 51–78. London: Routledge.

Fox Piven, Frances. 2002. Welfare policy and American politics. In *Work, welfare, and politics: Confronting poverty in the wake of welfare reform*, ed. F. Fox Piven, J. Acker, M. Hallock, and S. Morgen, 19–23. Eugene: University of Oregon Press.

Friedan, B. 1963. *The feminine mystique*. New York: Dell.

Fuller, S. 1998. From content to context: A social epistemology of the structure-agency craze. *What is social theory? The philosophical debates*, ed. A. Sica, 92–117. Malden, Mass.: Blackwell.

Gadamer, H. G. 1975. *Truth and method*. London: Sheed & Ward.

Gardiner, Michael. 1992. *The dialogics of critique: M. M. Bakhtin and the theory of ideology*. New York: Routledge.

Garfinkel, Harold. 1967. *Studies in ethnomethodology*. Englewood Cliffs, N.J.: Prentice Hall.

———. 2002. *Ethnomethodology's program: Working out Durkheim's aphorism*. Ed. and intro. Anne Warfield Rawls. Lanham, Md.: Rowman and Littlefield.

Giddens, A. 1984. *The constitution of society*. Berkeley: University of California Press.

Gilens, Martin. 1999. *Why Americans hate welfare: Race, media, and the politics of antipoverty policy*. Chicago: University of Chicago Press.

Giltrow, J. 1998. Modernizing authority, management studies, and the grammaticalization of controlling interests. *Technical Writing and Communication* 28(4): 337–58.

Glaser, B. G., and A. L. Strauss. 1967. *The discovery of grounded theory: Strategies for qualitative research*. Chicago: Aldine.

Glazer, N. Y. 1993. *Women's paid and unpaid labor: The work transfer in health care and retailing*. Philadelphia: Temple University Press.

Goffman, E. 1963. *Behavior in public places: Notes on the social organization of gatherings.* [New York]: Free Press of Glencoe.

———. 1974. *Frame analysis: An essay on the organization of experience.* New York: Harper Colophon Books.

Goodwin, Marjorie Harness. 1990. *He-said-she-said: Talk as social organization among black children.* Bloomington: Indiana University Press.

Grahame, Kamini. 1998. Feminist organizing and the politics of inclusion. *Human Studies* 21:377–93.

———. 1999. State, community and Asian immigrant women's work: A study in labor market organization. PhD diss., University of Toronto.

Grahame, Peter R. 1998. Ethnography, institutions, and the problematic of the everyday world. *Human Studies* 21:360–60.

Griffith, Alison. 1984. Ideology, education, and single parent families: The normative ordering of families through schooling. PhD diss., Department of Education, University of Toronto.

———. 1986. Reporting the facts: Media accounts of single parent families. *Resources for Feminist Research* 15 (1): 32–43.

———. 1995. Mothering, schooling and children's development. In *Knowledge, experience, and ruling relations: Studies in the social organization of knowledge,* ed. M. Campbell and A. Manicom, 108–22. Toronto, Ont.: University of Toronto Press.

Griffith, A., and D. E. Smith. 1987. Constructing cultural knowledge: Mothering as discourse. *Women and education: A Canadian perspective,* ed. J. Gaskell and A. McLaren, 87–103. Calgary, Alberta: Detselig.

———. 1990a. Coordinating the uncoordinated: Mothering, schooling, and the family wage. In *Perspectives on social problems,* ed. G. Miller and J. Holstein, 2:25–34. Greenwich, Conn.: JAI Press.

———. 1990b. "What did you do in school today?" Mothering, schooling and social class. In *Perspectives on social problems,* ed. G. Miller and J. Holstein, 2:3–24. Greenwich, Conn.: JAI Press.

———. 2004. *Mothering for schooling.* New York: Routledge.

Grosz, Elizabeth A. 1995. *Space, time, perversion: Essays on the politics of bodies.* New York: Routledge.

Gurwitsch, A. 1964. *Field of consciousness.* Pittsburgh, Pa.: Duquesne University Press.

Habermas, Jürgen 1992. *The structural transformation of the public sphere: An inquiry into a category of bourgeois society.* Trans. Thomas Burger with the assistance of Frederick Lawrence. Cambridge, Mass.: MIT Press.

Halliday, M. A. K. 1994. *Introduction to functional grammar.* London: E. Arnold.

Halliday, M. A. K., and R. Hasan. 1989. *Language, context, and text: Aspects of language in a social-semiotic perspective.* Oxford: Oxford University Press.

Halliday, M. A. K., and J. R. Martin. 1993. *Writing science: Literacy and discursive power.* Pittsburgh: University of Pittsburgh Press.

Hammersley, M., and P. Atkinson. 1995. *Ethnography: Principles in practice.* London: Routledge.

3Harding, S. 1988. *The science question in feminism.* Ithaca, N.Y.: Cornell University Press.

Harney, Stefano. 2002. *State work: Public administration and mass intellectuality.* Durham, N.C.: Duke University Press.

Hartsock, Nancy. 1998. *The feminist standpoint revisited and other essays.* Boulder, Colo.: Westview Press.

Hays, Sharon. 2003. *Flat broke with children: Women in the age of welfare reform.* Oxford: Oxford University Press.

Hempel, Carl G. 1966. *The philosophy of natural science.* Englewood Cliffs, N.J.: Prentice Hall.

Holquist, M. 1990. *Dialogism: Bakhtin and his world.* London: Routledge.

Horton, John, and Linda Shaw. 2002. Opportunity, control and resistance. In *Work, welfare, and politics: Confronting poverty in the wake of welfare reform,* ed. F. Fox Piven, J. Acker, M. Hallock, and S. Morgen, 197–212. Eugene: University of Oregon Press.

Ingram, J. 1993. *Talk talk talk: An investigation into the mystery of speech.* Harmondsworth, U.K.: Penguin Books.

Jackendoff, Ray. 2002. *Foundations of language: Brain, meaning, grammar, evolution.* Oxford: Oxford University Press.

Jackson, Nancy. 1974. Describing news: Toward an alternative account. Master's thesis, University of British Columbia.

Keller, Helen [Adams]. 1909. *The story of my life.* With her letters (1887–1901) and a supplementary account of her education, including passages from the reports and letters of her teacher, Anne Mansfield Sullivan [Anne Sullivan Macy], by John Albert Macy. New York: Grosset and Dunlap.

Keller, Helen Adams. 1955. *Teacher: Anne Sullivan Macy; A tribute by the fosterchild of her mind.* Garden City, N.Y.: Doubleday.

Kristeva, Julia. 1986. *The Kristeva reader.* ed. Toril Moi. New York: Columbia.

Kuhn, Thomas. 1970. *The structure of scientific revolutions.* Chicago: University of Chicago Press.

Labov, W., and J. Waletzky. 1967. Narrative analysis: Oral versions of personal experience. In *Essays on verbal and visual arts,* ed. J. Helm. Seattle: University of Washington Press.

Landes, Joan B. 1996. *Feminists read Habermas: Gendering the subject of discourse.* New York: Routledge.

Lapham, Lewis. 2004. Tentacles of rage: The Republican propaganda mill, a brief history. *Harper's* 309 (1882): 31–41.

Larson, M. S. 1977. *The rise of professionalism: A sociological analysis.* Berkeley: University of California Press.

Latour, Bruno, and Steve Woolgar. 1986. *Laboratory life: The construction of scientific facts.* Princeton, N.J.: Princeton University Press.

Leont'ev, A. N. 1978. *Activity, consciousness, and personality.* Englewood Cliffs, N.J.: Prentice Hall.

——. 1981. *Problems of the development of the mind.* Moscow: Progress Publishers.

Leys, C. 2001. *Market-driven politics: Neoliberal democracy and the public interest.* London: Verso.

Lioncelli, Stephanie A. 2002. "Some of us are excellent at babies": Paid work, mothering, and the construction of "need" in a Welfare-to-Work. In *Work, welfare, and politics: Confronting poverty in the wake of welfare reform,* ed. F. Fox Piven, J. Acker, M. Hallock, and S. Morgen, 81–94. Eugene: University of Oregon Press.

Lipietz, A. 1986. Behind the crisis: The exhaustion of a regime of accumulation. A regulation school perspective on some French empirical works. *Review of Radical Political Economics* 18 (1/2): 13–32.

———. 1987. *Mirages and miracles: The crisis of global Fordism*. London: Verso.

Luria, A. R. 1961. *The role of speech in the regulation of normal and abnormal behaviour*. New York: Pergamon Press.

———. 1976. *Cognitive development: Its cultural and social foundations*. Cambridge, Mass.: Harvard University Press.

Luria. A. R., and R. Ia. Yudovich. 1971. *Speech and the development of mental processes in the child*. New York: Penguin Books.

Lynch, M. 1983. Discipline and the material forms of images: An analysis of scientific visibility. Paper presented at the Canadian Sociology and Anthropology Association annual meeting, Vancouver, British Columbia.

Lynch, M., and D. Bogen. 1996. *The spectacle of history: Speech, text, and memory at the Iran-Contra hearings*. Durham, N.C.: Duke University Press.

Lyotard, J.-F. 1984. *The post-modern condition*. Minneapolis: University of Minnesota Press.

Macdonnell, Diane. 1986. *Theories of discourse: An introduction*. Oxford: Basil Blackwell.

Manicom, A. 1988. Constituting class relations: The social organization of teachers' work. In *Sociology in education*. Toronto, Ont.: University of Toronto Press.

———. 1995. What's health got to do with it? Class, gender, and teachers' work. In *Knowledge, experience and ruling relations: Essays in the social organization of knowledge*, ed. M. Campbell and A. Manicom, 135–48. Toronto, Ont.: University of Toronto Press.

March, J. G., M. Schulz, and X. Zhou. 2000. *The dynamics of rules: Change in written organizational codes*. Stanford, Calif.: Stanford University Press.

Martinez, Elizabeth, and Arnoldo Garcia. 1997. What is neoliberalism? A brief definition for activists. From CorpWatch.org, www.corpwatch.org/article.php?id=376 (retrieved December 13, 2004).

Marx, K. 1973. *Grundrisse: Foundations of the critique of political economy*. Trans. Martin Nicolaus. New York: Vintage.

———. 1976. *Capital: A critique of political economy*. London: Penguin Books.

Marx, K., and F. Engels. 1976. *The German ideology*. Moscow: Progress Publishers.

Maurer, David W. 1981. The argot of pickpockets. In *Language of the underworld*, ed. Allan W. Futrell and Charles B. Wordell, 234–56. Lexington: University of Kentucky Press.

McCarthy, E. Doyle. 1993. George Herbert Mead and *Wissenssoziologies:* A reexamination. In *In search of community: Essays in memory of Werner Stark, 1909–1985*, ed. Eileen Leonard, Hermann Strasser, and Kenneth Westhues, 97–115. New York: Fordham University Press.

McCoy, L. 1995. Activating the photographic text. In *Knowledge, experience, and ruling relations: Essays in the social organization of knowledge*, ed. M. Campbell and A. Manicom, 181–92. Toronto, Ont.: University of Toronto Press.

———. 1999. Accounting discourse and textual practices of ruling: A study of institutional transformation and restructuring in higher education. PhD diss., University of Toronto.

———. 2002. Dealing with doctors. In *Making care visible: Antiretroviral therapy and the health work of people living with HIV/AIDS*, ed. M. Bresalier, L. Gillis, C. Mc-Clure, L. McCoy, E. Mykhalovskiy, D. Taylor, and M. Webber, 1–36. Toronto, Ont.: Making Care Visible Group.

McCoy, Liza. Forthcoming. Keeping social organization in view: A data analysis in institutional ethnography. In *Institutional ethnography as practice*, ed. D. E. Smith. Walnut Creek, Calif.: AltaMira Press.

McDermid, V. 2002. *The last temptation*. London: Harper Collins.

McGann, Jerome J. 1993. *The textual condition*. Princeton, N.J.: Princeton University Press.

McHoul, A. W. 1982. Rule, occasion, reading the news. In *Telling how texts talk: Essays on reading and ethnomethodology*, 110–37. London: Routledge & Kegan Paul.

McKeon, M. 1987. *The origins of the English novel, 1600–1740*. Baltimore: Johns Hopkins University Press.

McLean, C., and K. Hoskin. 1998. Organizing madness: Reflections on the forms of the form. *Organization: The Interdisciplinary Journal of Organization, Theory, and Society* 5 (4): 519–41.

McRobbie, A. 1982. The politics of feminist research: Between talk, text, and action. *Feminist Review* 12:46–57.

Mead, G. H. 1959. *The philosophy of the present*. La Salle, Ill.: Open Court.

———. 1962. *Mind, self, and society from the perspective of a social behaviorist*. Chicago: University of Chicago Press.

Mehan, Hugh. 1996. The construction of an LD student: A case study in the politics of representation. In *Natural histories of discourse*, ed. M. Silverstein and G. Urban, 253–76. Chicago: University of Chicago Press.

Merleau-Ponty, Maurice. 1966. *The phenomenology of perception*. London: Routledge & Kegan Paul.

Messer-Davidow, Ellen. 1993. Manufacturing the attack on liberalized higher education. *Social Text* 36:40–79.

———. 2002. *Disciplining feminism: From social activism to academic discourse*. Durham, N.C.: Duke University Press.

Mills, C. Wright. 1951. *White collar: The American middle classes*. New York: Oxford University Press.

Moya, M. L. 2000. Postmodernism, "realism," and the politics of identity: Cherrie Moraga and Chicana feminism. In *Realist theory and the predicament of postmodernism*, ed. M. L. Moya, 67–101. Berkeley: University of California Press.

Mykhavlovskiy, Eric. 2001. On the uses of health services research: Troubled hearts, care pathways and hospital restructuring. *Studies in Cultures, Organizations, and Societies* 7 (1): 269–98.

———. 2002. Understanding the social character of treatment decision-making. In *Making care visible: Antiretroviral therapy and the health work of people living with HIV/AIDS*, ed. M. Bresalier, L. Gillis, C. McClure, L. McCoy, E. Mykhalovskiy, D. Taylor, and M. Webber, 37–63. Toronto, Ont.: Making Care Visible Group.

Mykhavlovskiy, Eric, and Liza McCoy. 2002. Troubling ruling discourses of health: Using institutional ethnography in community-based research. *Critical Public Health* 12 (1): 17–37.

Naples, N. A. 2003. *Feminism and method: Ethnography, discourse analysis, and activist research*. New York: Routledge.

Naples, Nancy A. 1997. The "new consensus" on the gendered "social contract": The 1987–1988 U. S. congressional hearings on welfare reform. *Signs: Journal of Women in Culture and Society* 22 (4): 907–43.

Neubeck, Kenneth J., and Noel A. Cazenave. 2002. Welfare racism and its consequences: The demise of AFDC and the return of the states' rights era. In *Work, welfare, and politics: Confronting poverty in the wake of welfare reform*, ed. F. Fox Piven, J. Acker, M. Hallock, and S. Morgen, 35–53. Eugene: University of Oregon Press.

New School of Social Research. n.d. History of economic thought. http/cepa .newschool.edu/het/profiles/jamesmill.htm (reviewed November 2003).

Ng, R. 1995. Multiculturalism as ideology: A textual analysis. *Knowledge, experience, and ruling relations: Explorations in the social organization of knowledge*, ed. M. Cambell and A. Manicom, 35–38. Toronto, Ont.: University of Toronto Press.

Ng, Roxanna. 1986. *Politics of community services: Immigrant women, class, and state.* Toronto, Ont.: Garamond Press.

Noble, David. 1977. *America by design: Science, technology, and the rise of corporate capitalism.* Oxford: Oxford University Press.

Ogden, C. K., and I. A. Richards. 1923. *The meaning of meaning: A study of the influence of language on thought and of the science of symbolism.* London: Routledge & Kegan Paul.

Parada, H. 2002. The restructuring of the child welfare system in Ontario: A study in the social organization of knowledge. PhD diss., Ontario Institute for Studies in Education, University of Toronto.

Parsons, T. 1937. *The structure of social action.* New York: McGraw-Hill.

Pence, E. 1996. Safety for battered women in a textually mediated legal system. PhD diss., University of Toronto.

———. 2001. Safety for battered women in a textually mediated legal system. *Studies in Cultures, Organizations, and Societies* 7(2): 199–229.

Perkin, Harold. 1989. *The rise of professional society: England since 1880.* London: Routledge.

Perrow, C. 1986. *Complex organizations: A critical essay.* New York: McGraw Hill.

Pinker, Steven. 2000. *Words and rules: The ingredients of language.* New York: Harper-Collins.

Prior, Lindsay. 2003. *Using documents in social research.* London: Sage Publications.

Rankin, J. 2003. How nurses practise health care reform: An institutional ethnography. PhD diss., University of Victoria.

Rankin, Janet M. 1998. Health care reform and restructuring of nursing in British Columbia. Paper presented at Exploring the Restructuring and Transformation of Institutional Processes: Applications of Institutional Ethnography, York University, Toronto, October.

———. 2001. Texts in action: How nurses are doing the fiscal work of health care reform. In *Institutional ethnography*, special issue, *Studies in Cultures, Organizations, and Societies* 7 (2): 251–67.

Reimer, M. 1988. The social organization of the labour process: A case study of the documentary management of clerical labour in the public service. PhD diss., University of Toronto.

Reynolds, Tracey. 2002. On relations between black female researchers and participants. In *Qualitative research in action*, ed. Tim May, 300–309. London: Sage.

Ridzi, Frank. 2003. Processing private lives in public: An institutional ethnography of front-line welfare intake staff post welfare reform. PhD diss., Maxwell School of Citizenship and Public Affairs, Syracuse University, New York.

Rinehart, James, Christopher Huxley, and David Robertson. 1997. *Just another car factory: Lean production and its discontents*. Ithaca, N.Y.: Cornell University Press.

Rosdolsky, Roman. 1977. *The making of Marx's "Capital."* London: Pluto Press.

Rothman, S. M. 1978. *Woman's proper place: A history of changing ideals and practices, 1870 to the present*. New York: Basic Books.

Rousseau, J.-J. 1966. *Emile*. Trans. B. Foxley. New York: Dutton.

Rowbotham, Sheila. 1979. *Dutiful daughters: Women talk about their lives*. London: Allen Lane.

Roy, William G. 1997. *Socializing capital: The rise of the large industrial corporation in America*. Princeton, N.J.: Princeton University Press.

Rubin, I. I. 1975. *Essays on Marx's theory of value*. Montreal: Black Rose Books.

Ryan, Mary P. 1993. Gender and public access: Women's politics in nineteenth-century America. In *Habermas and the public sphere*, ed. Craig Calhoun. Cambridge, Mass.: MIT Press.

Sacks, H., E. Schegloff, and G. Jefferson. 1974. A simplest systematics for the organization of turntaking for conversation. *Language* 50:696–735.

Salzinger, Leslie. 1991. A maid by any other name: The transformation of "dirty work" by Central American immigrants. In *Ethnography unbound*, ed. Michael Burawoy, A. Burton, et al. Berkeley: University of California Press.

Saussure, Ferdinand de. 1966. *Course in general linguistics*. New York: McGraw-Hill.

Schatzmann, A., and A. L. Strauss. 1966. Social class and modes of communication. In *Communication and culture: Reading in the codes of human interaction*, ed. A. Smith, 442–55. New York: Holt, Rinehart and Winston.

Schegloff, Emmanuel A. 1987. Between micro and macro: Contexts and other connections. In *The micro-macro link*, ed. J. Alexander et al. Berkeley: University of California Press.

———. 1991. Reflections on talk and social structure. In *Talk and social structure: Studies in ethnomethodology and conversation analysis*, ed. D. Boden and D. H. Zimmerman, 45–70. Berkeley: University of California Press.

Schiller, Herbert I. 1996. *Information inequality: The deepening social crisis in America*. New York: Routledge.

Schmid, H.-J. 2000. *English abstract nouns as conceptual shells: From corpus to cognition*. Berlin: Mouton de Gruyter.

Schutz, A. 1962a. *Collected papers*, vol. 1, *The problem of social reality*. The Hague: Martinus Nijhoff.

———. 1962b. On multiple realities. In *Collected Papers*, 1:207–59. The Hague: Martinus Nijhoff.

Scott, J. W. 1992. Experience. In *Feminists theorize the political*, ed. J. Butler and J. W. Scott, 22–40. New York: Routledge.

Searle, John R. 1969. *Speech acts: An essay in the philosophy of language*. London: Cambridge University Press.

Simmel, G. 1950. *The sociology of Georg Simmel*. Ed. K. H. Wolff. New York: Free Press.

Sloan, Afred. 1964. *My years with General Motors*. Garden City, N.Y.: Doubleday.

Smith, D. E. 1974a. Women's perspective as a radical critique of sociology. *Sociological Inquiry* 4 (1): 1–13.

——. 1974b. The ideological practice of sociology. *Catalyst*, no. 8 (Winter): 39–54.

——. 1987. *The everyday world as problematic: A feminist sociology.* Toronto, Ont.: University of Toronto Press.

——. 1990a. *The conceptual practices of power: A feminist sociology of knowledge.* Boston: Northeastern University Press.

——. 1990b. K is mentally ill: The anatomy of a factual account. In *Texts, facts, and femininity: Exploring the relations of ruling*, ed. Dorothy E. Smith, 12–51. London: Routledge.

——. 1990c. On sociological description: A method from Marx. In *Texts, facts, and femininity: Exploring the relations of ruling*, ed. Dorothy E. Smith, 86–119. London: Routledge.

——. 1990d. *Texts, facts, and femininity: Exploring the relations of ruling.* London: Routledge.

——. 1997. The underside of schooling: Restructuring, privatization, and women's unpaid work. *Journal for a Just and Caring Education* 4 (1): 11–29.

——. 1999a. Discourse as social relations: Sociological theory and the dialogic of sociology. In *Writing the social: Critique, theory, and investigations*, ed. Dorothy E. Smith, 133–56. Toronto, Ont.: University of Toronto Press.

——. 1999b. The ruling relations. In *Writing the social: Critique, theory, and investigations*, ed. D. E. Smith. Toronto, Ont.: University of Toronto Press.

——. 1999c.The Standard North American Family: SNAF as an ideological code. In *Writing the social: Critique, theory, and investigations*, ed. D. E. Smith. Toronto, Ont.: University of Toronto Press.

——. 1999d. Telling the truth after postmodernism. In *Writing the social: Critique, theory, and investigations*, ed. D. E. Smith. Toronto, Ont.: University of Toronto Press.

——. 2001a. Institutional ethnography. In *Qualitative research in action*, ed. T. May, 17–52. London: Routledge.

——. 2001b. Texts and the ontology of institutions and organizations. *Studies in Cultures, Organizations, and Societies* 7 (2): 159–98.

——. 2003. Making sense of what people do: A sociological perspective. *Journal of Occupational Science* 10 (1): 64-67.

——. 2003. Resisting institutional capture: A research practice. In *Our studies, our selves*, ed. B. Glassner and R. Hertz. New York: Oxford University Press.

——. 2004. Ideology, science, and social relations: A reinterpretation of Marx's epistemology. *European Journal of Social Theory* 7 (1): 445–62.

——, ed. Forthcoming. *Institutional ethnography as practice.* Walnut Creek, Calif.: AltaMira Press.

Smith, D. E., and S. Dobson. 2002. Storing and transmitting skills: The expropriation of working class control. New Approaches to Lifelong Learning (NALL), www.oise.utoronto.ca/depts/sese/csew/nall, 91 pages.

Smith, D. E., and J. Whalen. 1996. Texts in action. Unpublished paper, University of Victoria.

Smith, G. W. 1988. Policing the gay community: An inquiry into textually mediated relations. *International Journal of Sociology and the Law* 16:163–83.

———. 1990. Political activist as ethnographer. *Social Problems* 37:401–21.

———. 1995. Accessing treatments: Managing the AIDS epidemic in Toronto, in Campbell, M., and Manicom, A. eds. *Knowledge, experience and ruling relations: Essays in the social organization of knowledge,* Toronto, Ont.: University of Toronto Press, 18–34.

Smith, George W. 1998. The ideology of "fag": Barriers to education for gay students. *Sociological Quarterly* 39 (2): 309–35.

Spradley, J. 1979. *The ethnographic interview.* New York: Holt, Rinehart and Winston.

Stock, Andree. 2002. An ethnography of assessment in elementary schools. EdD diss., University of Toronto.

Stoll, D. 1999. *Rigoberta Menchú and the story of all poor Guatemalans.* Boulder, Colo.: Westview Press.

Thompson, J. B. 1990. *Ideology and modern culture: Critical social theory in the era of mass communication.* Stanford, Calif.: Stanford University Press.

Turner, J., ed. 1989. *Theory building in sociology: Assessing theoretical cumulation.* Newbury City, Calif.: Sage.

Turner, S. 2001. Texts and the institutions of municipal planning government: The power of texts in the public process of land development. *Studies in Cultures, Organizations, and Societies* 7 (2): 297–325.

———. 2003. The social organization of planning: A study of institutional action as texts and work processes. PhD diss., University of Toronto.

———. Forthcoming. Mapping institutions as work and text. In *Institutional ethnography as practice,* ed. D. E. Smith. Walnut Creek, Calif.: AltaMira Press.

Uchitelle, Louis. 1993. How Clinton's economic strategy ended up looking like Bush's: A theory of growth that has never worked is now the sacred text. *New York Times,* August 1, 1 and 4.

Vaitkus, Steven. 2000. Phenomenology and sociology. In *The Blackwell companion to social theory,* ed. Bryan S. Turner, 270–98. Oxford: Blackwell.

Vallas, S. P., and J. Beck. 1996. The transformation of work revisited: The limits of flexibility in American manufacturing. *Social Problems* 43 (3): 339–61.

Veblen, Thorstein. 1954. *Absentee ownership and business enterprise in recent times.* New York: Viking Press.

———. 1957. *The higher learning in America.* New York: Hill & Wang.

Vološinov, V. I. 1973. *Marxism and the philosophy of language.* Trans. I. R. Titunik. New York: Academic Press.

von Glasersfeld, Ernst. 1995. *Radical constructivism: A way of knowing and learning.* London: Falmer Press.

Vygotsky, L. S. 1962. *Thought and language.* Cambridge, Mass.: MIT Press.

———. 1978. *Mind in society.* Cambridge, Mass.: Harvard University Press.

Walker, Gillian. 1990. *Family violence and the women's movement: The conceptual politics of struggle.* Toronto, Ont.: University of Toronto Press.

———. 1995. Violence and the relations of ruling: Lessons from the battered women's movement. In *Knowledge, experience, and ruling relations: Studies in the social organization of knowledge,* ed. M. Campbell and A. Manicom, Toronto, Ont.: University of Toronto Press, 65–79.

Waring, Stephen. 1991. *Taylorism transformed: Scientific management theory since 1945.* Chapel Hill: University of North Carolina Press.

Warren, Leanne D. 2001. Organizing creation: The role of musical text. *Studies in Cultures, Organizations, and Societies* 7 (2): 327–52.

Watson, R. 1992. The understanding of language use in everyday life: Is there a common ground? In *Text in context: Contributions to ethnomethdology*, ed. G. Watson and R. Seifer, 1–19. Newbury Park, Calif.: Sage.

———. 1997. Ethnomethodology and textual analysis. In *Qualitative research: Theory, method, and practice*, ed. David Silverman, 80–97. London: Sage.

Weber, Max. 1978. *Economy and society.* Ed. Guenther Roth and Claus Wittich. Trans. E. Fischoff et al. Berkeley: University of California Press.

Whalen, J. 1990. Processing "emergencies" in 9-1-1 communications. Unpublished paper, Department of Sociology, University of Oregon.

Whalen, M., and D. H. Zimmerman. 1987. Sequential and institutional contexts in calls for help. *Social Psychology Quarterly* 50 (2): 172–85.

Whyte, William H. 1956. *The organization man.* New York: Simon & Schuster.

Wieder, D. L. 1974. *Language and social reality: The case of telling the convict code.* The Hague, Neth.: Mouton.

Wilson, Alex, and Ellen Pence. Forthcoming. A Native community assesses U.S. legal interventions in the lives of battered women: Investigation, critique and vision. In *Institutional ethnography as practice*, ed. D. E. Smith. Walnut Creek, Calif.: AltaMira Press.

Wilson, T. P. 1991. Social structure and the sequential organization of interaction. In *Talk and social structure: Studies in ethnomethodology and conversation analysis*, ed. D. Boden and D. H. Zimmerman, 23–43. Berkeley: University of California Press.

Winter, Eugene. 1992. The notion of unspecific versus specific as one way of analysing the information of a fund-raising letter. In *Discourse description: Diverse linguistic analysis of a fund-raising text*, ed. W. C. Mann and S. A. Thompson. Philadelphia: John Benjamins Publishing Co., 131–70.

Yates, J. 1989. *Control through communication: The rise of system in American management.* Baltimore: Johns Hopkins University Press.

Zimmerman, Don. 1969. Record-keeping and the intake process in a public welfare agency. In *On records: Files and dossiers in American life*, ed. S. Wheeler, 319–54. New York: Russell Sage Foundation.

———. 1992. The interactional organization of calls for emergency assistance. In *Talk at work*, ed. Paul Drew and John Heritage, 418–69. Cambridge: Cambridge University Press.

Zimmerman, D. H., and D. Boden. 1991. Structure-in-action: An introduction. In *Talk and social structure: Studies in ethnomethodology and conversation analysis*, ed. D. Boden and D. H. Zimmerman. Berkeley: University of California Press.

accountability: circuits, 173–77, 180, 184, 193, 211, 219; institutional, 113, 118, 155, 156–57, 179, 185–86, 191, 216, 218; in institutional ethnography, 136; and work organization, 79, 174–77, 216

accounting, 174–77, 193, 211, 215; and organization, 15–16, 169

action, 53–54, 64–65, 72n16, 76; circuit of, 159, 162, 170, 211; coordination of, 58, 63, 84; institutional, 3, 186–87, 188, 190–91, 197, 199, 211; judicial sequences of, 67, 170–73, 174. *See also* activity; sequences of action

active text. *See* text

activation. *See* textual activation

activism, 28–29, 32, 39–40, 42, 44n2, 45n4, 118–19, 150–51, 160, 180, 208, 221

activity, 54–57, 104–5, 162, 166, 209; coordination of, 57–60, 63, 64, 68, 80, 90–92, 95, 104, 133

activity theory, 72n12

actual. *See* actualities

actualities, 2–3, 22, 31, 42, 54–57, 96n4, 113, 125–26, 194–95, 215, 219, 223; and categories, 188–89; and concepts, 54–56; and coordination, 69–70; and institutional discourse, 123, 156–57, 186, 195; and institutions, 34, 113, 188, 197; mapping, 160–61; and method of inquiry, 10, 22, 24, 29, 50, 51–53, 57, 68, 70, 209; and processing interchanges, 143, 171–73, 177–78, 180, 227

administration, 174–77, 179–80

agent. *See* agency

agency, 25, 44, 54–56, 111–13, 122n7, 123–24, 132, 173, 183, 187, 223; and institutional discourses, 117, 127; and the ruling relations, 10, 14, 22–23, 183–84; of women, 10, 22–23. *See also* reading; subject; subjectivity

AIDS, 150, 157, 207

alienation, 7, 21, 53

Alexander, Jeffrey, 50, 53, 55

Althusser, Louis, 38, 71n9, 71n10

Anderson, R. J., 156

Anyon, Jean, 29–31, 34, 43

Archimedean point, 29, 53

assembling work knowledge, 157–61, 166, 211

"assymetries of power" (Briggs), 136–38, 141

Austin, John L., 95n3

Bakhtin, Mikhail, 2, 50, 62, 65–66, 68, 86, 95, 123, 127, 129, 142, 210

Bal, Mieke, 109, 121n3

bathhouse raid, 40, 193–98, 199–200, 212

"bawdy house" laws, 194–98, 200, 211, 215

Bazerman, Charles, 55, 65

Beck, John, 213–14

bias, 42, 193

Blalock, Hubert, 55

blob-ontology, 56, 58–59

Blumer, Herbert, 64

Boden, Deirdre, 88–89, 94

bourgeoisie, 57, 62

Bourdieu, Pierre, 56, 59, 184–85

Briggs, Charles, 136–37

Brown, Deborah, 163n5

Burawoy, Michael, 29, 35–36, 37–38, 43, 49

bureaucracy, 10, 15, 17, 55–56

bus stop (Watson), 103–4, 106, 120

Butler, Judith, 124, 126, 142

Campbell, Marie, 4n1, 45n5, 189–90, 198

Canadian Broadcasting Corporation (CBC), 18

capital, 56–57, 60–62, 134, 219; "cultural," 56

capitalism, 14–17, 21, 152, 163n7, 215, 219; mode of production of, 56, 69

capture. *See* institutional capture
Cartesian dichotomy. *See* mind-body
   duality
case, 170–73, 180, 211; as genre, 171,
   173; judicial, 65, 67, 170–73, 174,
   180, 184, 211; as linear sequence,
   170–73, 180, 211; manager
   interview, 189–90, 198; needs
   assessment, 189–90, 198; studies in
   institutional ethnography, 51,
   213–19; union grievance, 117
categories, 31; criminal code, 197–98,
   199, 200, 211; institutional, 32–33,
   68, 117, 120, 122n9, 155, 188–89, 191,
   196–98, 199
Chandler, Norman, 15–16
Chomsky, Noam, 58, 79, 96
Cicourel, Aaron, 125, 142
Cable News Network (CNN), 18
circuit: of accountability, 173–77, 180,
   184, 193, 211, 219; of action, 159, 162,
   170, 211. *See also* sequences of action
class, 8, 10, 25n1, 30–31, 36, 61–62, 69,
   97n10, 117, 217; reproduction of,
   19–20, 37
code: convict, 66, 133; criminal, 193–98,
   199, 200, 211; restricted and
   elaborated (Bernstein), 97n10
Code, Lorraine, 27, 28, 186
colonialism, 8, 10, 62
commodity, 56–57, 60, 134, 163n8
community college, 174–76, 180, 193,
   211
complex: of discourses, 68;
   institutional, 51, 68, 162, 206, 213,
   217, 220; language as, 65; of
   organizations, 68
concept, 24, 43, 50, 54–57, 64, 70,
   76–77, 118, 134–35, 160, 209, 212,
   216; of consciousness, 14, 69; of
   discourse, 17–18, 25, 127; of "dog,"
   84, 87, 94, 111; of domination, 36; of
   economy, 56–57, 60, 134; of "family
   violence," 45n4, 118; of frame, 191;
   as generalizer, 135; in institutional
   processes, 32–33, 187, 191; and
   nominalization, 55; of "norms" 55,
   59, 64, 113; and ontology, 56, 209,
   226; of social organization, 160, 227;
   of "rules," 54–55, 58, 59, 64–67,

95n3, 113, 188; of the ruling
   relations, 13, 16, 69, 227; of "secret,"
   109–11, 114, 121n3; and social
   relations, 56–57; of social relations,
   158, 227–28; speech acts, 95n3; of
   "structure," 38, 54–56, 58–59, 60,
   209; of "system," 35–36, 37, 54, 58,
   209; of "table," 85, 87–88, 111; of
   text, 166, 228; of textual activation,
   105; and words, 85, 111–12; of work,
   125, 151–55, 157, 161, 210
conceptual practices, 31, 44n2, 55–56,
   68, 118
consciousness, 11, 14, 22, 25, 69, 79,
   108; disjuncture in, 11–13, 20–21;
   and language, 76–77; middle class,
   14, 19; objectification of, 17–18,
   25n1, 184; and the ruling relations,
   13–14, 20–21, 69; and the social,
   58–59, 75, 80, 94, 184; and texts, 167,
   184; universalized, 13, 62
context, 67, 73n18, 80, 135
conversational analysis, 60, 67, 71n2,
   73n17, 88, 98n11, 162, 168, 182n2
convicts, 66, 133
coordinate. *See* coordination, null
   point, system of coordination
coordination, 65–68, 71n11, 223; of
   action, 58, 63, 67, 84; of activities,
   57–60, 63–64, 68, 80, 90–92, 95, 104,
   133; and actualities, 69–70;
   dialogical, 65–68, 103; of the
   everyday, 18, 24, 36, 43, 129–30,
   132–33; of experience, 43–44, 60–62,
   125, 151, 209; and historical
   processes, 56, 65–68, 108; and
   institutions, 2, 63, 118–19, 132–33,
   142; and language, 2–3, 75–76,
   76–77, 79–80, 80–83, 86, 94–95, 185;
   of mother's work, 34, 133, 158; and
   the social, 57–60, 70, 80, 94, 96n4,
   211; and social relations, 36, 69; of
   subjectivity, 17–18, 75–76, 80–83,
   96n4, 185, 210; translocal, 2, 13, 37,
   41–42, 103, 166; of work, 111, 118,
   120, 132, 135, 151, 158, 160, 161–63,
   167, 170, 191, 211. *See also* textual
   coordination
corporations, 10, 69, 132, 163n7, 166,
   183, 214–15

courses of action. *See* sequences: of action
course of reading, 108–11
criminal code, 193–98, 199, 200, 211

Darville, Richard, 97n9, 121n4, 121n7, 121n8, 201n2
Darwin, Charles, 81, 97n6
data dialogue, 125, 135–42, 143, 145, 223; and work knowledge, 149, 150–51, 161–62. *See also* interviewing
Davidoff, Leonore, 14
"deep structure" (Chomsky), 79, 96n4
"defective" families, 32–33, 37, 41
de Montigny, Gerald, 45n4, 139–40, 185–86, 190, 198, 207
Derrida, Jacques, 24
Descartes, Rene, 23, 75, 79
determination, 10, 18, 36, 37, 44, 64–66, 126, 127, 184, 189, 206; "under-," (Bazerman), 55, 64–65
Devault, Marjorie, 152–54, 163n1, 163n6
devices. *See* textual devices
dialogic: 50, 57, 65–68, 119, 161; and coordination, 65–68, 103; and experience, 61, 124–28, 129–30, 135, 139, 142, 162; and interviewing, 128, 135–36; and utterance, 65, 126, 127–28. *See also* data dialogues
dialogue. *See* data dialogue, dialogic, primary dialogue, secondary dialogue
Diamond, Tim, 152, 178–80, 181, 208
difference, 31, 61–63, 87, 146, 211, 224; and language, 84; and perspective, 62–63, 70, 91, 209; power, 136–37, 138; and the social, 60–64, 70
discourse, 1, 17, 22, 25, 31, 68, 127, 135–36, 216–17, 224; academic, 104, 137, 206; concept of, 17–18, 25, 127; and experience, 7, 9, 105, 126; ideological, 217, 219, 224; of institutional ethnography, 40, 136; management, 111–12, 162, 206, 214–15, 217; mothering, 19–20, 51, 141; order of (Foucault), 17–18, 49, 71n1, 127, 224; and poststructuralism, 126; public, 9, 14, 18, 217–18; and regulation, 17, 105,

108, 187; ruling relations and, 10, 17, 22, 111; scientific, 111–12, 186–87; sociological, 10–11, 22, 31, 39, 49, 52–56, 137. *See also* ideology; institutional discourse
discourse analysis, 170
disjuncture, 11–13, 20–21, 176, 187–89, 194, 198, 199, 205
Dobson, Stephan, 117, 141, 153
"documents in action" (Prior), 102–3
domestic sphere, 14–15, 19–20, 62
domestic: abuse, 63–65, 67, 117, 159, 170–73, 174, 180, 188, 194, 199, 207, 211, 221; violence, 45n4, 118, 170
dominance, 24, 27, 36, 38, 71n11, 185, 220; male, 71n11, 124; racial, 62; white, 9, 19
Douglas, Mary, 26n6
DuPont, 15
Duranti, Alessandro, 73n18
Durkheim, Émile, 58

embodiment, 21–22, 23–25, 53–54, 126, 128, 167; and the ruling relations, 11–13, 28, 165
empiricism, 8
Engels, Frederick, 54, 56, 69, 72n12, 209
Engeström, Yrjö, 72n12
Enlightenment, 14, 62, 220
epistemology, 8, 52, 54, 62, 188; Harding's, 9–10. *See also* knowledge
essentialism, 9, 25n1
ethical review processes, 35, 45n3, 137. *See also* asymmetries of power
ethnography, 31, 35–36, 38–39, 42, 43–44, 49, 63–64, 102, 135, 150–51; of news room, 133–34; of reading, 92–93, 106
ethnomethodology, 2, 52, 60, 66, 67, 71n2, 72n15, 72n16, 88, 103–4, 121n2
everyday, 7, 12, 23, 33, 43, 61, 90, 135; coordination of the, 18, 24, 36, 43, 129–30, 132–33; as problematic, 39–41, 43, 49, 51, 104, 181, 207, 213; ruling relations and the, 10, 44, 101, 134, 213; worlds, 2–3, 24, 32, 34, 39, 51, 52, 123, 206–7. *See also* experience
events, 107, 131, 142, 191

experience, 1–3, 27, 80–81, 83–86, 105, 111, 114, 122n8, 124, 129, 151, 154–55, 191, 199, 224; as authorative, 126, 138–39, 141; beginning in, 11, 24, 31, 34, 41, 207; coordination of, 43–44, 60–62, 125, 151, 209; differences in, 60–63, 70; and dialogics, 61, 124–28, 129–30, 135, 139, 142, 162; and discourse, 7, 9, 105, 126; embodied, 23, 24, 53–54; and institutional ethnography, 3, 10–11, 43–44, 61, 123–26, 139–40, 142, 210; and interindividual territories, 86–87, 88–92, 95, 97n9, 97n10, 129, 210, 226; and knowledge, 64, 124–25, 142, 149; and language, 1, 78, 128–35; mapping, 29; and method of inquiry, 10–11, 24, 44, 125, 158, 221; and problematic, 38–43, 45n4, 49, 51, 68, 104, 157; and social organization, 128–35, 159–60; subsumption of, 115–16, 120–21, 155–56, 179; and texts, 28, 76, 86–95; and utterance, 127–28; of women, 7–9, 64; and the women's movement, 7–8, 11–12, 13, 18, 45n4, 78–79, 127
extended case study method (Burawoy), 29, 35–36, 37–38, 44n2, 49

facts, 27, 50, 107, 115, 131, 124, 191. *See also* events
"family violence," 45n4, 118
feminism, 8, 23, 25n1, 28, 136, 152, 154. *See also* women's movement
field notes, 136, 137–38, 142, 143
Fordism, 20
Foucault, Michel, 17–18; discourse concept of, 17–18, 49, 71n1, 127, 224
Fox News Channel, 218
frame, 50, 53, 191; institutional, 115–16, 118–19, 216. *See also* regulatory frames
Friedan, Betty, 19, 78–79
Fulton College, 174–77, 180

Gardiner, Michael, 62
Garfinkel, Harold, 50, 71n8, 72n15, 113
gay men, 40, 193–98

generalization, 42, 86, 166–67; in institutional ethnography, 51, 135, 219; and institutions, 44, 113, 186, 206
gender, 8, 10, 24, 62, 67, 117; historical trajectory of, 13–20, 20–21; order, 14–15, 109; organization, 10, 14–15; and the ruling relations, 19, 20, 165
General Motors, 15, 16
generative grammar (Chomsky), 58, 79, 96n4
gesture, 80–82, 97n7, 153–54
Giddens, Anthony, 53, 54, 58, 59, 64
Giltrow, Janet, 111–13, 120, 162
Goodwin, Charles, 71n2, 73n18
Goodwin, Majorie Harness, 71n2, 75–76, 79, 88–90, 98n11
"ghetto schooling," 29, 34
Glaser, Barney G., 135, 160
Glazer, Nona, 154
Goffman, Erving, 201n4
grading, 145–49, 161
Grahame, Kamini, 45n4, 139
Grahame, Peter, 4n1
Gregor, Frances, 4n1, 45n5
Griffith, Alison, 32–33, 36–37, 40–41, 45n4, 51, 132–33, 136, 141, 158, 207, 210
Grosz, Elizabeth, 23–24
grounded theory, 63, 135, 160

Habermas, Jürgen, 14, 19
habitus (Bourdieu), 59
Hall, Catherine, 14
Halliday, Michael A. K., 75, 80, 86, 97n5, 111, 122n5
Hanks, William E., 85, 93
Harding, Sandra, 8, 9–10
Hartsock, Nancy, 8, 10, 25n1
health and safety, 130–32
Hegel, George W. F., 8, 52
Heidegger, Martin, 52
Hempel, Carl, 54
hermeneutics, 35, 50–51
historical materialism, 25n1
historical trajectory: of the ruling relations, 13–20, 20–25, 26n1; of gender, 13–20, 20–21
history, 56–57, 62, 124, 129, 134; and dialogics, 65–68

Hobbes, Thomas, 64
hooking, 66, 215, 198, 228; into discourses, 136, 216; into institutional relations, 207, 208; into larger organization, 39–41, 87, 143, 169
housewives, 13, 20–21, 22, 43, 62, 152, 153, 210

idealism, 54, 69, 184
ideology, 14, 25, 33, 45n4, 94, 143n1, 140, 154, 201n5, 209; and discourse, 217, 219, 224; German, 54, 71n7
immigrant women, 45n4, 139
imperialism, 10, 62
indexicality, 224; mapping and, 29, 52, 161
inequality, 34, 41
individuation, 57–59, 67, 79, 95n3
informal learning, 130, 139, 140–41, 144n2
inquiry. *See* method of inquiry
institutional action, 3, 186–87, 188, 190–91, 197, 199, 211
institutional capture, 127, 119, 155–57, 214, 225. *See also* subsumption of experience
institutional complexes, 51, 68, 162, 206, 213, 217, 220. *See also* ruling relations
institutional discourse, 3, 104, 105, 118–19, 120–21, 127, 140, 179, 187, 206, 210, 216, 225; and actualities, 123, 156–57, 186, 195; and institutional capture, 155–57; monologies of, 123–24; and nominalization, 111–12, 120; and power, 120, 191, 193; and subjectivity, 155; text-reader conversations of, 111–17, 120, 187, 210; and shells, 112–13. *See also* regulatory frames
institutional ethnography, 1–3, 29–38, 49–50, 68, 94, 101, 103–4, 160–61, 180–81, 205–6, 225; and concepts, 55–56, 70, 160; case studies in, 51, 213–19; collective work of, 3, 212, 219–22; and data, 210–11; discourse of, 40, 136; and discovery, 1–3, 10, 21, 24, 41, 49, 51, 55, 104, 134, 139–40, 142–43, 151, 162, 207–8, 218; and experience, 3, 10–11, 43–44, 61, 123–26, 139–40, 142, 210; generalization in, 51, 135, 219; goals of, 1, 29, 49–51, 55, 59, 206, 209, 219; and history, 56–57, 129; ontology and, 2, 4n1, 57–58, 59, 69–70, 123–24, 158, 181, 219; and power, 183–85, 199–200; as practice, 3, 55–56, 57, 95, 119, 218; and the ruling relations, 205–6; and the social, 29, 59, 80; and standpoint, 32, 42, 68, 104; teaching, 70; and texts, 167–68, 170–73, 173–77, 177–80, 180–81, 182n4, 184; and theory, 49–50, 57, 70, 94, 206–7, 208–9; and universality, 62–63, 160. *See also* knowledge; method of inquiry; ontology
institutional processes, 31–32, 34–35, 40–44, 51, 60, 71, 207
institutional reality, 186, 187–91
institutional regime (G. W. Smith), 122n10
institutions, 17, 32–33, 71, 101, 104, 118–19, 132–33, 135, 137, 142, 155, 156–57, 163, 179, 183–87, 191, 196–98, 217, 220, 225; and the actual, 34, 113, 188, 197; as complexes, 51, 68, 162, 206, 213, 217, 220; and difference, 61; and generalization, 44, 113, 186, 206; language and, 2–3, 68–69; large-scale, 61, 184, 200, 206, 212; mapping of, 3, 157–58, 160–61; and power, 193–94, 199–200; as research focus, 33, 103–4; and standardization, 108, 113, 133, 135, 206, 219; and texts, 3, 44, 68–69, 108, 118–19, 181, 185, 212, 213; and work, 113, 135, 186. *See also* accountability; frame; organization
instructions for reading, 109–11, 114–16, 120, 187
Itard, Jean-Marc, 83–84
intelligentsia, 34, 219
intention, 28, 29, 53, 56, 65, 152, 154, 183–84, 210; writer's, 17, 124, 126, 127
interindividual territories, 76–79, 83–86, 86–94, 95, 210, 226;

experience-based, 88–92, 95, 97n9, 97n10, 129, 210, 226; text-based, 88, 90–94, 95, 97n10, 210, 226
interrogation, 138, 189–91
interrogatory devices, 191, 226
intersubjectivity (Schutz), 59, 77
intertextuality, 118, 185–87, 212, 213, 219, 221, 226
interviewing, 31; and dialogics, 128; and ignorance, 138–39, 141, 142, 153; institutional ethnography and, 33–34, 63, 125, 128, 135–42, 150, 158–60, 207; and preconceptions, 137–41, 142–43; and power asymmetries, 136–38, 138, 141. *See also* data dialogues; participant observation; primary dialogue; secondary dialogue

Jackendoff, Ray, 79–80
Jackson, Nancy, 133–34
judicial processes, 63–65, 67, 117, 159, 170–73, 174

Keller, Evelyn Fox, 109–11
Keller, Helen, 78, 86, 97n7, 111; Knowledge of, 1, 8, 17, 19, 44, 67, 121; as empirical, 55; as experiential, 64, 124–25, 142, 149; as expert, 24, 43, 52–53, 142–43, 154–55; and institutional ethnography, 1–2, 10, 29, 32, 36, 37–38, 42, 43, 49, 51, 52–53, 71, 129, 206; objectification and, 8, 18, 22–23, 62, 69, 206; and organization, 19, 27, 37–38, 206; and power, 19; standpoint and, 9, 24; and subjectivity, 17, 129. *See also* work knowledge
Kristeva, Julia, 107, 169
Kuhn, Thomas, 2

Landes, Joan, 14–15, 21
language, 2–3, 65, 68–69, 76–77, 93; and children, 83, 84–85; and coordination, 2–3, 65, 73n18, 75–76, 76–77, 79–80, 80–83, 86, 94–95, 185; experience and, 1, 78, 128–35; and gender, 67; "insufficiency of" (Devault), 153; and ontology, 3, 210; and the ruling relations, 69; and the

social, 70, 75–76, 76–86, 80; and social organization, 129–35, 138, 142, 210; and subjectivity, 3, 75–76, 76–77, 80–83, 185; and symbolic power (Bourdieu), 184–85; and texts, 68–69, 80, 184; and theory, 94, 126
langue, 65, 75
Lapham, Lewis, 218
law. *See* "bawdy house" law
Leont'ev, Alexei N., 72n12
lesbians, 8
linguistics, 65, 73n18, 75–76, 79, 87, 94, 96n4, 97n5, 111, 112, 166
Lioncelli, Stephanie, 216
Luria, Alexander R., 2, 83–86, 87, 95, 129, 210
Lynch, Michael, 186–87
Lyotard, Jean-François, 71n9

Manicom, Ann, 36, 41
Malinowski, Bronislaw, 80
mapping, 2, 3, 29, 151, 177–78, 206, 226; as indexical, 29, 52, 161; institutions, 3, 157–58, 160–61; the ruling relations, 51; sequences of action, 158–59, 160; social organization, 11, 29; social relations, 35; work knowledges, 157–61
Marco (steelworker), 130–32, 135, 138, 140, 151, 215
Martin, James, 111
Marx, Karl, 2, 15, 17, 25n1, 50, 54, 56–57, 60, 61–62, 71n7, 71n9, 71n10, 134, 209; concept of consciousness in, 14, 69; ontology of Engels and, 54, 56, 69, 72n12, 209
Marxism, 2, 154, 184, 217. *See also* historical materialism
mass media, 10, 18, 183, 219–20. *See also* news media
"masquerade of universality" (Landes), 14–15, 21
master-slave parable, 8
Maurer, David, 129–30
McCoy, Liza, 106, 121n1, 162, 163n1, 166, 174–77, 180, 193, 211, 215, 216, 218–19
McDermid, Val, 109–10, 114
McHoul, Alec, 92–93, 94, 106
McLean, C., 189, 191, 198
McRobbie, Angela, 136

Mead, George Herbert, 2, 11, 50, 59–60, 64, 72n13, 75–76, 80–82, 84–86, 87, 94, 95, 97n6, 110, 111, 162, 210
meaning, 55–56, 63, 65, 80–83, 93, 108, 110–11, 126, 132; "underdetermination of" (Bazerman), 55, 64–65
men, 40, 71n11, 118, 193–98, 124; work of, 14–15, 20, 36–37, 62, 153
Mending the Sacred Hoop, 188, 198
mental illness, 54, 58, 106, 114
Messer-Davidow, Ellen, 217–18
metaphors, 56, 71, 184
method of inquiry, 1–3, 10–11, 24–25, 29, 31–35, 36–38, 40, 49–51, 51–53, 63, 68–71, 104, 135; and actualities, 10, 22, 24, 29, 50, 51–53, 57, 68, 70, 209; and experience, 10–11, 24, 44, 125, 158, 221; and interviewing, 31, 33–34, 63, 125, 128, 135–42, 150, 158–60, 207; and observation, 52, 133, 135–38, 142, 145, 162–63, 199, 208–9; and power, 183–84; and problematic, 24–25, 31, 38, 49, 51, 68, 70, 104, 206–7; and the ruling relations, 185, 198, 200, 213. *See also* institutional ethnography
micro and macro division, 35–36, 62
middle class: 14–15, 19–20, 25n1, 97n10, 133, 138; parents, 37, 133; mothers, 133, 158–59; women, 8–9, 14–15, 19–20, 34, 136; white, 9, 19, 20
mind-body dichotomy, 23–25, 75–76, 165
models, 7–8, 51, 53, 58, 65–66, 72n12
monologic, 50, 62; and concepts, 160; of institutional discourse, 123–24; and the ruling relations, 123; of sociology, 50, 123–24
mothering discourse, 19–20, 51, 141
mothers' work, 10, 11–13, 36–37, 51, 132–33, 136; and schooling, 32–34, 132–33, 157–59, 162, 210–11
Moya, Paula, 125–26, 142
municipal land use planning, 39–41, 118–19, 151, 157–58, 177–80, 181, 183–84, 217
mystery novel, 109–11

naming, 7, 78–79, 111. *See also* nominalization

Naples, Nancy, 216
natural science, 27, 109, 206
Navaho filmmakers, 157
needs assessment, 189–90, 198–99
neoliberalism, 217, 220
new deal, 219
"new public managerialism," 217
news media, 18–19, 91–94, 98n12, 114–15, 134–35, 191–93, 217–18. *See also* mass media
newsroom ethnography, 133–34
Newton, Isaac, 111, 122n5
Ng, Roxana, 45n4
nominalization, 43, 85, 122n5, 134–35; and institutional discourse, 111–12, 120; in mainstream sociology, 54–55
"norms," 55, 59, 64, 113
null point (Schutz), 90
nurses, 40, 45n4, 178–80

"objective organization" (Sloan), 15
objectivity, 8, 43, 28–29, 148; of institutions, 44; social relations of, 28–29; and sociology, 42, 160
objectification, 11, 18, 31, 63, 67–68, 104, 186; of consciousness, 17–18, 25n1, 184; and institutional discourse, 120; and knowledge, 8, 10, 18, 22–23, 27–28, 58, 62, 69, 206; and representation, 27–28, 206; and the ruling relations, 13–14, 22–23, 25n1, 44, 69, 123; of the subject, 10, 22, 52–53; and texts, 28, 44; of the women's movement, 28
operationalization, 110, 199
ontology, 35, 58, 226; "blob," 56, 58–59; and concepts, 56, 209; and institutional ethnography, 2, 4n1, 50, 57–58, 59, 69–70, 123–24, 158, 181, 219; and language, 3, 210; of Marx and Engels, 54, 56, 69, 72n12, 209; of the social, 3, 51–54, 59, 75, 167, 208–10
order: gender, 14–15, 109; of discourse (Foucault), 17–18, 49, 71n1; institutional, 33, 43, 208; "problem" of, 64–65, 67, 72n15
organization, 5, 11–13, 32, 34, 55, 57, 61, 68, 73n18; of experience, 83–86; gendered, 10, 14–15; knowledge and, 19, 27, 37–38, 206; large-scale,

61, 184, 200, 206, 212; objectified, 13, 69; of perception, 84–85, 129; and power, 19, 44n1, 163, 200; and ruling relations, 69, 119; and text-mediation, 179, 181; translocal, 10, 13, 19, 22, 38, 41, 69, 103, 119, 169–70, 205; and words, 69, 84–85, 108, 129; work and, 69, 84–85, 108, 137, 146–48, 174–77, 179, 211, 216

Parent Corps, 31–32
parents, 11, 32–33, 37, 41, 45n4, 133
parole, 65, 75
Parsons, Talcott, 59, 64
participant observation, 30, 35, 125, 150, 160. *See also* interviewing
patriarchy, 25n1
Pence, Ellen, 32, 63, 67, 143, 170–73, 177, 180, 188, 194, 207, 221
performative utterance (Austin), 95n3
Personal Responsibility and Work Opportunity Reconciliation Act (1996), 216
people: 40, 60; sociology for, 10, 38, 220; standpoint of 1, 28, 38, 68, 70–71
perception, 84–85, 129
Perkin, Harold, 26n4
Perrow, Charles, 56
perspective, 10, 31, 34, 123, 156; and difference, 62–63, 70, 91, 209; "problem" of, 43. *See also* standpoint
phenomenology, 23, 58, 77; philosophy, 23–24, 87, 111, 123
photographs, 106–7, 121n1, 166
pickpockets, 129–30
Pierce, Charles, 85
police, 67, 71n11, 92; and Berkeley incident, 114–17; and domestic abuse, 63, 159, 199, 207, 211, 221; raid on bathhouse, 40, 193–98, 199–200, 211; report, 171–73, 193–98, 211, 221
"politico-administrative regime" (G. W. Smith), 151
political economy, 10, 31, 34, 36, 57, 71n6, 163n7
political orientation, 42, 44n2, 193, 207–8
positivism, 28, 54
postmodernism, 62, 71n9, 95n3, 220

poststructuralism, 126
power, 17, 19, 44n1, 25n1, 120, 163, 190–91, 193, 200, 226; assymetries in interviewing, 136–38, 141; and institutional ethnography, 183–85, 199–200; and institutions, 193–94, 199–200; and knowledge, 19; language and symbolic (Bourdieu), 184–85; and method of inquiry, 183–84; and sociological theory, 29, 55
primary dialogue, 136–37, 142–43
primary narrative, 143n1
"primitive accumulation," 62
print, 13–14, 15, 18, 20, 93, 166. *See also* texts
Prior, Lindsay, 102–3; problematic, 24, 31, 37–38, 45n5, 104, 145, 159–60, 161, 206–8, 227; everyday world as, 39–41, 43, 49, 51, 104, 181, 207, 213; and experience, 38–43, 45n4, 49, 51, 68, 104, 157; method of inquiry and, 24–25, 31, 38, 49, 51, 68, 70, 104, 206–7; and ontology, 51–52; and ruling relations, 41; and standpoint, 24–25, 38, 39, 70, 159, 206–7
processing interchange, 143, 171–73, 177–78, 180, 227
professions, 17, 25n1, 34, 190–91, 206
proletariat, 62. *See also* working class
psychology, 72n12, 83
public: discourse, 9, 14, 18, 217–18; service, 218, 219; sphere, 9, 14–15, 19, 21, 36–37, 92
pulp mills, 213–14, 218

race, 8–9, 10, 20, 30–31, 62, 117, 136, 139–40
Rankin, Janet, 45n4, 218
"rationality," 69, 113
reading, 19, 28, 82, 91–93, 97n9, 103–4, 105–8, 108–11, 119, 167; and agency, 105, 108–9, 111, 114–15, 116–17; instructions for, 109–11, 114–16, 120, 187. *See also* textual activation; course of reading
reification, 67–68. *See also* objectification
regulation, 50, 66, 105, 108, 132, 133, 140, 169, 173, 183, 187, 188, 198, 200, 215, 217

regulatory frames: 19, 34, 44, 50, 163n7, 191–98, 212, 213, 219, 227; concept of, 191; and discourse, 17, 187; and power, 191, 193, 199–200; sociological, 28, 50; reification, 2, 58–59, 60, 64. *See also* objectification
Reimer, Marilee, 191–92
representation, 28, 107, 123, 126, 146–47, 219; institutional, 186, 188, 197, 211, 215; in institutional ethnography, 40; objectified, 27–28, 206
reproduction, 23, 58; class, 19–20, 34, 37; of inequality, 34, 41
resistance, 36
responses (Mead), 87–88
restructuring, 29–30, 45n4, 174–77, 180, 211, 216, 220
Reynolds, Tracey, 138
"riot," 93–94, 98n12
risk assessment procedure, 155
"role," 55
Rose, Hilary, 8
Rousseau, Jean Jacques, 25n2
"rules," 54–55, 58, 59, 64–67, 95n3, 113, 188
ruling relations, 3, 58, 69, 111, 212, 205–6, 219–20; agency and, 10, 14, 22–23, 183–84; concept of the, 13, 16, 69, 227; and discourse, 10, 17, 22, 111; and the everyday, 10, 44, 101, 134, 213; extended, 29, 213, 218; and gender, 19, 20, 165; historical trajectory of the, 13–20, 20–25, 26n1; mapping, 51; and method of inquiry, 185, 198, 200, 213; and objectification, 13–14, 22–23, 25n1, 44, 69, 123; and ontology, 58, 68–69; and problematic, 41; standpoint and, 9–13, 20–25, 205; and texts, 18, 27–28, 86, 101, 103, 119, 163, 165–66, 181, 184–85, 187, 200, 219. *See also* institutional complexes

Salzinger, Leslie, 44n2
Saussure, Ferdinand de, 65, 75–76, 81, 85, 93, 97n6, 126
schema, 201n4
school, 17, 19–20, 29–34, 36, 45n4, 132–33, 211. *See also* mothers' work
Schiller, Herbert, 220

Schmid, Hans-Jörg, 112–13, 197, 201n4
Schutz, Alfred, 20–21, 59, 90
Scott, Joan, 124–26, 129, 142
scripts, 187, 189–90, 199
Searle, John, 95n3
secondary dialogue, 136, 137–38, 142–43
"secret," 109–11, 114, 121n3
Securities and Exchange Commission, 215
sequences of action, 97n4, 67, 103–4, 107, 110, 116–17, 136–37, 158–59, 174, 211; judicial sequences of, 67, 170–73, 174; and text-reader conversations, 112–13, 187, 212; and texts, 120, 167–68, 170–73, 177, 180–81, 199–200, 213
sequences of "communication," 97n6
"shell" (Schmid), 112–13, 116, 197, 200, 201n4
significant symbol (Mead), 78, 80–83, 86, 97n7
signs, 65, 78, 80–81, 103
Simmel, Georg, 58
Sloan, Alfred, 15, 16
Smith, Dorothy E., 4n1, 10, 11–13, 21–22, 32–33, 36–37, 40–41, 45n4, 51, 70, 132–34, 136, 138, 141, 153, 158, 207, 211
Smith, George W., 4n1, 40, 122n10, 123, 150–51, 151n3, 193–94, 197–98, 199, 207, 212, 219
social, the, 1, 10–11, 44, 50, 60–64, 65, 70, 76–77, 227; and consciousness, 58–59, 75, 80, 184; coordination of, 57–60, 70, 80, 96n4, 211; and goal of institutional ethnography, 29, 59; as happening, 64–68; and language, 70, 75–76, 76–86, 80; ontology of, 3, 51–54, 59, 75, 167, 208–10; reifications of, 58–59, 206
social organization, 15–18, 41, 124, 160, 227; and experience, 128–35, 159–60; generalization of, 166–67; and knowledge, 27, 206; and language, 129–35, 138, 142, 210; mapping, 11, 29
social relations, 1, 11, 14, 18, 28–29, 34–35, 69, 158, 227–28; capitalism and, 56–57, 61–62, 134; class and, 36; concepts and, 56–57;

disappearance of, 134; of the economy, 24, 31, 40, 213; extended, 39, 35–36, 37, 43, 213, 218; institutional ethnographic research and, 34–35, 136; of knowledge, 29; mapping, 35; problematic and, 41–42; of schooling, 31–32; ruling relations and, 13, 18, 24, 31, 40, 213, 218; texts and, 101, 199
"social-semiotics," 80
social structure. *See* structure
social system. *See* system
social work(ing), 139–40, 155, 185–86, 190, 199, 207
sociology, 36, 56, 62; alternative, 7, 10, 24; and epistemology, 62; for people, 10, 38, 220; mainstream, 1–3, 13, 21, 28–29, 31, 42, 44, 49–50, 52–54, 54–56, 58–59, 64–65, 70, 111, 123–24, 160, 206; metaphors in, 56; as monological, 50, 123–24; nominalization in, 54–55; objectification in, 28–29, 52–53, 54–56, 58–59, 60, 64, 209; objectivity of, 42, 160; phenomenological, 59, 77; for people, 10, 38, 220; as practice, 3, 13, 49, 55–56; qualitative, 2, 42, 50; and women, 10, 24. *See also* discourse; theory
social work(ing), 45n4
"Standard North American Family," 33–34
speech, 65, 91, 93, 97n5, 97n10
speech acts (Searle), 95n3
speech genre (Bakhtin), 126, 127, 129–30, 142, 180; primary, 86, 95; secondary, 86–87, 95
standardization, 85–86, 163n8, 186–87, 188–89; institutional, 108, 113, 133, 135, 206, 219; and interrogation, 189; and regulation, 188, 200; and report writing, 155; and texts, 155, 169, 186–87; translocal, 118
standpoint, 9–10, 12, 32–33, 39, 133, 147–48, 205–6, 206–8, 214; of academic discourse, 104; of the city, 98; feminist, 8, 10, 25n1; of gay men, 194; of immigrant women, 45n4; and institutional ethnography, 32, 42, 68, 104; of

mothers, 33; of people, 1, 28, 38, 68, 70–71, 206; as problematic, 24–25, 38, 39, 70, 159, 206–7; of women, 1, 7–9, 24, 33, 159, 165. *See also* women's standpoint
stasis of texts, 102, 104, 105, 112, 119, 167
steel work, 130–32, 135, 138, 139, 140–41, 144n2, 151
Stock, Andree, 155
stories: 18, 28, 33, 43, 63, 88–91, 95, 97n9, 97n10, 124, 143. *See also* news media
Strauss, Anselm L., 135, 160
"structure," 38, 54–56, 58–59, 60, 64–68, 71n9, 79–80, 96n4, 126, 209
"structuration" (Giddens), 58, 59
stylistics, 71n5
subject: disappearance of, 36, 43, 52–54, 55–56, 103, 111, 113, 117, 123–24, 122n7, 214; individuating the, 57–59, 67, 79, 95; objectified, 10, 22, 52–53; position and standpoint, 9–10, 13, 28, 41; universal, 8, 14–15, 21–23, 28–29, 62
"subjective organization" (Sloan), 15
subjectivity, 8–9, 11–13, 25, 41, 43, 52–53, 57–59, 117, 124, 187; coordination of, 17–18, 75–76, 80–83, 96n4, 185, 210; disjuncture in, 21–24, 205; and gender, 20–21; and institutional discourse, 155; and knowledge, 17, 129; and language, 3, 75–76, 76–77, 80–83, 185; and the social, 94; male, 14, 23, 25n1; of women, 22–23, 79; and work, 154–55
subsumption, 115–16, 120–21, 155–56, 179, 195, 198, 199–200. *See also* institutional capture
Suicide Prevention Center, 113
Sullivan, Anne Mansfield, 78
symbolic communication (Mead), 59–60, 77–78, 162
symbolic interactionism, 2
"symbolic power" (Bourdieu), 184–85
"system," 35–36, 37, 54, 58, 64, 80, 209; of signs, 65
systems of coordination (Schutz), 86, 90, 93

talk, 67, 76, 132–35, 137; of black children, 88–90; and "context," 67; media, 93–94; of people, 40, 60; of pickpockets, 129–30; and text, 76, 88, 91, 119; in the women's movement, 7
terms, 130, 132–35, 143n1. *See also* word
territories. *See* interindividual territories
text, 12, 13–15, 18, 21–22, 27–28, 44, 97n5, 199, 211–12; and accountability circuits, 173–77, 180; as active, 102–4, 120, 167, 174, 181; concept of, 166, 228; and consciousness, 167, 184; constancy of the, 107–8, 102; and experience, 28, 76, 86–95; hierarchical organization of, 185–87, 212, 213, 215, 216, 219; as institutional coordinators, 118–19; and institutional ethnography, 167–68, 170–73, 173–77, 177–80, 180–81, 182n4, 184; and institutions, 3, 44, 68–69, 108, 118–19, 181, 185, 212, 213; and language, 68–69, 80, 184; photographic, 106–7; replicability of, 19, 165–66, 169, 205–6; and rules, 65, 66, 191; and ruling relations, 18, 27–28, 86, 101, 103, 119, 163, 165–66, 181, 184–85, 187, 200, 219; as secondary speech genre, 86–87, 91; sequences of, 39–40; stasis of, 102, 104, 105, 112, 119, 167, 212; and work, 108, 151, 162–63, 167, 177–78, 181. *See also* interindividual territories; sequences of action; textual coordination
text-reader conversation, 104–11, 121n1, 166–67, 184, 228; as active, 105, 168, 170; and institutional capture, 119; and institutional discourse, 111–17, 120, 187, 210; observing, 106, 167–69; and ontology, 167; sequences of action, 112–13, 187, 212
textual activation, 91, 104, 105–7, 108–11, 120, 121n1, 168–69, 170, 176–77, 180–81. *See also* reading
textual coordination, 38, 102–4, 108, 162–63, 169, 170–80, 184, 212–13;

translocal, 166, 169–70, 173; of work, 166–67, 174, 180–81, 186, 200, 211; of work knowledge, 44, 166–67, 170, 173, 211, 220
textual devices, 56, 120, 188, 193, 199; and interrogation, 191
textual mediation, 104, 173–74, 178–79, 186–87, 199; and coordination, 104, 173, 211; and municipal land-use planning, 39–40; and organization, 179, 181, 205; and the ruling relations, 10, 22
textual reality, 94, 187, 191
theory, 25, 35–38, 52, 54, 76, 79, 134, 217; feminist, 8, 23, 136; of discourse, 127; and institutional ethnography, 49–50, 57, 70, 94, 206–7, 208–9; of language, 94, 126; literary, 65; and postmodernism, 62; sociological, 29, 43, 49–50, 53–56, 58–59, 60, 64–65, 206; standpoint, 8
Thompson, John B., 217
total quality management (TQM), 214
transcripts, 136, 137–38, 142, 143, 149
truth, 8, 15, 21–22, 95n3, 126
Turner, Susan, 39–41, 119, 151, 160, 162, 177–80, 181, 183–84, 217, 221

"underdetermination of meaning" (Bazerman), 55
union, 117, 130–32, 141, 191–93, 199
United Steelworkers of America (USWA) Local 1005, 141
universal grammar. *See* generative grammar
university, 10–11, 17, 19, 21, 22, 166, 217; grading, 145–49, 161
utterance: 77–78, 80, 82–83, 95n3, 112–13; and dialogics, 65, 126, 127–28; and speech genres, 86

Vaitkus, Steven, 77
Vallas, Steven, 213–14
Veblen, Thorstein, 16–17
verbal generalization system (Luria), 83–84, 86
Victor. *See* wild boy of Aveyron
violence, 45n4, 118, 71n11, 170
Vološinov, Valentin N., 2, 75–76, 76, 77, 80, 95, 210, 226

von Glasersfeld, Ernst, 87
Vygotsky, Lev, 75, 83

Wages for Housework, 152, 154
Walker, Gillian, 45n4, 118
Watson, Rod, 103–4, 105, 106, 120
Weber, Max, 15, 25n3, 56, 58, 69
welfare, 215–17, 219, 220
Whyte, William H., 19
Wieder, Lawrence, 66, 133
wild boy of Aveyron ("Victor"), 83–84, 86, 97n7
Wilson, Alex, 188
Wittgenstein, Ludwig, 96n4
Wolfe, Virginia, 152
Women's Christian Temperance Movement, 19
women, 10, 22–23; of color, 139–40; experience of, 7–9, 64; immigrant, 45n4, 139; middle-class, 8–9, 14–15, 19–20, 34, 136; Native, 8, 188, 198; sociology for, 10; white, 8, 9, 34, 139; work of 10, 11–13, 14, 25n1, 36–37, 62; working-class, 8, 20, 136
women's movement, 1, 3, 7–10, 19–21, 28, 53, 62, 118, 165; and agency, 23; and class, race, and gender, 8; and experience, 7–8, 11, 12, 13, 18, 45n4, 78–79, 127; and the naming of oppression, 7, 78–79; and women's standpoint, 7–9, 205–6. *See also* feminism
women's standpoint, 1, 228; and method of inquiry, 24–25; ruling relations and, 9–13, 20–25, 165; and sociology, 11–13; women's movement and, 7–9, 205–6
word, 69, 83, 95n2, 111–12, 108, 130; and objects, 85–86, 87, 210; and perception, 84–85, 129; as two-sided act, 77, 80–82, 84–85. *See also* terms
work: and accountability, 174–75, 79; of activism, 150–51; "caring," 163n6, 179; complementary, 159, 160, 166; coordination of, 111, 118,

120, 132, 135, 151, 158, 160, 161–63, 167, 170, 191, 211; of the consumer, 152, 154, 163n4, 163n8; disjunction in, 11–13; as employment, 35, 131, 151, 162; "generous" conception of, 125, 151–55, 157, 161, 210; of housewives, 13, 20–21, 22, 43, 62, 152, 153, 210; and institutions, 113, 135, 186; as intentional, 154; invisible, 152–53, 179; of men, 14–15, 20, 36–37, 62, 153; of mothers, 10, 11–13, 22, 32–34, 36–37, 51, 132–33, 136, 157–59, 162, 210–11; of nursing, 40, 178–80; and organization, 69, 79, 84–85, 108, 137, 146–48, 174–77, 211, 216; of pickpockets, 129–30; of police, 63, 71n11, 159, 197, 200; social, 139–40, 155, 185–86, 190; steel, 130–32, 135, 138, 140–41, 144n2, 151; of Suicide Prevention Center, 113; of teachers, 34, 36, 133, 155, 180; and texts, 108, 151, 162–63, 167, 177–78, 181; textual coordination of, 166–67, 174, 180–81, 186; of university, 11, 146–48; unpaid, 37, 163n4; of waiting, 152, 162, 208; of women, 10, 11–13, 14, 25n1, 36–37, 62. *See also* work knowledge
working class, 20, 45n4, 57, 98, 133, 214; mothers, 136, 158–59; women, 8, 20, 136
work knowledge, 1, 44, 125, 145–49, 161, 193, 210–11, 214; concept of, 151–55, 161, 210; and data dialogues, 149, 150–51, 161–62; of informants, 138–39, 140; and institutional capture, 155–57; mapping, 157–61; of parents and teachers, 133; textual coordination of, 44, 166–67, 170, 173, 211, 220. *See also* knowledge
workload form, 175–77
work-text-work sequence, 178, 184, 217, 221

Dorothy E. Smith is a professor emerita in the Department of Sociology and Equity Studies in Education of the University of Toronto and an adjunct professor in the Department of Sociology, University of Victoria, British Columbia. She has been preoccupied for the past thirty or so years with developing the implications of women's standpoint for sociology, problematizing the objectified forms of organization and social relations characteristic of contemporary society, and focusing more recently on the significance of texts for the organization of power. The approach, now called institutional ethnography, has become an established field of sociological endeavor whose practitioners are committed to mapping the social relations organizing the everyday world of people's experience so that they can better see the workings of which everyone is a part.

Breinigsville, PA USA
06 December 2010
250779BV00002B/2/P